Preparing Indonesian Youth

Preparing Indonesian Youth

A Review of Educational Research

Edited by

Anne Suryani, Isabella Tirtowalujo
and Hasriadi Masalam

BRILL
SENSE

LEIDEN | BOSTON

All chapters in this book have undergone peer review.

Library of Congress Cataloging-in-Publication Data

Names: Suryani, Anne, editor. | Tirtowalujo, Isabella, editor. | Masalam, Hasriadi, editor.
Title: Preparing Indonesian youth : a review of educational research / edited by Anne Suryani, Isabella Tirtowalujo and Hasriadi Masalam.
Description: Leiden ; Boston : Brill | Sense, 2020. | Includes bibliographical references and index.
Identifiers: LCCN 2020026217 (print) | LCCN 2020026218 (ebook) | ISBN 9789004393646 (paperback) | ISBN 9789004393653 (hardback) | ISBN 9789004436459 (ebook)
Subjects: LCSH: Education--Research--Indonesia. | Education--Aims and objectives--Indonesia. | Educational change--Indonesia.
Classification: LCC LA1271 .P67 2020 (print) | LCC LA1271 (ebook) | DDC 371.209598--dc23
LC record available at https://lccn.loc.gov/2020026217
LC ebook record available at https://lccn.loc.gov/2020026218

Typeface for the Latin, Greek, and Cyrillic scripts: "Brill". See and download: brill.com/brill-typeface.

ISBN 978-90-04-39364-6 (paperback)
ISBN 978-90-04-39365-3 (hardback)
ISBN 978-90-04-43645-9 (e-book)

Copyright 2020 by Koninklijke Brill NV, Leiden, The Netherlands.
Koninklijke Brill NV incorporates the imprints Brill, Brill Hes & De Graaf, Brill Nijhoff, Brill Rodopi, Brill Sense, Hotei Publishing, mentis Verlag, Verlag Ferdinand Schöningh and Wilhelm Fink Verlag.
All rights reserved. No part of this publication may be reproduced, translated, stored in a retrieval system, or transmitted in any form or by any means, electronic, mechanical, photocopying, recording or otherwise, without prior written permission from the publisher.
Authorization to photocopy items for internal or personal use is granted by Koninklijke Brill NV provided that the appropriate fees are paid directly to The Copyright Clearance Center, 222 Rosewood Drive, Suite 910, Danvers, MA 01923, USA. Fees are subject to change.

This book is printed on acid-free paper and produced in a sustainable manner.

Contents

Acknowledgements   VII
List of Figures and Tables   VIII
Notes on Contributors   X

1   Preparing Youth for Indonesia 4.0: Challenges and Prospects   1
Isabella Tirtowalujo, Anne Suryani and Hasriadi Masalam

PART 1
Teachers and Teaching

2   Science Teaching Practices in Indonesian Secondary Schools: A Portrait of Educational Quality and Equity-Based on PISA 2015   21
Anindito Aditomo

3   Governing Guru: The Political Economy of Teacher Distribution in Indonesia   48
Andrew Rosser

4   The Role of Religious Beliefs in Teacher Education Students' Career Aspirations   66
Anne Suryani

5   The Boundary Crossing of Indonesian Out-of-Field Teachers   89
Esti Rahayu and Shuki Osman

PART 2
School and Institutional Practices

6   The Implementation of Character Education Programs in Indonesian Schools   107
Wahyu Nurhayati

7   Fostering Quality Education and Global Engagement through Sister School Partnership: Perspectives of Teachers   124
Ahmad Bukhori Muslim

8   Politics of Gender and Gender Studies in Higher Education   145
    Widjajanti M. Santoso and Nina Widyawati

PART 3
Youth, Schooling, and Social Context of Education

9   Framing the Early School Leaving Policy Problem: Indonesian Rural Youth Engagement in Transnational Labour Migration as a Test Case   161
    Isabella Tirtowalujo

10 Significance of Sociocultural Factors in Attribution of Educational Outcomes and Motivation Goals   185
    Novita W. Sutantoputri, Aries Sutantoputra, Isabella Tirtowalujo, Juliana Murniati and Margaretha Purwanti

11 Successful Student Mobility: What Makes an Indonesian Alternative Education Beneficial for Internal Youth Migrants?   203
    Ila Rosmilawati and David Wright

12 Participatory Action Research on Education for Self-Reliance for Rural Youth in Indonesia   220
    Hasriadi Masalam

    Index   239

Acknowledgements

The collaborative and creative journey of developing this volume has been one that involved a group of hard-working and gracious individuals, who are not only achieved or tenured scholars, academics, researchers, and educators, but also young scholars, junior faculty, and recent doctoral graduates. The editors firstly wish to thank all of the contributors for their enthusiasm and persistence in developing this volume, including for the interesting and important research they are respectively doing addressing different educational and social issues while representing a diverse set of perspectives and research approaches. We appreciate all the contributors' patience, as well as readiness to follow up on our editorial requests.

We also express our gratitude to the Brill | Sense staff who supported this book from its ideation to completion, as well as the external reviewers who provided crucial feedback to strengthen the entire work. The editors would also like to thank Alex Lilley for the technical support in reviewing manuscript drafts and providing editorial input.

We appreciate our colleagues and friends who encouraged us in our work, and look forward to reading this book. We are also indebted to the members of our respective families—especially our parents, spouses, and children (and also pets)—who provided moral support and sustained our strength when we needed to persevere in our writing, reviewing, and editing.

We consider the publishing of this book timely, as the Ministry of Education and Culture recently laid out new directions, initiatives, and reforms to change and improve the system that shapes the learning, education, and schooling experiences of the young generation of Indonesia. The chapters here frame and highlight existing opportunities as well as persisting issues in the efforts to ensure children and youth are able access quality education, and develop to become independent, able, caring, and contributing members of the society and their respective communities. It is the contributors' and our hope that the collection of studies presented in this volume further the development of discourse and dissemination of knowledge surrounding different topics within education; and eventually provide a substantial basis for consideration for current and future policy development.

Figures and Tables

Figures

2.1 Regression lines for schools at the highest 25%, middle 50%, and the lowest 25% SES quartile, with 95% confidence intervals.   37
4.1 Theoretical framework: Indonesian teacher education students' motivations for choosing a teaching career (adapted from Watt & Richardson, 2007, p. 176; Suryani, Watt, & Richardson, 2016).   73
4.2 Different religious beliefs based on gender and religious groups.   75
4.3 Different religious influences on motivation to become teachers based on gender and religious groups.   76
4.4 Perception that teaching requires high expertise based on gender and religious groups.   77
4.5 Perception that teaching has high social status based on gender and religious groups.   78
4.6 Satisfaction with choice of becoming a teacher based on gender and religious groups.   78
4.7 Different aspirations based on religious groups.   79
4.8 Planned effort based on gender and religious groups.   80
4.9 Planned persistence based on gender and religious groups.   80
4.10 Professional development aspirations based on gender and religious groups.   81
4.11 Structural model for perceptions, religious beliefs and PECDA factors.   81
9.1 Conceptual illustration of the barrier-to-participation framework (Framework One).   166
9.2 Conceptual illustration of the sub-grouping framework (Framework Two).   169
9.3 Conceptual illustration of the governance framework (Framework Three).   170

Tables

1.1 The Indonesian educational system.   4
2.1 Number of participants.   29
2.2 Descriptive statistics.   33
2.3 Inter-correlations between predictor variables.   34
2.4 Results of the multilevel models predicting students' science literacy; number represent standardised coefficients, standard errors, and p values (1-tailed).   35
2.5 Interaction between teaching and SES (Models 4a–f).   37

FIGURES AND TABLES

3.1 Case studies. 54
5.1 Participants' qualification and teaching experience. 96
6.1 Summary of findings. 118
7.1 Teachers' accounts. 132
10.1 Regression for attribution, ethnic identity, religiosity, self-efficacy, intelligence beliefs on motivational goals. 192
11.1 Age, educational profile and employment status of in-migrant youth. 206
11.2 Education attainment of the in-migrant population (by percentage). 210
11.3 The integrating and inhibiting factors. 214

Notes on Contributors

Anindito Aditomo
is a lecturer at the Faculty of Psychology, University of Surabaya, Indonesia. He holds a bachelor degree from Universitas Gadjah Mada, Indonesia, and master and doctoral degrees from the University of Sydney, Australia. With a background in both psychology and education, he is particularly interested in how the sciences of learning can inform instruction and broader educational processes. Anindito is currently a guest researcher at the DIPF/Leibniz Institute for Research and Information in Education, Germany. His research at DIPF is funded by the Alexander von Humboldt Foundation and focuses on the analysis of international large-scale assessments of learning data.

Hasriadi Masalam
works on issues of rural education, youth as changemakers, rural development, capacity building, and knowledge management for two decades. He holds a PhD in Adult Education from University of Alberta, Canada, and MA from SIT, USA, where he receives prestigious awards including the Ford Foundation International Fellowship. Hasriadi is a co-founder of ININNAWA, which works in issues of rural transformation, agricultural innovations, traditional market revitalisation, literacy and education, and local culture publishing. He is also a co-founder of Rumah KAMU, an NGO focusing on youth critical thinking and awareness on rural issues. Hasriadi has contributed to more than dozen publications distributed in Indonesia, Europe and North America.

Juliana Murniati
has a PhD from Friedrich Schiller University, Jena-German, and has been actively involved in academic setting since 1991 at Atma Jaya Catholic University of Indonesia, Jakarta. She was the Vice Rector for Academic Affairs between 2015–2019. Her research interests include trust-building in organisational and intergroup context, intercultural competence, and global leadership, and she has several publications (books and articles) on these topics.

Ahmad Bukhori Muslim
is currently an Assistant Professor in the Department of English Education and the Director of the Office of International Education and Relations at Universitas Pendidikan Indonesia. He earned his Master's degree in Developmental Studies for Language and Literacy from Boston University, and a Doctoral degree in Educational Psychology from Monash University, Australia. His research interests and publications are on international education and partnership, intercultural language learning, language and identity, and English

education. Some of his works are published by Cambridge Scholars, Brill and Sense Publishers.

Wahyu Nurhayati
is a psychologist and a researcher at the Ministry of Education and Culture of Indonesia. She holds a PhD in early childhood education from Monash University, Australia. She was involved in the development of character education assessment instruments conducted by the Center for Educational Assessment, one of the departments in the Ministry of Education and Culture.

Shuki Osman
is an Associate professor at the School of Educational Studies, Universiti Sains Malaysia (USM). He received his PhD in 2003 from USM in Geography Education, an MSc (Education) in Curriculum, Instruction and Media in 1985 from Southern Illinois University, Carbondale, USA and a bachelor's degree in Geography from USM in 1983. Prior to his appointment at USM, he taught geography at MARA Junior Science Colleges. He has been teaching and supervising in the area of curriculum and instruction, presenting papers at national and international seminars, as well as writing for journals and books related to teaching and geography teaching. Previously, he was a Deputy Dean (Academic and Student Development) at USM.

Margaretha Purwanti
holds a PhD in Psychology from University of Indonesia in 2006. She has been with the Faculty of Psychology at the Atma Jaya Catholic University since 1993, and has held various positions with increasing responsibilities, such as Vice Dean. From 2016–2019, she was the Program Chair for the Masters of Psychology at Atma Jaya Catholic University. She is also a certified graphologist. Her research is on higher education learning and educational psychology. Her studies focus on students' motivation and also inclusiveness in academic setting.

Esti Rahayu
is a lecturer at Universitas Bina Nusantara, Jakarta where she teaches English for undergraduate students. She received her PhD in 2020 from Universiti Sains Malaysia in Professional and Teacher Education.

Ila Rosmilawati
holds a PhD in Education from Western Sydney University, Australia and is a Lecturer in the Department of Nonformal Education in the Faculty of Teacher Training and Education at Universitas Sultan Ageng Tirtayasa. Her research interests include the nonformal education sector, alternative education, trans-

formative learning and critical pedagogy. She teaches sociology of education, nonformal basic education, and lifelong education.

Andrew Rosser
is Professor of Southeast Asian Studies at the University of Melbourne. His research examines the political economy of Indonesia, with a particular focus on education, health, migration, and economic policy. His other work on Indonesia's education system has appeared in journals such as *Comparative Education, International Journal of Educational Development, Third World Quarterly, Asian Studies Review,* and *Journal of Development Studies* and edited books such as Juanita Elias and Lena Rethel (Eds.), *The Everyday Political Economy of Southeast Asia* (Cambridge University Press, 2016) and Darryl Jarvis and Ka Ho Mok (Eds.), *Transformations in Higher Education Governance in Asia* (Springer, 2019).

Widjajanti M. Santoso
is a senior researcher in the Research Centre for Society and Culture in the Indonesian Institute of Sciences. She holds a PhD in sociology from the University of Indonesia and a Master's degree from the Australian National University. Her research is on the sociology of everyday life among middle-class communities, gender, and media as a medium for social change and academic activities in books, journals and conferences. She contributes to the development of knowledge on women by supporting the Graduate Program on Gender Studies at the University of Indonesia, and serving as a reviewer of *Jurnal Perempuan*.

Anne Suryani
holds a PhD in Educational Psychology and MEd by Research from Monash University, Australia. She has received a number of awards and scholarships throughout her academic journey, including the Mollie Holman Doctoral Medal for outstanding contribution to research for PhD. Anne has been working in educational research projects in Australia and Indonesia focusing on teacher motivation, teacher education and professional development, vocational education, assessment and curriculum. Anne is currently a research fellow in the Centre for Vocational and Educational Policy, Melbourne Graduate School of Education, The University of Melbourne.

Aries Sutantoputra
earned his PhD in Management from Monash University, Australia and his MSc in International Financial Management from the University of Groningen, the Netherlands. Aries's research interests include strategy, sustainability issues, corporate social responsibility, corporate governance, cross-cultural is-

sues, education management, and international development. Currently, Aries is a Faculty in the Management program at the School of Business in Southern Alberta Institute of Technology, Calgary, Canada. He is a firm believer in the transformative power of education and has been providing consultancy to improve the quality of education to a network of schools that serves marginalised communities in Indonesia.

Novita W. Sutantoputri
holds a PhD in Educational Psychology from the Faculty of Education, Monash University, Australia. Her main research interests are intercultural studies, students' motivation, and gender differences in academic settings. Her studies on students' motivation also relate to studies of teaching and learning, and students' aspiration and attributions based on cultural differences. Beyond her work in education, she studies psychological application methods for chronic pain patients, particularly among patients with Fibromyalgia syndrome.

Isabella Tirtowalujo
holds a PhD in Curriculum, Instruction, and Teacher Education from Michigan State University. Her research on the social context of schooling focused on the intersection of education, rurality, youth, and labour migration. Her more recent work explores issues of out-of-school children and capacity development in the context of decentralisation of education in Indonesia. Isabella has worked in education development projects supporting central and local governments, and development partners including UNICEF and the Asian Development Bank, in areas of capacity building, knowledge management, report development, and preparation of background studies and sectoral reviews for strategic planning in education. She is currently the Assistant Director of the MSU Asian Studies Center.

Nina Widyawati
is a senior researcher at the Research Centre for Society and Culture in the Indonesian Institute of Sciences. She completed her doctoral and master degrees in communication studies from the University of Indonesia. Her research interests are media and minority; information technology and social changes; and comparative studies of Indonesia and Malaysia. Her current work is on disinformation issues. She also teaches research methodology in the Communication Studies Program at Bakrie University in Jakarta.

David Wright
is a Senior Lecturer in the School of Education at Western Sydney University, Australia. He teaches in the overlapping areas of social ecology and transfor-

mative learning. He is especially interested in learning processes and the contexts within which new learning arises. These contexts include the changing world environment, as a consequence of hyper-capitalism and its contribution to climate change. He is co-editor of the recent Routledge publication *Social Ecology: Transforming Worldviews and Practices* (2020).

CHAPTER 1

Preparing Youth for Indonesia 4.0: Challenges and Prospects

Isabella Tirtowalujo, Anne Suryani and Hasriadi Masalam

Abstract

The introductory chapter recognises firstly the prevalence and uses of the "Indonesia 4.0" discourse in directing attention to whether and how youths in Indonesia are both benefiting and underserved educationally. This chapter frames the studies in the book from a macro perspective of the education system, as contributing to conversations on a range of issues toward preparing Indonesian youth for the envisioned present and future pertaining to: educational participation, quality, and equity; teaching and learning; and youth's skills and employment. The book highlights cases that emphasise, critique, and delineate progresses, as well as new and persisting challenges. This chapter proposes ways the empirical studies contribute with insights to especially three aspects of the education system: teachers and teaching; programs and curricular offering in education especially at the secondary and tertiary levels; and the social and cultural contexts of education implicating youth's encounters with schooling and educational experiences. This chapter foregrounds that the case studies bring into their analyses how larger social forces and phenomena—for example, political and education decentralisation, internal rural-urban and transnational migration, and the global feminist and women's movement—shape and interact with visions of preparing all Indonesian youth for meaningful participation in the society.

Keywords

education research – education policy – elementary secondary education – higher education – education quality – cultural and education

Indonesia's recently launched 2020–2024 National Mid-Term Development Plan (*Rencana Pembangunan Jangka Menengah Nasional*, RPJMN) underlines renewed commitment to investment in human resource development. Growth in human capital through labour force and worker skill development is front and centre in the government's policy priorities and the "Making Indonesia 4.0" roadmap publicly announced in early 2018 by President Joko "Jokowi" Widodo. The roadmap envisions revolutionising and expanding big industries such as the electronics, automotive, chemicals, textile, and food and beverage industries, and creating more than 10 million new skilled jobs by 2030 (Aisyah, 2019; Industry Ministry launches making Indonesia 4.0, 2018). It involves multiple stakeholders and aims to have a much larger proportion of the population positioned and poised to participate in and capitalise on the digital revolution. With about one-third of the current Indonesian labour force still engaging in low-skill and low-productivity jobs in agriculture and informal sector (Manning & Pratomo, 2018), the charted obstacle-laden course has been laid out.

Clear implications involve the need to transform major components of the education system so as to align it with the Indonesia 4.0 roadmap and the demands to prepare individuals who are highly adaptable to the rapidly changing and globalising society and to raise up a future generation able to address societal challenges of the 21st century. Further, in light of religious polarisation rampant in recent political discourse; the prevalence of hostility, hatred, and fake news in social media; and incidents involving racial discriminatory acts spurring recent regional tensions, the vision for societal progress includes an ideal whereby all children and youth gain educational experiences that would enable them to be at the forefront of social restoration and advancement. This includes efforts to eradicate social and economic disparities and to ameliorate tensions that threaten the social cohesion and integrity of the diverse Indonesian people across the archipelagic nation. Education development moving forward needs to respond to the urgency to address education participation- and achievement-gap among different segments of the population, which exacerbates disparities and further marginalises the members of Indonesia's heterogeneous society who are most vulnerable.

Framed as Indonesia's future and rising leaders holding the key to the nation's development and progress, the youth are invited to step up to the challenge of furthering the new digital technology era and the democratic society, while contributing to the development of an equitable and thriving society. The central inquiry presented in this book is whether and how Indonesia's youth may be prepared, equipped, and benefitting from their experience and engagement with the vast Indonesian education system, its policies, institutions, educators, and programs. The book also contributes to an understanding of the extent to which larger segments of children and youth are able to meaningfully participate and benefit from education and training, highlighting contextual factors that shape the personal growth, educational, and work or career trajectories of the young.

This review of education research in Indonesia features empirically-based studies in Indonesia, highlighting the challenges and prospects within the educational system serving one of the largest school-age population globally, and the system's interaction with the wider social and political context of a rapidly changing society. The studies included highlights three particular aspects of education: teachers and teaching; innovative programs and curricular offering in education at the secondary and tertiary levels; and social identities of the youth learners and the social context of education. The analyses points to opportunities and potentials, as well as barriers and obstacles in increasing the quality and impact of teaching and teachers, and shaping educational programs that help learners and youths develop in knowledge, character, and crucial competencies.

1   Educating Youth in Indonesia

1.1   *Youth within the Indonesian Education System: A Brief Overview*

Stretched across more than 17,000 islands along the equator, Indonesia's multiplicities of diversity come with significant challenges in the task of managing the vast population of 267 million people, and an education system consisting of 45 million students, over 3 million teachers, 270,000 primary and secondary schools, and 4,670 degree-granting post-secondary institutions.[1]

Three major central government agencies—the Ministry of Education and Culture (MoEC), the Ministry of Religious Affairs (MoRA), and the Ministry of Research, Technology, and Higher Education (MoRTHE)—oversee students along the system and education levels of pre-primary (for students ages 3–6 years), primary (7–12 years), junior secondary (13–15 years), senior secondary (16–18 years), and tertiary (18 years and above) (see Table 1.1).

Denoting a public-private collaboration in the endeavours of providing mass education, public and private schools and madrasahs serve students at all levels. The education system under MoEC is predominantly decentralised, while MoRA has maintained centralised oversight of Islamic public and private madrasahs. Eighty per cent of all primary and secondary schools are "regular" schools managed by MoEC, and the rest are Islamic schools (madrasahs) managed by MoRA. All schools implement the national curriculum: *Kurikulum 2013*.

Reflecting the nature of secondary education in Indonesia, according to MoEC education data, in 2020 two thirds (66%) of Indonesia's secondary students attend public schools (MoEC, 2020b), even though only 38% of secondary schools are public (MoEC, 2020a). Further disaggregating between the

TABLE 1.1   The Indonesian educational system

Education level	Ages	School types
Primary education (Grades 1–6)	7–12 years	Primary school (*Sekolah Dasar*)
		Formal education (public and private) -Regular primary schools (MoEC) (Non-religious and religious schools—Islamic, Protestant, Catholic, Buddhist, Hindu, Confucius, and other) -Programs: National curriculum, National curriculum + English (*Nasional Plus*), and International curriculum -Islamic primary school (*Madrasah Ibtidaiyah*) (MoRA) *Non-Formal Education* -Equivalency education "A" program (*Paket A*)
Junior secondary education (Grades 7–9)	13–15 years	Junior secondary school (*Sekolah Menengah Pertama*)
		Formal education (public & private) -Regular junior secondary school (religious and non-religious) (MoEC) -Islamic junior secondary school (*Madrasah Tsanawiyah*) (MoRA) *Non-Formal education* -Equivalency education "B" program (*Paket B*)

(cont.)

TABLE 1.1   The Indonesian educational system (*cont.*)

Education level	Ages	School types
Senior secondary education (Grades 10–12)	16–18 years	Senior secondary school (*Sekolah Menengah Atas*)
		Formal education (public and private)
		University preparation
		-Regular senior secondary school (religious and non-religious) (MoEC)
		-Islamic senior secondary school (*Madrasah Aliyah*) (MoRA)
		Vocational education
		-Vocational school (*Sekolah Menengah Kejuruan*)
		-Islamic vocational school (*Madrasah Aliyah Kejuruan*)
		Non-Formal education
		-Equivalency education "C" program (*Paket C*)
Tertiary education	≥ 18 years	Higher education (*Pendidikan Tinggi*) (public and private)
		-University (*Universitas*)
		-Institute (*Institut*)
		-School of Higher Learning (*Sekolah Tinggi*)
		-Academy (*Akademi*) (1–3-year Diploma)
		-Community College (*Akademi Komunitas*)
		-Polytechnic (*Politeknik*) (Diploma in Sciences)
		Degrees: 1–4 years Diploma (D1–D4), Bachelor's (S-1), Master's (S-2), Doctoral (S-3), Professional (*Profesi*), and Specialist (*Spesialis*)

SOURCE: ADAPTED FROM SURYANI (2017)

secondary levels, almost three quarters (74%) of senior secondary students attend public schools (including in madrasahs), when only a third (33%) of all senior secondary schools are public. This highlights a stark contrast between the relatively small number of public senior secondary schools (excluding vocational schools) and madrasahs in Indonesia (about 7,700) serving a significantly large number of senior secondary students (3.5 million), and twice the number of smaller private senior secondary institutions across the country (about 15,000) serving a third fewer students (1.2 million) in various predominantly rural and remote communities. The data set up the stage for an understanding of the wide range of educational experiences among youth, and persisting gaps in education quality, achievements, and outcomes further discussed below and throughout the book.

In addition to schools and madrasahs, at the senior secondary level, youths also have the option to attend senior secondary vocational schools, which similarly are public and private. Based on 2019 data, half of the senior secondary students in Indonesia do attend vocational schools, which are overwhelmingly (75%) private and relatively also much smaller.

1.1.1 Education Funding

All schools and madrasahs regardless of public or private status receive funding from the central government in the form of school grant (called *Bantuan Operasional Sekolah* [BOS], School Operational Assistance). However, a vast majority of private schools are run by community- and faith-based organisations with limited financial capacities. Many of them serve populations in under-resourced areas.

Indonesia has implemented pro-education fiscal policies, adhering to the Education Law 2003 which ensures an education budget minimum of 20% of the Annual State Budget. Education spending has, in fact, continued to increase. For example, the $36 billion education budget for the year 2020 (Negara, 2019) is a 133% increase from the 2010 education budget of IDR 216.7 trillion (Ministry of Finance, 2019). Supporting decentralisation of education, about 60% of this budget will be directly transferred to the 514 districts and municipalities within the 34 provinces across the archipelago. These achievements and sustained fiscal commitments to education development have served as a strong basis in the expansion of compulsory education to 12 years.

1.1.2 Teachers

Indonesia has one of the largest and most diverse teacher workforces worldwide (Chang et al., 2014). In 2019 there are over 3 million teachers in Indonesia with 2.1 million of them in public schools and the remaining 900,000 in private schools (MoEC, 2019). In terms of teacher certification status, almost 1.8 million civil servant teachers have been certified, and about 200,000 non-civil servant teachers have also received their certification. For those in-service teachers without certification, most likely they have not completed their undergraduate or four-year university study (MoEC, 2019).

In 2005, Indonesia passed the Teacher Law (14/2005). A major component of this legislation was the implementation of a teacher certification program, which aimed to certify over two million teachers by 2015. This program is delivered to approximately 200,000 teachers per year and as of 2012, government statistics show that 1.15 million teachers have been formally certified. To qualify for this program, teachers are required to hold a university bachelor's degree or equivalent (although exemptions are allowed for senior teachers). Those who have completed the certification process were eligible for a certification allowance that equalled to their base salary in the civil service. For most teachers, certification meant a doubling of their take-home pay. However, the implementation of this program costs the government more than USD 5 billion each year, corresponding to approximately a quarter of the overall education budget.

1.2 Preparing Youth: Progress, Achievements, and Remaining Challenges

1.2.1 Issues in Participation, Quality, and Equity

In the last few decades, the government's efforts in the expansion of education have displayed commendable achievements. Based on 2018 data, primary education completion rate in Indonesia is close to universal (95%) with gender parity (Ministry of National Development Planning/National Development Planning Agency [Bappenas], 2019). Secondary education Net Enrolment Rate (NER) has also displayed a generally upward trend, from 50% in 2001 to 77% in 2015 (The World Bank Data, 2015).

Junior secondary education completion rates among youths 16–18 years old[2] have increased significantly from 64% in the year 2000 to 84% in 2016 (Bappenas, 2019). However, it has relatively stagnated and increased only slightly to 85% by 2018. Based on 2018 data, almost 1 out of 4 (23%) of youths in this age group are not in school. This is equivalent to 3 million youths ages 16–18 years old who for various reasons have dropped out of the education system. When looking into an older cohort, senior secondary completion rates among youths 19–21 years old[3] have been and are still on the rise, from 38% in 2000 to 62% in 2018, despite a diminishing rate of increase over the last 3 years.

Various indicators triangulate a pattern of a plateauing in the expansion of participation at the secondary education level, suggesting the need for a more rigorous and comprehensive efforts to integrate the rest of the youth population in those age groups into education, whether through formal or informal programs. The fact remains that there is more than one-third of youths ages 19–21 years with only a junior secondary education or lower (Bappenas, 2019). If the age group is expanded in the estimation to include older youths, it would reveal an even larger proportion of youths who lack a senior secondary diploma, suggesting limitations faced by a significant proportion of Indonesian youths in their ability to further and realise their academic, professional, and work aspirations.

Concerns over the current education participation and attainment levels of youths 16 years and older are warranted. However, equally concerning are children and youths' competencies and display of learning outcomes. For example, results from international competency assessments such as PISA (Programme for International Student Assessment), which targets 15-year old adolescents display low proportions of Indonesian students who performed at least at a minimum proficiency level in reading and mathematics. In 2015, while 45% of Indonesian students at the end of junior secondary who participated in PISA achieved at least a minimum proficiency level in reading, only about 31% achieved them in mathematics. PISA aims to assess the efficiency of the education system as it impacts adolescent competency development. It tests students to assess their reading, mathematics, and science literacies, and their abilities to display their competencies for tasks relevant in adult life (Kurniawati, Suryadarma, Bima, & Yusrina, 2018). The most recent 2018 test involved about half a million 15-year olds from 80 countries and economies.

Participation and learning outcomes measures such as those mentioned above point consistently to issues of disparity putting at a disadvantage those from lower socioeconomic backgrounds and from rural areas (MoEC & UNICEF, 2018). Youths' experience and engagement with the education system significantly shape the trajectories of the pursuit of successful adulthood and participation as contributing members of the society. Sound education policies, quality schools, and effective teachers within the system hold potentials to expand these opportunities for youth. However, they are ridden with issues.

1.2.2 *Issues on Teacher Quality and Teaching in Indonesian Classrooms*

A crucial issue posing as a major challenge in the effort of improving educational and learning outcomes of all learners is teacher quality. The majority of 3 million Indonesian teachers did not pass a national teacher competency test in 2015. Only seven provinces achieved the minimum targeted competency standard[4] (MoEC, 2016). This challenge is complicated by the fact that teacher management is a joint responsibility of the central government and over 500 autonomous districts. Although in 2001 Indonesia has decentralised basic education to the district level, a large share of the education budget and regulations is still managed at the central level.

Teachers play a significant role in student learning. Attracting the right candidates for teaching and improving the quality of teachers are the main problems faced by Indonesia. In a previous study investigating teacher education students' motivation to become teachers, it was found that social utility values (contributing to the society by working as a teacher), prior teaching and learning experiences, intrinsic career values (interest and enjoyment from working as a teacher), and influence from religious beliefs were some of their main motivations for entering teacher education and to become teachers (Suryani, Watt, & Richardson, 2016).

A recent World Bank study investigating the implementation and outcomes of the teacher certification program suggests that increasing teacher remuneration decreased teachers' intention to undertake additional jobs and reduced their (self-reported) financial stress, but it does not make teachers teach better (De Ree, 2016). The study also revealed that teachers with bachelor's degrees are only moderately better teachers than teachers without bachelor's degrees (p. 9). This was more evident for primary school teachers. Another finding was that teachers with a reasonable level of subject-matter knowledge are much better teachers than those who have difficulties with even the most basic mathematical exercises (p. 9). Hundreds of thousands of Indonesian teachers in primary schools struggle with even the most basic mathematical exercises. The World Bank study also confirmed the problem of teacher supply in Indonesia, where 250,000 pre-service teachers graduate from university/teacher training colleges each year, but the school system needs only 50,000–100,000 teachers (p. 9).

The teacher certification program also aims to financially entice accomplished high school graduates to pursue a career in teaching. While appealing in theory, in reality, schools and districts still overlook the best or most trained candidates. Government statistics indicate that around 12% of primary school teachers still do not hold a bachelor's degree (MoEC & UNICEF, forthcoming). Due to the overproduction of teachers with ambiguous and potentially unfair hiring rules, even high-calibre candidates have difficulties in finding a secure and well-paid teaching position and are likely to seek other opportunities outside of teaching. Hence, the current system *deters* rather than *attracts* high-achieving high school graduates to become teachers.

1.2.3   Issues in Youth, Skill, and Employment

The demographic bonus in Indonesia—a condition whereby the population of individuals in productive ages (15–64 years) are larger than the children and elderly population combined—has been hailed by the World Bank as a window of opportunity. With youth making up a quarter of the total population (64.2 million) (Statistics Indonesia, 2019), the Indonesian youth bulge will hypothetically drive further investing in basic and secondary education. The extent to which the Indonesian government can unleash the potential and productive capacities of the young, especially those between the ages of 16- and 30 years remains in question.

Challenges abound. According to 2012 data, 23% of urban and 33% of rural youth between the ages of 15–24 years were reported unemployed (Tanu, 2014, p. 51), with young women being three times more likely to be economically idle. A fiercely competitive labour market and one that is in transition contribute to long term unemployment. The report found that 42% of the unemployed youth had been jobless for on average at least 12 months, with longer periods experienced by those living in Eastern Indonesia (Kring & Breglia, 2015, p. xi). The issue of educated unemployment and underemployment among youth with secondary and even tertiary degrees is also rampant, highlighting the issues of the relevance of their educational investments in helping the school-to-work transition, as well as of the slow pace of the job creation growth.

As they find that their formal employment prospects are shrinking, young people often redirect their aspirations to self-employment and entrepreneurship, a direction readily supported by the government. The 2016–2019 National Youth Action Plan highlights the priority of promoting youth employment and youth entrepreneurship. President Jokowi himself is a big promoter of a youth-driven creative economy, particularly out of the digital industry sector. Jokowi's move seek to tap into the "hyper-connectivity" of young population evidenced by the fact that: 84% of Indonesians own at least one cell phone; one out ten online users are active on social media (higher than the U.S. at only seven out of ten); and 56% of the 64 million Facebook users in Indonesia are 16–24 years old (Picard & Chang, 2013).

Despite the potentials of youth as pioneers in adopting and creating business opportunities out of new technologies, the appealing image of a thriving creativity-based digital industry which has attracted many highly educated and tech-savvy urban millennials and their cosmopolitan career aspirations, however, hides the "informality traps" (Kring & Breglia, 2015, p. xiii) and the precarious nature of creative work, due to a dependence on fluctuating freelance projects (Azali, 2015). Indonesia's standing continues to climb in the

World Bank's *Ease of Doing Business Index* (2019), signalling how the infrastructures are responding to aspiring entrepreneurs, bettering individuals' and organisations' experiences in dealing with the complex environment in starting up their ventures and improving access to business development services.

As for rural youth, their experiences of school-to-work transition seem rather grim. Despite increasingly being more educated than former generations, some observe that rural youth undergo a "deskilling process" during their formal schooling experiences, which have led them to neglect farming skills and devalue rural livelihood (White, 2012). Further, youth participation in the agriculture sector are made more complex by various structural and practical obstacles, such as limited access to land, volatile market of agricultural products, and vulnerability of farming to climate change risks. These phenomena have often left them to resort to urban migration, where they end up in low-paying jobs in urban areas or as overseas migrant workers.

Particular attention and sustained efforts are needed to ensure that Indonesia is is spared from turning the "demographic bonus" euphoria into a "demographic tragedy", through effective policies and programs that can ensure that young people are adequately equipped with appropriate skills to increase their employability and fulfil their productive aspirations as citizens.

2   Review of Education Research: Teachers, School Practices and Innovative Programs, and Social Context of Schooling

The case study chapters presented in this book feature empirically-based studies focusing on three issue areas in education in Indonesia: teaching and teachers; school and institutional programs and innovative practices; and the social contexts of youth, schooling, and education. A majority of the studies rely mainly on primary sourced data. Further, the range of epistemologies and methodological approaches to data construction and analysis in the chapters seeks to capture insights on the way particular cases and context-specific information speak to the larger contexts in which education occurs, and youths live and learn. These contexts include national, local, and institutional policy contexts; the global and regional discourses and forces framing and inspiring, for instance, teacher quality and science teaching improvements, and internationalisation of education initiatives; and socio-economic and -cultural forces shaping teaching, development and implementation of particular education programs, and youths' educational outcomes and work aspirations.

The case studies also provide insights on how larger social phenomenon—for example, political and education decentralisation, internal rural-urban and transnational migration, and the global feminist and women's movement—negatively and positively impact and interact with enacted visions of preparing all youth for meaningful participation in the society. A short review and mapping of the chapters are included below.

Four chapters in Part 1 open the volume and offer discussions on various issues on teacher quality and teachers in Indonesia. In an investigation of the quality of science education teaching in secondary schools, *Anindito Aditomo* addresses the types and effectiveness of teaching practices in science education, particularly as it translates to Indonesian students' science literacy across different Socio-Economic Status (SES) . Through quantitative analysis of the OECD's Programme for International Student Assessment (PISA) data, this study found that interactive instruction together with orderly classroom management results were linked to higher science literacy at both individual (student) and collective (school) levels. Addressing equity issues in science competencies development, the study makes the case for additional support required by disadvantaged students to adequately benefit from science education in schools.

Andrew Rosser offers a political economy perspective shaping the realities of governing teacher distribution in Indonesia, based on case studies in four locales. The author explores the origins and political obstacles blocking reforms towards promoting more equitable teacher distribution across Indonesia. The chapter makes the case for tension between central government initiatives to reform teacher distribution systems, and local politics involving district bureaucratic elites and their educational patronage networks largely undermining the central government's efforts. The author suggests a combination of disciplinary measures, "working with the grain" approach, and facilitative components as holding potentials in teacher redistribution, particularly for disadvantaged areas.

Investigating the role of religious beliefs in future teachers' career aspirations, *Anne Suryani* foregrounds a core trait of Indonesians as a collectivist and religious society. The chapter examines how religion influences students' motivations to become teachers based on a quantitative analysis of 802 final-year undergraduate teacher education students from four universities in Indonesia. It was found that Muslim participants experienced a stronger influence from their religion to enter teacher education compared to Protestant and Catholic participants. Additionally, those who perceived themselves as more religious were likely to persist longer in their teaching careers and invest more effort into their future teaching.

In their chapter, *Esti Rahayu* and *Shuki Osman* examine the concept of out-of-field teachers—those who teach either without a teaching qualification or a subject beyond their expertise. Often arising from organisational issues within a school, it often results in less effective teaching and teacher burnout. However, some teachers have proven to undergo "identity expansion" (Hobbs, 2013) where they take advantage of the opportunity and consequently flourish in their new field. This qualitative study follows four Indonesian out-of-field teachers from local joint cooperation schools (*Satuan Pendidikan Kerjasama* [SPK]) and found that all four teachers had similar motivations, support networks, and ongoing reflection to undergo boundary-crossing to become accomplished teachers with over ten years of experience.

Shifting to a focus on education offerings and innovative institutional practices in Part 2, in a chapter on character education in Indonesian schools *Wahyu Nurhayati* utilises the 7E's Framework of assessing the implementation of character education, and how it shapes the rest of the school curriculum and culture. The qualitative study involves focus group discussions with six teachers from three private schools in Jakarta, all of which have implemented character education programs. The faith-based nature of these schools meant that their programs are largely based on religious values interspersed with self and peer evaluations to track students' progress.

The next chapter discusses the internationalisation of education and school improvement initiatives. *Ahmad Bukhori Muslim's* study focuses on the practice of sister school partnerships between Australian and Indonesian schools to promote quality education and students' global engagement. A series of 20 interviews with teachers, ten from each country, were conducted investigating their understanding, perspectives, and implementation of sister school partnerships within their home schools as well as its perceived benefits and disadvantages. This study suggests that teachers view such partnerships positively, with schools generally receiving adequate support from the government and community. The author discusses the benefits of student engagement with their foreign counterparts including in the area of development of foreign language competencies and cross-cultural understanding, both crucial components of 21st-century living.

Addressing gender mainstreaming in education at the higher education level, *Widjajanti Santoso* and *Nina Widyawati* present a comparative case study evaluating the politics and position of gender knowledge—or knowledge regarding the concept of gender, as well as gender issues—in higher education. The chapter examines the social contexts shaping supportive and prohibitive institutional policies and practices regarding the place of gender studies, and dissemination of gender knowledge in higher education institutions. The comparative case is based on two programs: a graduate-level gender studies program, and a communications studies program offered at both undergraduate and graduate levels, respectively illustrating the phenomenon of "ghettoisation" of gender knowledge, and "diffusion" of gender perspectives and knowledge via integration of gender topics within disciplinary studies.

The chapters in Part 3 present multiple vantage points and perspectives in understanding the social contexts shaping student academic experiences, and youths' successful and failed encounters with schooling. In an analysis of a forthcoming government policy document laying out a national strategy to address the early school-leaving and out-of-school issues in Indonesia, *Isabella Tirtowalujo* investigates the multiple framings of the policy problem inherent in the frameworks used to map public policies addressing these issues within the policy document. The chapter analyses the potentials and limitations of the frameworks in addressing the real-life situation, utilising a case involving youth labour force participation. The author folds into the analysis a test case based on findings from a larger ethnographic case study on rural youth overseas work aspirations, foregrounding the role of ethnography in not only informing policy design and evaluation, but also in providing nuances in understanding the issues at hand, with the potential of disrupting dominant framing of the issues.

Examining identities and family backgrounds of the learner, *Novita Sutantoputri, Aries Sutantoputra, Isabella Tirtowalujo, Juliana Murniati*, and *Margaretha Purwanti*'s joint study aims to understand the influence of students' sociocultural backgrounds on their educational motivation and attribution of outcomes. Through a quantitative study involving 1,006 Indonesian students from three public universities, it was found that ethnic and religious backgrounds did not significantly affect educational outcomes, whereas gender significantly affects the extent to which a student exerts themselves academically and the subsequent responses from the community. Culturally relevant pedagogies and role models and aid students in positively increasing their motivation and educational aspirations.

Ila Rosmilawati and David Wright's chapter uniquely highlights the potentials and challenges of the non-formal education system in Indonesia, while illuminating issues in the state of education programs serving marginalised youth populations. The authors examine how the Indonesian equivalency education system mitigates the unfavourable yet profound educational impact internal migration has on migrant youth. This qualitative study interviewed 15 in-migrant adolescents and concluded that their decision to re-enrol into education is influenced by an understanding of their current life situation and desire to improve their future. The authors make the case that a greater flexibility in equivalency programs is required to strategically meet the needs of all students, most of whom are in different stages of education.

Concluding the volume with an investigation of a vision of education that is more sustainable for rural communities, Hasriadi Masalam reflects on educational practices that can initiate self-reliance activities and projects in a rural community. The urban bias and elitist nature of the rural education hidden curriculum contribute to the growing perception among parents to see school as alienating institution and the deskilling of rural youth and their retreat from the agriculture sector. Based on the author's series of Participatory Action Research (PAR) engagements (2006–2011) in a remote mountainous village in South Sulawesi, the eastern part of Indonesia, the PAR participants rethought aspects of current learning and knowledge reproduction practices in their village. The study argues and advocates for the need to address factors contributing to the diminishing of the self-reliant practices and advance collective action and commons in generating rural youth agency.

3   Conclusion and Implication

The collection of recent studies in this edited volume aims to highlight the prospects of existing practices and policies, as well as new knowledge developed through education research.

They serve to further understandings of remaining and anticipated challenges faced by educators, education practitioners, policy-makers, non-governmental entities involved in education development in Indonesia as they manifest in different locals and communities, institutions, as well as within the nation at large. The authors of each chapter also offer future directions and agendas that can enhance and frame current and future dialogues on issues with high practical concern in Indonesia, with potential implications on shaping teacher and school development efforts, and larger educational reform agendas, while adding to current issue-specific bodies of research knowledge.

Notes

1 Primary and secondary data is taken from MoEC (2019) Education Management Information System data available online, and post-secondary data is based on the 2018 Higher Education Statistics Year Book (Ministry of Research, Technology, 2018)
2 Junior secondary completion rate is calculated on the basis of the proportion of youths ages 16–18 years (or 1–3 years above official junior secondary school completion of 15 years), who

have completed junior secondary, suggesting that they entered junior secondary school generally on time and progressed through the education system without excessive delays (UIS, 2019).
3   Senior secondary completion rate is calculated on the basis of the proportion of youths ages 19–21 years (or 1–3 years above official senior secondary school completion of 18 years), who have completed senior secondary, similarly suggesting that they entered senior secondary school generally on time and progressed through without excessive delays (UIS, 2019).
4   The minimum standard competencies set by MoEC is 55. The seven provinces include Yogyakarta, Central Java, Jakarta, East Java, Bali, Bangka Belitung, and West Java.

References

Aisyah, R. (2019, January 18). Indonesia rolls out index to assess progress on Industry 4.0. *The Jakarta Post*. Retrieved from https://www.thejakartapost.com/news/2019/01/18/indonesia-rolls-out-index-to-assess-progress-on-industry-4-0.html

Azali, K. (2015). Boosting youth entrepreneurship in creative industries. *Inside Indonesia, 120*, April–June. Retrieved from https://www.insideindonesia.org/boosting-youth-entrepreneurship-in-creative-industries-2

De Ree, J. J. (2016). *Indonesia – Teacher certification and beyond: An empirical evaluation of the teacher certification program and education quality improvements in Indonesia*. World Bank.

Industry Ministry launches making Indonesia 4.0. (2018, September 2). *The president post (Jakarta, Indonesia)*. Retrieved from https://link.gale.com/apps/doc/A536856337/STND?u=msu_main&sid=STND&xid=e28097ec

Kring, S. A., & Breglia, M. G. (2015). *Jobs and skills for youth: Review of policies for youth employment of Indonesia*. ILO.

Kurniawati, S., Suryadarma, D., Bima, L., & Yusrina, A. (2018). Education in Indonesia: A white elephant? *Journal of Southeast Asian Economies, 35*(2), 185–199. https://doi.org/10.1355/ae35-2e

Manning, C., & Pratomo, D. (2018). Labour market developments in the Jokowi years. *Journal of Southeast Asian Economies, 35*(2), 165–184. https://doi.org/10.1355/ae35-2d

Ministry of Education and Culture [MoEC]. (2016). *7 provinces achieved the best score in 2015 teacher competency test*. Retrieved September 6, 2019, from https://www.kemdikbud.go.id/main/blog/2016/01/7-provinsi-raih-nilai-terbaik-uji-kompetensi-guru-2015

Ministry of Education and Culture [MoEC]. (2019). *The government improves teacher capacity and welfare*. Retrieved September 6, 2019, from https://www.kemdikbud.go.id/main/blog/2019/03/pemerintah-terus-tingkatkan-kapasitas-dan-kesejahteraan-guru

Ministry of Education and Culture [MoEC]. (2020a). Jumlah data satuan pendidikan (sekolah) per provinsi berdasarkan seluruh bentuk pendidikan [Number of schools by province and education level]. *Data Referensi Pendidikan [Education Reference Data]*. Retrieved from https://referensi.data.kemdikbud.go.id/index11.php

Ministry of Education and Culture [MoEC]. (2020b). Jumlah data peserta didik per provinsi berdasarkan seluruh bentuk pendidikan [Number of students by province and education level]. *Data Referensi Pendidikan [Education Reference Data]*. Retrieved from https://referensi.data.kemdikbud.go.id/pd_index.php

Ministry of Education and Culture [MoEC] & UNICEF. (forthcoming). *Laporan Monitoring SDG4 untuk Indonesia [SDG4 Monitoring Report for Indonesia]*. Kemdikbud & UNICEF.

Ministry of Education and Culture [MoEC] & UNICEF. (2018). *SDG4 baseline report for Indonesia*. Kemdikbud & UNICEF.

Ministry of Finance, State Annual Budget Data Portal. (2019). *Anggaran pendidikan, 2010–2019* [Education budget] [Data file]. Retrieved from http://www.data-apbn.kemenkeu.go.id/Dataset/Details/1007

Ministry of National Development Planning/National Development Planning Agency [Bappenas]. (2019). *Republic of Indonesia Voluntary National Reviews (VNR): Empowering people and ensuring inclusiveness and equality*. Jakarta.

Ministry of Research, Technology, and Higher Education [MoRTHE]. (2018). *Higher education statistical year book 2018*. Pusdatin Iptek Dikti, Setjen, Kemristekdikti. https://doi.org/10.1002/chem.200802548

Negara, S. D. (2019, September 1). Indonesia has big plans for education but severely lacks good teachers. *Channel News Asia*. Retrieved from https://www.channelnewsasia.com/news/commentary/indonesia-education-quality-teachers-budget-jokowi-schools-11852570

Picard, N., & Chang, M. (2013). *Will Indonesia's online youth shape 2014 elections?* Retrieved from http://asiafoundation.org/in-asia/2013/10/16/will-indonesias-online-youth-shape-2014-elections/

Statistics Indonesia [Badan Pusat Statistik]. (2019). *Statistik Pemuda Indonesia 2019 [2019 Indonesia Youth Statistics]*. Author.

Suryani, A. (2017). Motivations and aspirations of teacher education students in Indonesia. In H. M. G. Watt, P. W. Richardson, & K. Smith (Eds.), *Global perspectives on teacher motivation* (pp. 248–296). Cambridge University Press.

Suryani, A., Watt, H. M. G., & Richardson, P. W. (2016). Students' motivations to become teachers: FIT-Choice findings from Indonesia. *International Journal of Quantitative Research in Education, 3*(3), 179–203.

Tanu, D. (2014). Engaging Indonesia's youth. In *New perspective on Indonesia*. Perth USAsia Centre.

White, B. (2012). Indonesian rural youth transitions: Employment, mobility and the future of agriculture. In Booth, Manning, & T. K. Wie (Eds.), *Land, livelihood, environment, and the economy in Indonesia: Essays in honour of Joan Hardjono* (pp. 1–14). Yayasan Pustaka Obor Indonesia.

World Bank. (2019). *Doing business 2019: Training for reform: comparing business regulation for domestic firms in 190 economies.* Retrieved from https://www.worldbank.org/content/dam/doingBusiness/media/Annual-Reports/English/DB2019-report_web-version.pdf

PART 1

Teachers and Teaching

∵

CHAPTER 2

Science Teaching Practices in Indonesian Secondary Schools: A Portrait of Educational Quality and Equity-Based on PISA 2015

Anindito Aditomo

Abstract

This study seeks to identify instructional practices which have positive effects on Indonesian students' scientific literacy, and examine whether those practices mitigate the impacts of family socio-cultural-economic background and improve equity. Drawing upon the 2015 cycle of the Programme for International Student Assessment (PISA), this study applies multilevel regression to nationally representative data from 6,513 students from more than 200 schools. Three instructional practices were examined: interactive teaching, inquiry-based learning, and traditional lecture. Interactive teaching is an approach that encourages students to debate and explain their ideas, in combination with teacher explanations of how concepts relate with and can be applied to daily life. The second approach, inquiry-based learning, refers to the use of activities related to scientific investigations which are enacted independently by students. The third approach, traditional lecture, reflects teacher-centred exposition of content. The study finds little difference in the frequency of implementation of these instructional approaches across the types of schools examined. Consistent with constructivist theories, interactive teaching was found to be associated with higher scientific literacy. In contrast, both inquiry and traditional teaching were associated with lower literacy. None of the three instructional approaches moderated the effect of family socio-cultural-economic background on students' scientific literacy.

Keywords

science teaching – international assessment – science literacy – constructivism (learning) – instructional effectiveness

1   Introduction

> Teaching is recognised as among the most important determinants of educational quality. (Muijs et al., 2014)

This chapter discusses teaching quality issue in the context of science education in Indonesian secondary schools. Research on educational effectiveness in developing countries often focuses on input variables such as expenditure, school facilities, and teacher qualifications (Scheerens, 2001). Comparatively few studies examine teaching practices in nationally representative samples of schools and students. To help remedy this gap, this chapter aims to generate insights about what characterises good science teaching in Indonesia.

The issue of teaching quality is addressed from two complementary perspectives. First, good teaching should be positively associated with important learning outcomes. In other words, good teaching is characterised by practices which facilitate the overall level of achievement and other learning outcomes. Second, good teaching can be defined in terms of equity, i.e. effectiveness for students from different Socio-Economic Status (SES). Decades of research has shown that low SES is associated with poorer learning outcomes (Entwisle, Alexander, & Olson, 2010; Sirin, 2005; van Ewijk & Sleegers, 2010). Thus, good teaching should at least be equally effective for all students and in various schools, regardless of their level of SES. Better still would be teaching practices which are especially effective for lower-SES students and schools, thereby reducing the influence of family background on learning outcomes.

This chapter addresses two questions:
1. What kinds of teaching practices are associated with better science achievement in Indonesian secondary schools?
2. Are these practices equally effective for students from various SES backgrounds?

These are addressed by capitalising on the 2015 cycle of the Programme for International Student Assessment (PISA) which provided rich data on teaching practices and students' literacy in science (OECD, 2016b). Before elaborating on this study's method, the following sections clarify what is meant by "teaching", how teaching should relate to science learning, the notion of equity in education, and how teaching may influence educational equity.

1.1   *Dimensions of Teaching*

The practice of teaching is complex and multidimensional. While it can be characterised in various ways, this chapter focuses on three important dimensions: classroom management, emotional climate, and instruction.

This description is based on a framework developed in observational studies of teaching quality in mathematics, but it can be applied to other domains including science (Fauth, Decristan, Rieser, Klieme, & Büttner, 2014; Klieme, Pauli, & Reusser, 2009; Neumann, Kauertz, & Fischer, 2012). I will discuss each dimension briefly, beginning with classroom management.

Classroom management refers to teachers' actions intended to establish and maintain order. Much of early research on teaching focused on classroom management because an orderly classroom was considered to be a pre-requisite for student learning (Brophy, 1983). In a disorderly classroom, teachers are forced to spend more time on controlling disruptions which would divert attention away from the main learning agenda. Orderly classrooms enable students to focus on learning tasks and allow teachers to attend to students who need more individual feedback. In short, the basic assumption is that orderly classrooms can increase "time on task", which should improve students understanding of the content and subsequently influence their achievement.

If classroom management is more about behaviour, emotional climate has more to do with how the classroom is perceived to support students' psychological needs. To create a supportive emotional climate in the classroom, teachers need to attend to three basic needs: autonomy, belongingness, and competence (Deci, Ryan, Vallerand, & Pelletier, 1991; Ryan & Deci, 2000). Autonomy refers to a students' need to feel that they have control over learning activities in the classroom. Belongingness refers to feelings of being safe and of having positive personal relations among students and teachers. Competence has to do with feelings of mastery, of having the ability to accomplish important goals. When students feel that they have autonomy, that they belong to the classroom community, and that they can increase their competencies, they should be engaged and enjoy the learning activities (Ryan & Deci, 2000). The more students are intrinsically engaged, the more likely they are to understand and improve their academic performance.

The third dimension of teaching, instruction, refers to teachers' actions intended to facilitate interactions between students and curriculum content. Traditionally, instruction has meant transmitting or "delivering" content to students. Contemporary theories of learning make clear that this traditional model of instruction is erroneous. Knowledge cannot be transferred from teachers to students. Rather, knowledge must be actively constructed by the student through a process in which new information is made sense of based on prior knowledge (Bransford, Brown, & Cocking, 2000; Derry, 1996). From this constructivist view, instruction can be defined as actions intended to activate cognitive processes which produce learning. Instruction should be effective when it elicits relevant prior knowledge and provides adequate structure/

guidance which help process new information and build deeper, more powerful understandings.

Of these dimensions, classroom management and emotional climate are defined more as domain-general, meaning that good practices associated with them are similar across various subject matter. Instruction has both domain-general and domain-specific aspects. One can use questions to elicit a students' relevant prior knowledge; this is a prime example of a domain-general aspect of good instruction. Educators can also use analogies to help students connect prior knowledge to new information and can be applied across all domains. Yet another method is to provide timely and relevant feedback to help students recognise gaps in their knowledge.

In addition, each subject often has "signature pedagogies" or unique instructional forms. For science, it is instruction that incorporates aspects of scientific inquiry: formulating questions and hypotheses, designing and conducting systematic observations and experiments, as well as collecting and analysing data. Participation in inquiry activities can help students see how abstract concepts can help explain natural phenomena and predict future events (Chinn & Malhotra, 2002; Windschitl, Thompson, & Braaten, 2008). Experimental studies have generally shown that inquiry-based instruction is more effective than more traditional ones (Furtak, Seidel, Iverson, & Briggs, 2016; Lazonder & Harmsen, 2016). However, inquiry activities can pose heavy cognitive load which hamper learning (Aditomo, 2009; Kirschner, Sweller, & Clark, 2006). For inquiry-based instruction to be effective, they need to incorporate adequate structure and guidance, e.g. in the form of conceptual explanations, epistemic scaffolds, or help with group roles and collaborative processes (Hmelo-silver, Duncan, & Chinn, 2007).

1.2 *Educational Equity*

Educational equity is the idea that every student, regardless of their background, has equal right to learn in schools. This implies not only equal opportunity to access education, but also to benefit from schooling. The value of educational equity is closely linked to the ideal of a meritocratic society in which a person's position is determined more by their talent and effort, rather than their family's wealth, occupation, and social standing. Schools are quite often seen to play a critical role to achieve this meritocratic ideal by providing the opportunity for all members of society to acquire the knowledge and skills needed to lead a successful life. In other words, schools should enable poor but talented and hardworking students to climb up the socio-economic ladder.

From this "equal opportunities" perspective, equity can be quantified by estimating the relationship between students' socio-economic status (SES) and some measure of important learning outcomes (most often, achievement test scores which represent the mastery of a curriculum's content). SES is an umbrella concept meant to capture a person's relative position within the social hierarchy. A student's SES is typically operationalised as a composite measure of the parents' level of education and occupational prestige, possession of cultural resources at home, and overall family income and wealth. Many studies indicate that higher SES is associated with higher academic performance at both the student/individual and school/collective levels (Aditomo & Hasugian, 2018; Entwisle et al., 2010; Sirin, 2005; van Ewijk & Sleegers, 2010). The stronger this association, the lower/poorer equity is in an educational system.

Several mechanisms have been proposed to explain the link between SES and academic outcomes at the individual level. First, students from higher SES families tend to have access to more cultural resources at home (De Graaf, De Graaf, & Kraaykamp, 2000; Edgerton & Roberts, 2014). This is more a reflection of "taste" or ways of thinking rather than income or wealth (economic capital). Thus, high SES families invest more in cultural products (e.g. books, news media, encyclopaedia) and experiences (visits to museums, libraries, new places). These things are not necessarily expensive, but they expose children to the academic language and enable them to see the world through the lenses of knowledgeable others. These experiences also cultivate an interest in knowledge and enjoyment of learning, which are important motivational resources for academic life.

Another mechanism has to do with how parents interact with their children. High SES parents tend to engage in more verbal interactions with their infant children. Higher SES parents also often model and encourage ways of thinking and problem solving which are in line with the academic culture (Entwisle et al., 2010). For example, when solving problems together, high SES parents often allow their children to try alternative solutions, provide more specific and positive feedback, use more complex language, and are more receptive to questions (Bee, Van Egeren, Pytkowicz Streissguth, Nyman, & Leckie, 1969; Hess & Shipman, 1965). As a result of such interactions, by the age of 6–7 years, children from high SES families tend to have a larger vocabulary and are more familiar with the ways of talking, thinking, and behaving expected in schools. Compared to lower SES students, they are better prepared to perform in school from the very start. Such early successes further strengthen positive academic self-concept and self-efficacy, as well as foster higher aspirations.

Beyond the family, the wider community and societal contexts also shape socialisation processes in ways which contribute to inequalities in educational outcomes. The influence of these wider contexts is especially pertinent when learning is considered from sociocultural perspectives (Sfard, 1998). According to these perspectives, learning is not so much an individual process of acquiring abstract knowledge, but more a process of enculturation into communities of practice. Learning to participate in the academic practices valued at school entails seeing one's self as a (future) scientist, mathematician, literary critique, etc. Without the development of such identities and aspirations, schoolwork tends to be experienced as mechanical chores which are bereft of meaning. This observation is crucial for the present discussion; that the development of academic identities is facilitated and constrained by the kinds of cultural resources that are available in a student's home and wider community (Esmonde, 2009; Sirin, Diemer, Jackson, & Howell, 2004). One can surmise that this process would be considerably more difficult for students coming from low SES communities; that they would be unfamiliar with professions that require higher levels of academic knowledge (professors, scientists, lawyers, etc.).

At the school level, at least two mechanisms have been proposed to explain why high SES schools tend to perform better than lower SES ones (Armor, Marks, & Malatinszky, 2018; van Ewijk & Sleegers, 2010).

The first mechanism operates through school or institutional factors. In higher SES schools, parents can provide more financial contributions and also exert higher academic expectations, which in turn improve the school resources, teacher qualifications, and curriculum/teaching quality (Agirdag, 2018; Agirdag, Van Houtte, & Van Avermaet, 2012).

The second mechanism operates through factors related to student characteristics. Students in lower SES schools have, on average, lower aspirations, motivation, and academic self-concept. Overall, this tends to create a poor academic climate which drags down students who may have initially high motivation/aspirations/self-concept. Conversely, peer pressure and competition may encourage students with initially lower motivation to work harder and adopt better learning strategies.

Studies have confirmed that there is a positive association between school SES and student achievement (van Ewijk & Sleegers, 2010). Based on cross-sectional data from Programme for International Student Assessment (PISA) and (Trends in International Mathematics and Science Study) TIMSS, school SES composition is estimated to have a moderate effect on achievement in many countries. For example, an analysis of 28 countries in PISA 2003 found substantial effects of a school's SES using a composite score (reflecting the combination of various indicators such as parental education, home cultural resources, and overall wealth) (Liu, Van Damme, Gielen, & Van Den Noortgate, 2015). An analysis of the TIMSS 2003 data showed that school-level SES still predicts math scores even after controlling individual differences in motivation and family SES (Dumay & Dupriez, 2007). Longitudinal studies, which take into account prior achievement, indicate the effect of school SES on performance from cross-sectional studies may be over-estimated, but still significant (Dumay & Dupriez, 2008; Rjosk et al., 2014).

1.3 Teaching and Educational Equity

Good teaching practices are defined as practices that reliably facilitate student learning. As described previously, with regards to classroom management this refers to practices which create an orderly climate where students can focus on learning-related activities. With regards to emotional climate, good teaching refers to practices which fulfil students' needs for autonomy, belongingness, and competence. With regards to instruction, good teaching is reflected in practices which elicit relevant prior knowledge and provide the necessary structure to help students make sense of new information.

Furthermore, good teaching should be effective for all students in all schools, regardless of their SES background. The relevant question here is whether there are reasons to suggest that the effects of teaching depend on students' SES. With regards to classroom management, theoretical considerations suggest that an orderly classroom is a prerequisite for learning and thus should benefit all students (Brophy, 1983; Emmer & Stough, 2001). Similarly, because autonomy, belongingness and competence are regarded as universal psychological needs (Ryan & Deci, 2000), a supportive emotional climate should also benefit students from different SES backgrounds. However, a recent review suggests that a positive emotional climate may benefit lower SES students more than for their affluent peers (Berkowitz, Moore, Astor, & Benbenishty, 2017).

A few studies have suggested that student-centred instruction may benefit students from affluent families but can be detrimental for lower SES students (Andersen & Andersen, 2017). This argument is based upon sociological theories regarding the incompatibility between the school's linguistic/cultural codes and the linguistic/cultural codes of lower SES families (Sadovnik, 1991). According to this argument, student-centred instruction represents an "invisible pedagogy" in which norms, expectations, and criteria of evaluation are rendered implicit to encourage students to self-regulate their learning. This may benefit high SES students because they are more intrinsically motivated and already possess the necessary dispositions for academic self-regulation. However, students from low SES backgrounds may fail to profit from student-centred instruction as they lack these dispositions. Andersen and Andersen (2017) found that student-centred instruction is negatively associated with mathematics achievement among low SES Norwegian high school students, but not among their higher SES peers.

Unfortunately, there is scant research on how instructional effects are influenced by students' SES. Moreover, the research results are inconsistent. Contrary to the findings of Andersen and Andersen (2017), a study of kindergarten students in the US found that student-centred group/collaborative learning methods are effective in increasing math achievement, regardless of SES background, and even reduced the SES gap among African-American students (Bodovski & Farkas, 2007). Thus, the current study is designed to contribute by examining this issue in the context of science learning in Indonesia.

1.4   The Current Study

To investigate links between teaching, SES, and science learning outcome, this study utilises the Indonesian sample from PISA 2015. Coordinated by the Organisation for Economic Cooperation and Development (OECD), PISA is a tri-annual international study which assesses reading, math, and science literacy among 15-year-old students in participating countries. PISA also collects data on a student's background, their school characteristics and educational processes (including teaching practices) for a target domain. In 2015, the target domain was science (OECD, 2016b).

For PISA 2015, science literacy referred to a students' ability to understand and reason using scientific concepts and information to solve problems in various contexts. This definition was driven by PISA's interest in how well education prepares young people to participate in the 21st-century economy and society. Consequently, PISA's cognitive tests are not tied to (school) curriculum content; rather, they are based on contexts relevant to contemporary issues and problems.

As for teaching practices, this study examines PISA data which reflects on classroom management, emotional climate, and the four instructional practices (teacher feedback, teacher-directed instruction, interactive instruction, and inquiry-based instruction). These dimensions were assessed from the students' perception, i.e. by asking students to report their feelings, thoughts, or experiences of certain classroom activities. The use of student perceptions to assess teaching quality has advantages, especially regarding efficiency. Compared to collecting observational data, assessing students' perceptions is much cheaper and quicker. In addition, student perception is arguably the most appropriate source of information regarding a classroom's teaching climate. On the other hand, students can only be asked to report observable events; they cannot comment on things like pedagogical intent which drives certain learning tasks. Overall, student perceptions of teaching produce useful and reliable data (Lüdtke, Trautwein, Kunter, & Baumert, 2006).

2 Method

2.1 *Participants*

PISA adopts a two-stage stratified sampling strategy. First, schools are randomly sampled from a list of schools in each participating country. Second, around 30 students are sampled randomly from a list of 15-year old students enrolled in each school. For Indonesia in 2015, this resulted in a sample of 6,513 students (51.3% female) from 236 schools (see Table 2.1). Data were obtained from the PISA database website.[1] The average sample size in each school was 27.60 students.

TABLE 2.1   Number of participants

School type		Students	School
Level	Junior secondary (SMP)	3,116	118
	Senior secondary (SMA)	3,397	116
Status	Public	4,032	131
	Private	2,481	105
	TOTAL	6,513	236

2.2 *Learning Outcome Variables*

2.2.1 Science Literacy

Science literacy is the ability to use science concepts to explain natural phenomena, to design and evaluate scientific inquiry, and to interpret data in a scientific method (OECD, 2016a). Combining multiple-choice and open-ended questions, the PISA science literacy test contains items referring to problems related to health, natural resources, environmental quality, hazards, and frontiers in science and technology. The test (as well as all background questionnaires) was translated into Bahasa Indonesia. Item-response theory scoring procedures were applied by the OECD to yield 10 plausible values representing each student's science literacy (OECD, 2016b). The scores were scaled to have a mean value of 500 (across the OECD countries) and a standard deviation of 100. Values below 500 indicate literacy levels below that of the average student in OECD countries.

2.3 *Predictor Variables*

2.3.1 Classroom Management

Classroom management refers to the extent to which the classroom environment is orderly enabling students to concentrate on learning activities. It is measured using 5 items with response options from 1 = "Every lesson" to 4 = "Never or hardly ever".

Example item: "There are noise and disorder". Reliability (alpha) was 0.77.

2.3.2 Emotional Support

Emotional support reflects the extent to which students feel emotionally supported by the teacher to succeed in their learning. It is measured using 5 items with response options from 1 = "Hardly ever" to 4 = "In all lessons".

Example items: "The teacher shows interest in every student's learning" and "Teacher allows expressing opinions". Reliability (alpha) was 0.69.

2.3.3 Teacher-Directed Instruction

Teacher-directed instruction reflects a form of lecturing in which the teacher provides explanations and discusses students' questions. It is measured using 4 items with response options from 1 = "Never or almost never" to 4 = "Every lesson or almost every lesson". The items were:
- The teacher explains scientific ideas.
- The teacher demonstrates an idea.
- The teacher discusses our questions.
- A whole-class discussion takes place with the teacher.

Reliability (alpha) was 0.70.

2.3.4 Interactive Instruction

Interactive instruction refers to an interactive form of concept-focused instruction that combines teacher explanations (about how science ideas are relevant and can be applied) with student explanations and argumentation. While indicators of Teacher-directed Instruction are activities which are controlled or led by the teacher, indicators of Interactive Instruction include student-centred activities. Interactive Instruction was measured using 4 items with response options from 1 = "Never" to 4 = "In all lessons". The items were:
- The teacher explains how <school science> idea can be applied.
- Students are given opportunities to explain their ideas.
- The teachers clearly explain the relevance of science concepts to our lives.
- Students are required to argue about science questions.

Reliability (alpha) was 0.68.

2.3.5 Inquiry-Based Instruction

Inquiry-based instruction illustrates the implementation of inquiry activities (conducting and debating experiments/investigations) performed independently by students, without a teachers' guidance. It is measured using 5 items also with response options from 1 = "Never" to 4 = "In all lessons". An example item is "Students are allowed to design their experiments". Reliability (alpha) was 0.70.

2.3.6 Teacher Feedback

Teacher feedback describes the feedback students received from their science teacher regarding performance, areas of strength, areas of improvement, and how to progress. It is measured by 4 items with response options from 1 = "Never or almost never" to 4 = " Every lesson or almost every lesson". An example item is "The teacher tells me how I can improve my performance". Reliability (alpha) was 0.79.

2.3.7 Socio-Economic Status (SES)

Socio-economic status reflects parents' highest level of education, occupational prestige, cultural possessions at home, and overall family wealth. Scores were IRT-scaled by the OECD. A value of zero represents the average SES of students from OECD countries.

2.4 *Control Variables*

2.4.1 Motivation

Instrumental motivation refers to students' perceptions regarding the utility of learning science. It is measured using four items with response options from 1 = "Strongly agree" to 4 = "Strongly disagree". Scores were reversed so that higher scores reflect stronger motivation. An example item is "Many things I learn in my <school science> subject(s) will help me to get a job". Internal reliability (alpha) was 0.98.

2.4.2 Grade Repetition

Grade repetition measures whether a student has repeated a grade (0 = "No", 1 = "Yes"). Grade repetition, in most cases, indicates the failure to perform at the required level at a certain grade.

2.4.3 School Level

School level differentiates between junior secondary (SMP) and senior secondary schooling (SMA). Senior-secondary students in the sample, on average, have one-year additional schooling compared to junior-secondary students.

2.4.4 School Status

School status differentiates between private and public (government-owned) schools.

2.5 *Analysis*

Multilevel modelling (hierarchical linear regression) was employed to account for the clustered nature of the data (Hox, 2010). SES, teaching variables, and science literacy were treated at both the student (L1) and second levels (L2) of analyses. At L1, scores represent individual differences between students in the same school. Thus, L1 instructional practices reflect differences in how often students (from the same school) experienced each form of instruction (e.g. inquiry-based instruction). Individual differences in the experience of instruction are possible because students in one school come from different classes and may be taught by different science teachers. L1 classroom discipline and emotional climate represent individual differences in perceptions of the classroom environment. Such variation is possible because each student may have different perceptions about the quality of discipline and support a teacher/classroom provides. At L2, variance in these variables represent differences between schools in average levels of each variable.

Multilevel modelling was implemented using the CLUSTER and TYPE = TWOLEVEL options in Mplus v.8 (Muthén & Muthén, 2017). The final student weight provided by the OECD was incorporated to account for sampling bias due to stratification. All analyses to predict science literacy were performed 10 times (each of the 10 plausible values) and integrated through Mplus' TYPE = IMPUTATION data command. To help control for individual differences which may influence students' science literacy, motivation and grade repetition were included as covariates at L1. In addition, school level (junior vs. senior secondary) and type (public vs. private) were used as control variables at L2.

In summary, the following models were analysed. The first research question is addressed by Model 3, while the second question by Models 4a–f.
- Null model (no predictors)
- Model 1: motivation, grade repetition, senior secondary school, and private school
- Model 2: all predictors in Model 1 + SES
- Model 3: all predictors in Model 1 + SES + teaching variables
- Model 4a–f: all predictors in Model 1 + SES + teaching variables + interaction term

To facilitate interpretation, interactions between SES and teaching were tested separately for each teaching dimension (thus the six sub-models in Model 4). SES and teaching dimensions examined for their interaction were centred at the grand mean.

3 Findings

Descriptive statistics for SES, teaching variables and covariates are displayed in Table 2.2. The low SES scores indicate the sample's position compared to the average student from OECD countries.

TABLE 2.2   Descriptive statistics

Variable	Minimum	Maximum	Mean	Std. Dev.
Main predictors				
SES	−5.5762	1.8734	−1.79	1.11
Interactive instruction	1	4	2.86	0.65
Inquiry-based instruction	1	4	2.03	0.60
Teacher-directed instruction	1	4	2.42	0.65
Teacher feedback	1	4	2.27	0.67
Emotional support	1	4	3.11	0.59
Classroom management	1	4	3.08	0.60
Covariates				
Motivation	1	4	1.69	0.56
Grade repetition	0	1	0.14	0.35

Zero-order correlations between predictors are displayed in Table 2.3. The correlation strengths are mostly weak to moderate. The strongest correlation is between interactive instruction and inquiry-based instruction, most likely because both constructs reflect instruction which involves student-centred activities. Nonetheless, the size of the correlation (0.495) suggests that they can be differentiated and should not pose multicollinearity problems for the regression models.

3.1   *Multilevel Modelling*

Based on the null model, the student level variance was estimated at 2749.617, while the school level variance was 1946.842. This resulted in an Intraclass Correlation (ICC) of 0.422, indicating that a substantial portion (42.2%) of the variation in science literacy existed at the school level. Meanwhile, the intercept, reflecting the average science literacy score—was estimated at 405.747.

Standardised coefficients, standard errors, and p values from subsequent models are displayed in Table 2.4. Models 1 and 2 show the effects of the

TABLE 2.3   Inter-correlations between predictor variables

Variable	SES	Interact.	Inquiry	T. dir.	T. feed.	Em. sup	Class. M	Motiv.
SES								
Interact. inst.	0.065**							
Inquiry. inst.	0.061**	0.495**						
Teach-dir. inst.	0.066**	0.286**	0.278**					
Teacher feed.	−0.052**	0.250**	0.266**	0.395**				
Emot. support	0.038**	0.494**	0.347**	0.280**	0.278**			
Class. manag.	−0.012	−0.023	−0.087**	0.078**	0.053**	0.029*		
Motivation	−0.022	−.138**	−0.089**	−0.091**	−0.088**	−0.147**	−0.037**	
Grade rep.	−0.174**	0.009	0.061**	0.014	0.050**	−0.023	−0.075**	0.002

** $p < 0.01$; * $p < 0.05$

covariates and SES on a students' science literacy. As predicted, SES is associated with better performance at the student and school levels. Students who repeated grades tended to perform worse, while those who report stronger motivation tended to perform better. Senior secondary schools exhibited higher scores compared to junior secondary schools. Private schools on average had lower scores than public ones.

3.1.1   Main Effects of Teaching Practices (Research Question 1)

The effects of teaching practices are revealed in Model 3. Two practices were associated with higher science literacy at the individual and school levels: classroom management and interactive instruction. Inquiry-based instruction was associated with lower literacy also at both levels of analysis. Teacher-directed instruction and feedback were both negatively associated with literacy at the individual level. Emotional support was also negatively associated with literacy but at the school level.

3.1.2   Interaction between Teaching and SES (Research Question 2)

The interaction terms from Models 4a-f are displayed in Table 2.5. Only the interaction between interactive instruction and SES was found to be significant at the school level (Model 4a, complete results from this model is shown in Table 2.4). The positive value of the interaction indicates that the association between interactive instruction and science literacy becomes

TABLE 2.4 Results of the multilevel models predicting students' science literacy; number represent standardised coefficients, standard errors, and p values (1-tailed)

Predictors	Model 1			Model 2			Model 3			Model 4a: Interactive X SES		
	Estimate	s.e.	p	Estimate	s.e.	p	Estimate	s.e.	p	Estimate	s.e.	p
L1: Student level												
Grade repetition	−0.151	0.018	0.000	−0.146	0.018	0.000	−0.122	0.018	0.000	−0.121	0.018	0.000
Motivation	0.053	0.015	0.000	0.052	0.015	0.000	0.054	0.016	0.001	0.054	0.016	0.000
SES	—	—	—	0.068	0.015	0.000	0.078	0.016	0.000	0.078	0.016	0.000
Interactive instruction	—	—	—	—	—	—	0.118	0.018	0.000	0.118	0.018	0.000
Inquiry-based instruction	—	—	—	—	—	—	−0.166	0.021	0.000	−0.167	0.021	0.000
Teacher-directed instruction	—	—	—	—	—	—	−0.031	0.019	0.048	−0.031	0.019	0.050
Teacher feedback	—	—	—	—	—	—	−0.084	0.016	0.000	−0.083	0.016	0.000
Classroom management	—	—	—	—	—	—	0.092	0.019	0.000	0.092	0.019	0.000
Emotional support	—	—	—	—	—	—	0.008	0.020	0.349	0.008	0.020	0.342
Interaction term	—	—	—	—	—	—	—	—	—	−0.009	0.016	0.295
L2: School level												
Senior secondary	0.381	0.058	0.000	0.100	0.053	0.029	0.092	0.053	0.044	0.157	0.065	0.008

(*cont.*)

TABLE 2.4 Results of the multilevel models predicting students' science literacy; number represent standardised coefficients, standard errors, and p values (1-tailed) (Cont.)

Predictors	Model 1			Model 2			Model 3			Model 4a: Interactive X SES		
	Estimate	s.e.	p	Estimate	s.e.	p	Estimate	s.e.	p	Estimate	s.e.	p
Private school	−0.218	0.064	0.000	−0.180	0.050	0.000	−0.207	0.053	0.000	−0.220	0.055	0.000
SES	—	—	—	0.682	0.047	0.000	0.580	0.076	0.000	0.568	0.076	0.000
Interactive instruction	—	—	—	—	—	—	0.313	0.16	0.028	0.449	0.189	0.009
Inquiry-based instruction	—	—	—	—	—	—	−0.365	0.112	0.001	−0.478	0.129	0.000
Teacher-directed instruction	—	—	—	—	—	—	−0.108	0.122	0.187	0.188	0.224	0.200
Teacher feedback	—	—	—	—	—	—	−27.15	30.60	0.190	−0.113	0.124	0.183
Classroom management	—	—	—	—	—	—	0.200	0.058	0.001	0.159	0.063	0.006
Emotional support	—	—	—	—	—	—	−0.214	0.097	0.014	−0.184	0.100	0.033
Interaction term	—	—	—	—	—	—	—	—	—	0.231	0.139	0.043
Explained variance												
L1 (student level)	2.6%			3.0%			7.2%			7.2%		
L2 (school level)	18.0%			56.6%			75.4%			79.1%		

Note: Values in bold indicate statistically significant estimates ($p < 0.05$)

SCIENCE TEACHING PRACTICES IN INDONESIAN SECONDARY SCHOOLS

TABLE 2.5   Interaction between teaching and SES (Models 4a–f)

Interaction term	Estimate	s.e.	p
L1 (*Student level*)			
a. Interactive inst. X SES	−0.009	0.016	0.295
b. Inq.based inst. X SES	0.000	0.017	0.493
c. Teacher-dir. inst. X SES	−0.013	0.015	0.184
d. Teacher feedback X SES	−0.023	0.016	0.174
e. Classroom manag. X SES	−0.014	0.014	0.167
f. Emotional support X SES	−0.019	0.015	0.104
L2 (*School level*)			
a. Interactive inst. X SES	**0.231**	**0.139**	**0.043**
b. Inq.based inst. X SES	0.050	0.062	0.210
c. Teacher-dir. inst. X SES	0.164	0.109	0.065
d. Teacher feedback X SES	−0.047	0.089	0.299
e. Classroom manag. X SES	0.025	0.079	0.375
f. Emotional support X SES	0.013	0.073	0.429

Note: Values in bold indicate statistically significant estimates ($p < 0.05$)

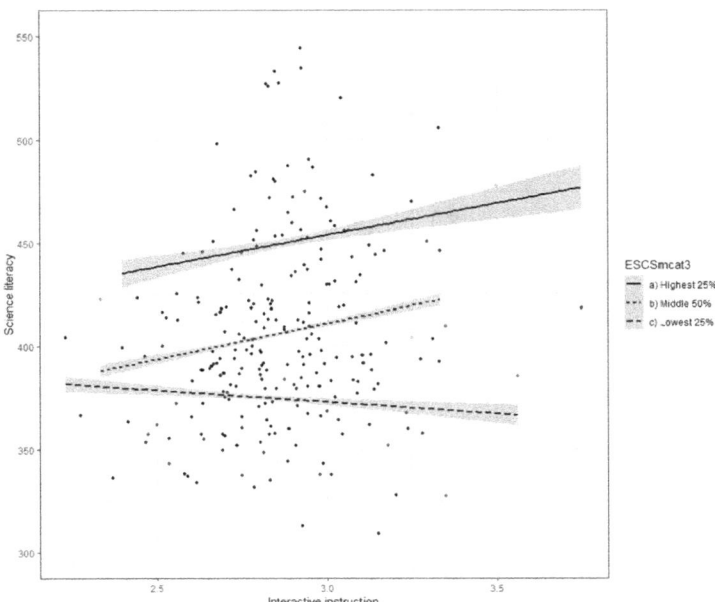

FIGURE 2.1   Regression lines for schools at the highest 25%, middle 50%, and the lowest 25% SES quartile, with 95% confidence intervals

stronger as school SES increases. Put differently, interactive instruction is more effective among higher SES schools than lower SES ones, as illustrated in Figure 2.1.

4 Discussion

This study seeks to generate evidence-based insights regarding good science teaching practices in Indonesian secondary schools. More specifically, two questions were addressed, the first regarding associations between teaching and learning outcomes generally, and the second regarding whether teaching interacts with students' family background (SES).

4.1 Associations between Teaching Practices and Learning Outcome

Controlling for individual differences in the family background (SES), motivation, and grade repetition, two teaching practices were found to be associated with higher learning outcomes at both the student and school levels: classroom management and interactive instruction. Thus, within the same school, students who reported that their science lessons were orderly also tended to perform better at PISA's science literacy test. Schools where students reported experiencing more orderly science lessons also showed higher than average performance compared to other schools. Similarly, within the same school, students who reported to have experienced more interactive science instruction tended to obtain better science literacy scores. Schools where students reported higher frequencies of interactive science instruction also performed better than other schools in PISA's science literacy test. These findings are consistent with prior research as well as with contemporary theories of learning.

Conversely, inquiry-based instruction was found to be negatively associated with science literacy at both the student and school levels. This finding is consistent with previous studies based on large-scale assessments of learning such as PISA and TIMSS. Given the strong emphasis on the use of inquiry in contemporary science education reforms, this may seem disconcerting (Sjøberg, 2018). However, it is useful to note that inquiry-based instruction in this study refers to unstructured or unguided inquiry activities; that the five items forming the inquiry-based instruction variable in this study referred to student-led activities without reference to any teacher or expert guidance. From a cognitive theory perspective, unstructured inquiry posed a heavy cognitive load, much of which may not be relevant for learning about the intended content (Kirschner et al., 2006; Mayer, 2004). Thus, the negative association between unguided inquiry activities and science literacy is to be expected. It does not mean that inquiry-based science instruction should be abandoned. Indeed, there is strong evidence to suggest that guided inquiry approaches are effective to foster science learning (Furtak et al., 2016; Lazonder & Harmsen, 2016).

Teacher-directed instruction, teacher feedback, and emotional support were also associated with lower science literacy at either the student or school level. Teacher-directed instruction refers to a teacher-centred, content-focused approach. It was found to be associated with lower science literacy only at the student level, and only affected a small percentage of students. That is to say, within the same school, students who reported experiencing more teacher-directed instruction also tended to obtain slightly lower scores on PISA's science literacy test. From a constructivist perspective, this negative association is unsurprising: learning occurs when learners are prompted/facilitated to actively process new information (Bransford et al., 2000; Derry, 1996). Thus, instruction which emphasises the delivery of content from teacher to student is unlikely to be effective.

The other negative associations between teaching practices and learning outcomes observed in this study are unexpected and more difficult to explain theoretically. Teacher feedback during instruction was found to be associated with lower science literacy at the individual level. Thus, within the same school, students who often received feedback regarding their performance and areas of improvement also tended to obtain lower science literacy scores. Given the strong body of research showing that feedback facilitates learning, it seems imprudent to conclude that the provision of feedback by Indonesian science teachers is detrimental. Another possibility for this negative association is that teachers tended to provide more individual feedback for students with lower science abilities. In other words, it is a students' prior abilities which prompted teachers to provide more frequent feedback. Further research, preferably utilising longitudinal or experimental designs, would need to be conducted to examine this possibility.

Emotional support was also found to be related to lower science literacy but at the school level. Schools with more positive emotional climate tended to perform poorly in PISA's science literacy test compared to other schools. Again, it would be hasty to conclude that Indonesian science teachers should refrain from creating a positive emotional climate in their classrooms (Becker & Luthar, 2002; Good, Wiley, & Florez, 2009). A closer examination of PISA's emotional support items ("the teacher gives extra help" or "the teacher continues teaching until students understand") suggest that this variable may reflect teachers' perception of students' learning needs. Similar to the provision of individual feedback, teachers may feel a stronger need to provide emotional support when teaching students with lower abilities; longitudinal and/or experimental research is needed to be conducted to test this conjecture.

4.2 Teaching and Educational Equity

Good teaching should be effective for all students, regardless of their family background. In technical terms, this condition would be reflected in a non-significant interaction between teaching practice and a students' SES. Of the two teaching practices found to associate positively with science literacy, only classroom management met this criterion. Findings in the same school showed that students who reported experiencing an orderly "better managed" science lesson (regardless of their SES background) tended to perform better than their peers. This was also true at the school level: classroom management is positively associated with school performance, regardless of the school's SES composition.

As illustrated in Figure 2.1, an increased frequency of interactive instruction is directly linked to better performance in schools catering to students from the mid to high SES backgrounds. However, this is not so with students from low SES backgrounds; the study shows that interactive instruction did not seem to add to an improved learning outcome. One can safely assume that unlike their peers in higher SES schools, students attending low SES schools fail to benefit from interactive science instruction.

While unfortunate, this finding is to be expected; social stratification theories have long suggested that schools play an important role in reproducing inequalities between socio-economic classes (Collins, 2009). One proposed mechanism involves discussing how instruction is experienced by students from different social classes (Sadovnik, 1991). The academic culture that is dominant in many schools is often incongruent with the dispositions and identities of students from disadvantaged families. Compared to peers from more advantaged backgrounds, these students are often less interested in academic subjects, less confident in their academic ability, have poorer study skills, and possess incongruent beliefs about the kinds of expected behaviour in class. In addition, they may also perceive that educational institutions favour their wealthier peers and hence tend to adopt lower academic aspirations (e.g. obtaining vocational as opposed to academic degrees). Due to these reasons, students from lower SES families may be less prepared and less willing to take initiative and participate actively in the context of interactive instruction, which requires students to express their ideas and engage in argumentation about science questions.

5 Implications for Practice and Future Research

This study highlights the importance of classroom management to create an orderly climate for learning to occur. How can teachers create orderly classrooms? Emmer and Stough (2001, p. 105) identified two principles which underlie good classroom management. First, classroom management should be preventive rather than reactive. Desirable and undesirable behaviours need to be made clear to students at the start of a school year. In other words, classroom rules need to be established at the outset, and not made up on the fly in response to specific events. Second, desirable behaviours need to be explicitly taught: students need help to understand, adhere to, and enact classroom rules. This can also involve careful monitoring so that problematic behaviours can be detected and addressed before they become entrenched (Emmer & Stough, 2001).

It needs to be noted that classroom management should not be equated with a controlling style of teaching. The notion of classroom management has evolved from an authoritarian view which emphasises teacher control over student behaviour, to more egalitarian views which emphasise student involvement in co-constructing a climate conducive for learning (Egeberg, Mcconney, & Price, 2016). In this more contemporary perspective, classroom management is implemented in a participatory manner (e.g. by involving students in formulating classroom rules and help monitor their implementation). Orderly behaviour is considered to be a by-product of an underlying positive emotional climate and intellectually stimulating instruction. To generate appropriate guidelines and professional development related to effective classroom management, more in-depth research in the Indonesian context is needed.

With regards to instruction, on the one hand, the current findings should caution against using unstructured or unguided inquiry activities. Asking students to independently perform science experiments or investigations may seem like a good, student-centred teaching practice. However, student-centred teaching should not be translated as simply allowing students to perform complex activities without scaffolding. Without proper structure and guidance, students will tend to enact inquiry in a hands-on manner, without processing the underlying science concepts. This is not to say that a more traditional style of instruction is the antidote. Instruction which emphasises content delivery through teacher-centred lectures was found to be ineffective (and even slightly negatively associated with poorer learning).

What should be promoted as good teaching is what I refer to as "interactive instruction", a style of instruction which combines teacher explanations with student-centred discussions and argumentation. More specifically, rather than focus on abstract definitions (declarative knowledge per se), the teacher explanations in interactive instruction focus on how science concepts relate to everyday life, on how they can be applied to understand familiar phenomena and solve important problems. Furthermore, interactive instruction involves allowing students to explain their ideas about science, and to argue about science questions. Thus, to implement interactive instruction, teachers need to value students' ideas, to be skilled at eliciting and productively responding to those ideas. Teachers also need to value and understand science argumentation as a learning method. These needs should be prime targets for professional development programs intended for the science teacher.

This study also indicates that while interactive instruction seems to be effective for middle and high SES schools, it is less so for students in low SES schools. In other words, the implementation of interactive instruction does little to rectify the achievement gap between rich and poor secondary school students in Indonesia. Social stratification theories propose that students often lack the dispositions required to benefit from instruction that demands active participation and initiative. Further research should investigate this issue to examine the interaction between family SES, student dispositions, and experiences of instruction in the Indonesian context. A deeper understanding of the underlying mechanism would be useful for teachers, school managers, and policymakers who wish to address the issue of educational inequity.

6   Limitations and Conclusions

As a secondary analysis, the current study is constrained by the characteristics of the primary study. In this case, the cross-sectional nature of PISA data prevents causal inferences to be made regarding the effects of teaching. Even so, the current analysis yielded some findings which are theoretically and practically meaningful. In particular, classroom management and interactive instruction emerged as practices which were associated with higher science literacy, both at the individual/student and collective/school levels. Furthermore, the findings also highlight the challenge of addressing educational inequality by showing that students from disadvantaged families may need additional support to benefit from science instruction at school. On the flip side, instructional practices which seem to be effective in general (i.e. interactive instruction) need to be adjusted to make it beneficial for all students regardless of their socioeconomic background.

Acknowledgements

I would like to thank the Alexander von Humboldt Foundation for supporting this research. I would also like to thank Dr. Nina Jude and Dr. Nina Roczen for suggestions regarding data analysis, as well as Professor Dr. Eckhard Klieme for supporting my stay at the Leibniz Institute of Research and Information on Education, Frankfurt, Germany.

Note

1 See http://www.oecd.org/pisa/data/2015database/

References

Aditomo, A. (2009). Cognitive load theory and mathematics learning: A systematic review. *Indonesian Psychological Journal, 24*(3), 207–217.

Aditomo, A., & Hasugian, E. J. (2018). Indonesian adolescents' EFL reading comprehension: Gender differences and the influence of parental background. *Indonesian Journal of Applied Linguistics, 8*(2), 325–335. https://doi.org/10.17509/ijal.v8i2.13279

Agirdag, O. (2018). The impact of school SES composition on science achievement and achievement growth: Mediating role of teachers' teachability culture. *Educational Research and Evaluation, 24*(3–5), 264–276. https://doi.org/10.1080/13803611.2018.1550838

Agirdag, O., Van Houtte, M., & Van Avermaet, P. (2012). Why does the ethnic and socio-economic composition of schools influence math achievement? The role of sense of futility and futility culture. *European Sociological Review, 28*(3), 366–378. https://doi.org/10.1093/esr/jcq070

Andersen, I. G., & Andersen, S. C. (2017). Student-centered instruction and academic achievement: Linking mechanisms of educational inequality to schools' instructional strategy. *British Journal of Sociology of Education, 38*(4), 533–550. https://doi.org/10.1080/01425692.2015.1093409

Armor, D. J., Marks, G. N., & Malatinszky, A. (2018). The impact of school SES on student achievement: evidence from U.S. statewide achievement data. *Educational Evaluation and Policy Analysis, 40*(4), https://doi.org/10.3102/0162373718787917

Becker, B. E., & Luthar, S. S. (2002). Social-emotional factors affecting academic outcomes among disadvantaged students: Closing the achievement gap. *Educational Psychologist, 27*(4), 197–214. https://doi.org/10.1207/S15326985EP3704

Bee, H. L., Van Egeren, L. F., Pytkowicz Streissguth, A., Nyman, B. A., & Leckie, M. S. (1969). Social class differences in maternal teaching strategies and speech patterns. *Developmental Psychology, 1*(6), 726–734. https://doi.org/10.1037/h0028257

Berkowitz, R., Moore, H., Astor, R. A., & Benbenishty, R. (2017). A research synthesis of the associations between socioeconomic background, inequality, school climate, and academic achievement. *Review of Educational Research, 87*(2), 425–469. https://doi.org/10.3102/0034654316669821

Bodovski, K., & Farkas, G. (2007). Do instructional practices contribute to inequality in achievement? The case of mathematics instruction in kindergarten. *Journal of Early Childhood Research, 5*(3), 301–322. https://doi.org/10.1177/1476718X07080476

Bransford, J. D., Brown, A. L., & Cocking, R. R. (Eds.). (2000). *How people learn: Brain, mind, experience, and school*. National Academies Press.

Brophy, J. E. (1983). Classroom organisation and management. *The Elementary School Journal, 83*(4), 265–285. https://doi.org/10.1086/461318

Chinn, C. A., & Malhotra, B. A. (2002). Epistemologically authentic inquiry in schools: A theoretical framework for evaluating inquiry tasks. *Science Education, 86*, 175–218. https://doi.org/10.1002/sce.10001

Collins, J. (2009). Social reproduction in classrooms and schools. *Annual Review of Anthropology, 38*, 33–48. https://doi.org/10.1146/annurev.anthro.37.081407.085242

Deci, E. L., Ryan, R. M., Vallerand, R. J., & Pelletier, L. G. (1991). Motivation and education: The self-determination perspective. *Educational Psychologist, 26*(3–4), 325–346. https://doi.org/10.1080/00461520.1991.9653137

De Graaf, N. D., De Graaf, P. M., & Kraaykamp, G. (2000). Parental cultural capital and educational attainment in the Netherlands: A refinement of the cultural capital perspective. *Sociology of Education, 73*, 92–111.

Derry, S. J. (1996). Cognitive schema theory in the constructivist debate. *Educational Psychologist, 31*(3–4), 163–174. https://doi.org/10.1080/00461520.1996.9653264

Dumay, X., & Dupriez, V. (2007). Accounting for class effect using the TIMSS 2003 eighth-grade database: Net effect of group composition, net effect of class process, and joint effect. *School Effectiveness and School Improvement, 18*(4), 383–408. https://doi.org/10.1080/09243450601146371

Dumay, X., & Dupriez, V. (2008). Does the school composition effect matter? Evidence from Belgian data. *British Journal of Educational Studies, 56*(4), 440–477. https://doi.org/10.1111/j.1467-8527.2008.00418.x

Edgerton, J. D., & Roberts, L. W. (2014). Cultural capital or habitus? Bourdieu and beyond in the explanation of enduring educational inequality. *Theory and Research in Education, 12*(2), 193–220. https://doi.org/10.1177/1477878514530231

Egeberg, H. M., Mcconney, A., & Price, A. (2016). Classroom management and national professional standards for teachers: A review of the literature on theory and practice. *Australian Journal of Teacher Education, 41*(7), 1–18.

Emmer, E. T., & Stough, L. M. (2001). Classroom management: A critical part of educational psychology, with implications for teacher education. *Educational Psychologist, 36*(2), 103–112. https://doi.org/10.1207/S15326985EP3602

Entwisle, D. R., Alexander, K. L., & Olson, L. S. (2010). Socioeconomic status: Its broad sweep and long reach in education. In J. L. Meece & J. S. Eccles (Eds.), *Handbook of research on schools, schooling, and human development* (pp. 237–255). Routledge.

Esmonde, I. (2009). Ideas and identities: Supporting equity in cooperative mathematics learning. *Review of Educational Research, 79*(2), 1008–1043. https://doi.org/10.3102/0034654309332562

Fauth, B., Decristan, J., Rieser, S., Klieme, E., & Büttner, G. (2014). Student ratings of teaching quality in primary school: Dimensions and prediction of student outcomes. *Learning and Instruction, 29*, 1–9. https://doi.org/10.1016/j.learninstruc.2013.07.001

Furtak, E. M., Seidel, T., Iverson, H., & Briggs, D. C. (2016). Experimental and quasi-experimental studies of inquiry-based science teaching: A meta-analysis. *Review of Educational Research, 82*(3), 300–329. https://doi.org/10.3102/0034654312457206

Good, T. L., Wiley, C. R. H., & Florez, I. R. (2009). Effective teaching: An emerging synthesis. In G. Dworkin (Ed.), *International handbook of research on teachers and teaching* (pp. 803–816). https://doi.org/10.1007/978-0-387-73317-3_51

Hess, R. D., & Shipman, V. C. (1965). Early experience and the socialisation of cognitive modes in children. *Child Development, 36*(4), 869–886.

Hmelo-silver, C. E., Duncan, R. G., & Chinn, C. A. (2007). Scaffolding and achievement in problem-based and inquiry learning: A response to Kirschner, Sweller, and Clark (2006). *Educational Psychologist, 42*(2), 99–107.

Hox, J. J. (2010). *Multilevel analysis: Techniques and applications*. Routledge.

Kirschner, P. A., Sweller, J., & Clark, R. E. (2006). Why minimal guidance during instruction does not work: An analysis of the failure of constructivist, discovery, problem-based, experiential, and inquiry-based teaching. *Educational Psychologist, 41*(2), 75–86. https://doi.org/10.1207/s15326985ep4102

Klieme, E., Pauli, C., & Reusser, K. (2009). *The pythagoras study: Investigating effects of teaching and learning in Swiss and German mathematics classrooms* (pp. 137–160). Munster: Waxmann Verlag.

Lazonder, A. W., & Harmsen, R. (2016). Meta-analysis of inquiry-based learning: Effects of guidance. *Review of Educational Research, 86*(3), 681–718. https://doi.org/10.3102/0034654315627366

Liu, H., Van Damme, J., Gielen, S., & Van Den Noortgate, W. (2015). School processes mediate school compositional effects: Model specification and estimation. *British Educational Research Journal, 41*(3), 423–447. https://doi.org/10.1002/berj.3147

Lüdtke, O., Trautwein, U., Kunter, M., & Baumert, J. (2006). Reliability and agreement of student ratings of the classroom environment: A reanalysis of TIMSS data. *Learning Environments Research, 9*(3), 215–230. https://doi.org/10.1007/s10984-006-9014-8

Mayer, R. E. (2004). Should there be a three-strikes rule against pure the case for guided methods of instruction. *American Psychologist, 59*(1), 14–19. https://doi.org/10.1037/0003-066X.59.1.14

Muijs, D., Kyriakides, L., van der Werf, G., Creemers, B., Timperley, H., & Earl, L. (2014). State of the art-teacher effectiveness and professional learning. *School Effectiveness and School Improvement, 25*(2), 231–256. https://doi.org/10.1080/09243453.2014.885451

Muthén, L. K., & Muthén, B. O. (2017). *Mplus user's guide* (8th ed.). Muthén & Muthén.

Neumann, K., Kauertz, A., & Fischer, H. E. (2012). Quality of instruction in science education. In B. J. Fraser, K. Tobin, & C. J. McRobbie (Eds.), *Second international handbook of science education* (pp. 247–258). Springer.

OECD. (2016a). *PISA 2015 assessment and analytical framework: Science, reading, mathematic and financial literacy*. OECD Publishing. https://doi.org/10.1787/9789264255425-en

OECD. (2016b). *PISA 2015 results: Excellence and equity in education* (Vol. I). OECD Publishing.

Rjosk, C., Richter, D., Hochweber, J., Lüdtke, O., Klieme, E., & Stanat, P. (2014). Socioeconomic and language minority classroom composition and individual reading achievement: The mediating role of instructional quality. *Learning and Instruction, 32*, 63–72. https://doi.org/10.1016/j.learninstruc.2014.01.007

Ryan, R. M., & Deci, E. L. (2000). Self-determination theory and the facilitation of intrinsic motivation, social development, and well-being. *American Psychologist, 55*(1), 68–78. https://doi.org/10.1037/0003-066X.55.1.68

Sadovnik, A. R. (1991). Basil Bernstein's theory of pedagogic practice: A structuralist approach. *Sociology of Education, 64*(1), 48. https://doi.org/10.2307/2112891

Scheerens, J. (2001). Monitoring school effectiveness in developing countries. *School Effectiveness and School Improvement: An International Journal of Research, 12*(4), 359–384. https://doi.org/10.1076/sesi.12.4.359.3447

Sfard, A. (1998, March). On two metaphors for learning and the dangers of choosing just one. *Educational Researcher*, 4–13.

Sirin, S. R. (2005). Socioeconomic status and academic achievement: A meta-analytic review of research. *Review of Educational Research, 75*(3), 417–453.

Sirin, S. R., Diemer, M. A., Jackson, L. R., & Howell, A. (2004). Future aspirations of urban adolescents: A person-in-context model. *International Journal of Qualitative Studies in Education, 17*(3), 437–459. https://doi.org/10.1080/0951839042000204607

Sjøberg, S. (2018). The power and paradoxes of PISA: Should inquiry-based science education be sacrificed to climb on the rankings? *Nordic Studies in Science, 14*(2), 186–202. https://doi.org/10.5617/nordina.6185

van Ewijk, R., & Sleegers, P. (2010). The effect of peer socioeconomic status on student achievement: A meta-analysis. *Educational Research Review, 5*(2), 134–150. https://doi.org/10.1016/j.edurev.2010.02.001

Windschitl, M., Thompson, J., & Braaten, M. (2008). Beyond the scientific method: Model-based inquiry as a new paradigm of preference for school science investigations. *Science Education*, 1–27. https://doi.org/10.1002/sce

CHAPTER 3

Governing Guru: The Political Economy of Teacher Distribution in Indonesia

Andrew Rosser

Abstract

Indonesia has an enormous number of teachers. But they are poorly distributed between and within regions. At the same time, this maldistribution involves not simply unevenness in the supply of teachers but also in their quality, with more qualified and experienced teachers tending to be concentrated in more affluent urban areas. To address this problem, the central government issued a joint ministerial regulation instructing regional governments to redistribute teachers more equitably. However, this regulation appears to have had little effect at the local level. Regional governments have in general taken little action in response. Drawing on fieldwork in four Indonesian districts or municipalities, this chapter examines the reasons for this outcome. It argues that the underlying causes of the regional governments' non-responsiveness to the regulation have been political in nature, reflecting the way in which regional elites have long used the local school system—and teacher management in particular—to accumulate resources, distribute patronage, mobilize political support, and exercise political control. The chapter also examines the political dynamics surrounding redistribution in two cases where this happened.

Keywords

teachers – teacher distribution – political economy – predatory elites – Indonesia

Indonesia has an abundance of teachers—around 3 million by one estimate (The Economist, 2014)—giving it one of the most enviable teacher-student ratios in the world (USAID Prioritas, 2015). But these teachers are poorly distributed between schools, and especially between schools in urban areas and rural and remote areas. As Al-Samarrai et al. (2012, p. 2) have explained, this maldistribution has involved not simply unevenness in the supply of teachers but also in their quality: '[M]ore qualified and experienced teachers are frequently concentrated in wealthier urban areas'. As one measure of the scale of the problem, USAID (2015) found that teacher-student ratios in a set of 23 districts and municipalities ranged from 10 in urban Madiun to 25 in the remote rural district of Nias Selatan. There is also a marked maldistribution of teachers *within* districts and municipalities, with the urban-rural divide again being the central dimension of inequality (Al-Samarrai et al., 2012; Heyward et al., 2017, p. 252). Al-Samarrai et al. (2012) illustrate that the Indonesian government's standards on teacher numbers at the school level could be largely met by redistributing teachers more equitably within these districts/municipalities.

This maldistribution of teachers is widely considered to have undermined the country's performance in promoting learning. For instance, in a recent study, the World Bank (2013, p. 80) found that teacher maldistribution had contributed to diminished educational performance in *Bahasa Indonesia* amongst students in rural and remote areas compared to students in urban areas. More generally, Indonesia has consistently achieved dismal results in international standardized tests such as the Program for International Student Assessment (PISA) and Trends in International Mathematics and Science Study (TIMSS) since it started participating in these tests in the late 1990s.[1]

Indonesia's central government has introduced a range of reform initiatives in recent years to address teacher mal-distribution but these have had little effect. Recent government statements and media reports suggest that the problem remains largely unsolved (e.g. Warta Ekonomi, 2018).

What explains the maldistribution of teachers in Indonesia? Most analysis of teacher distribution in developing countries has focused on mapping the distribution of teachers within countries, identifying areas of over- and under-supply, assessing the effects on learning outcomes and government budgets, and devising programs for redistributing teachers (Mulkeen, 2010; Al-Samarrai et al., 2012). It has given relatively little attention to the underlying causes of teacher maldistribution and, in particular, the role of politico-economic factors in this respect.[2]

This chapter focuses on precisely these factors. It suggests that teacher maldistribution in Indonesia has its origins in the way in which predatory political and bureaucratic elites, at both the national and local levels, have for decades used the school system—and teacher management in particular—to accumulate resources, distribute patronage, mobilize political support, and exercise political control. This orientation has meant that teacher numbers, quality, and distribution have been managed to maximize flows of rents and votes from schools to these elites, lubricate patronage and political networks, and ensure that these elites maintain political control rather than to maximize educational performance and equity, notwithstanding their rhetoric in support of the latter. Democratization and decentralization since the fall of the New Order, the authoritarian and centralized regime that ruled Indonesia from 1965 to 1998, have done little to change this situation. They have consolidated the formal authority of district governments in relation to teacher management and created genuine competition within the local elite for teachers' votes. But schools' role as a source of rents and votes and a mechanism for distributing patronage and exercising political control has remained more or less unchanged.

In this context, central government initiatives to promote a more equitable distribution of teachers have represented a direct assault on elite interests. In particular, given that local elites play the dominant role in teacher management, the central government's efforts have represented an assault on the interests of local elites. Central government reform initiatives have consequently encountered considerable—if often subterranean—resistance except in a few exceptional cases where specific conditions conducive to reform have emerged. The chapter argues—on the basis of an analysis of the political dynamics surrounding teacher distribution in four regional cases—that these conditions are: (i) where mid-level government officials, especially officials in the local education agency, judge that reform initiatives can be exploited for patronage purposes; secure support from more senior officials; and they devise effective strategies for managing the politics of reform; (ii) where reform-minded district leaders are elected providing an imperative for education agency officials to design reform programs and the latter have access to relevant ideas and policy advice as a result of contact with donors; and (iii) the central government devises and implements policy instruments that, accidently or otherwise, provide regional governments with firm incentives to carry out teacher redistribution.

In presenting this argument, the chapter begins by providing a general overview of the political economy of teacher management in Indonesia. It then examines the experiences of four districts with regards to teacher redistribution in an attempt to understand both the political obstacles to this policy and the conditions under which, to the extent teacher redistribution has occurred, it has been possible. The final section of the chapter draws out the policy implications of the analysis.

1   The Political Economy of Teacher Management[3]

The New Order invested heavily in promoting improved access to education, especially basic education. It dramatically expanded the scope of the public school system, especially during the oil boom years of the 1970s and early 1980s when the government was awash in petrodollars, achieving universal primary enrolment in the early 1980s (Prawiro, 1998, p.180). However, corruption undermined the educational effectiveness of this investment. Indonesian schools became part of the larger 'franchise' structure that characterized the New Order's rule, the key feature of which was the purchase of government positions in exchange for access to the rents they could generate (McLeod, 2000). As such, teachers became incorporated into networks of corruption and patronage as both generators and beneficiaries of the rents that education budgets and teaching positions made available (Irawan et al., 2004, p. 50; Rosser & Joshi, 2013).

At the same time, the New Order used schools as vehicles for mobilizing votes at election time and exercising political control (Schiller, 1999, p. 11; Bjork, 2003, pp. 192–193). The school system was one of few national institutional structures that reached all the way down to the village level, making it an extremely important link between the predatory political and bureaucratic elites who dominated the New Order and the masses. As civil servants, teachers were required to support Golkar, the New Order's electoral vehicle; display 'mono-loyalty' to the state; and both take and teach compulsory courses in the state ideology, *Pancasila*. If they failed to perform these responsibilities, they risked demotion or transfer to less attractive schools, particularly in remote areas. Teachers were also required to be members of the Indonesian Teachers Union (PGRI), the sole recognized teachers' trade union. Established in 1945 as part of the nationalist resistance to Dutch rule, the PGRI operated during the New Order period as a mechanism for controlling teachers rather than the articulation of their collective interests. Its political subordination was made transparent by its incorporation into Golkar in 1970 (Kompas, 1970). In exchange for its allegiance to the New Order, the PGRI was given a monopoly on the representation of teachers and the authority to extract fees from teachers' salaries with little or no accountability over use of the associated funds (Reeve, 1985, p. 328).

In this context, there was little political will within the government to address issues related to teacher quality, teacher distribution, or teacher numbers and cost. Rather the dominant logic at work was to expand and consolidate networks of corruption and patronage and enhance political control. This meant maximizing teacher numbers to provide additional patronage opportunities while expecting little of teachers in terms of accountability for educational outcomes. One consequence was maldistribution of teachers as political and bureaucratic elites ensured that their friends, family and political allies gained teaching positions at schools in urban areas near their family and social networks. Particularly privileged in this respect were the 'favourite schools' attended by children of local government officials and other members of the middle class.

The Asian economic crisis in 1997 and demise of the New Order regime in 1998 produced a political context that was slightly more conducive to teacher management reform and teacher redistribution in particular. The crisis undermined the economic base of predatory New Order elites and their corporate clients and forced the government to negotiate a rescue package with the International Monetary Fund (IMF) and accept increased aid. In this context, government technocrats, particularly in the National Development Planning Agency (Bappenas) and the Ministry of Education and Culture (MoEC), pushed hard for teacher management reform, leveraging the support of the World Bank and other members of the donor community. In September 1998, the Bank published a major report on Indonesia's education system which argued that: "A key part of quality improvement is teachers—having them equitably distributed, giving them appropriate incentives, and ensuring they are adequately trained" (World Bank, 1998, p. x). Immediately afterward, it then co-funded with Bappenas the establishment of a series of Task Forces to prepare reports on key education policy issues including teacher management (Jalal & Musthafa, 2001). Over the next few years, donors provided loans and grants to the Indonesian government for a series of projects related to teacher management including USAID's Kinerja and Prioritas projects, both of which had an explicit concern with teacher distribution.

In seeking to promote teacher management reform, however, government technocrats and their allies in the donor community were constrained by three factors. The first was the fact that they had little direct authority over the implementation of teacher management policy. Under the New Order, district and municipal governments already had primary responsibility for implementing teacher management policy notwithstanding the centralized nature of New Order rule (King, 1995, pp. 80–84). The introduction of new decentralization laws in 1999 and their implementation in 2001 consolidated the role of these governments in this respect by granting them formal authority over education policy. The second constraint was the continued political dominance during the post-New Order period of predatory military and bureaucratic officials and their corporate clients; at both national and regional levels, long-standing patronage and political networks have consequently remained an entrenched feature of Indonesia's system of education governance. The third constraint was the fact that democratization opened up new opportunities for teachers to challenge teacher management reform by allowing the PGRI greater autonomy from government, enabling the establishment of new teacher organisations, and creating greater scope for these organisations to lobby policy-makers and use courts to achieve their ends.

The overall effect of this political context was to severely limit the extent to which technocratic elements and their donor supporters were able to promote teacher management reform including teacher redistribution. For instance, in an attempt to promote teacher redistribution, the central government's Education Committee chaired by Vice-President Boediono, a former economics professor and a prominent technocrat, agreed that five government ministers (the Minister of National Education, the State Minister for the Empowerment of the State Apparatus and Bureaucratic Reform, the Minister of the Interior, the Minister of Finance, and the Minister of Religious Affairs), all of whom were represented on the Committee, should issue a joint regulation instructing regional (and especially district/municipal) governments[4] to redistribute teachers more equitably (Kompas, 2010). Issued in 2011, the Five Ministerial Decree, as the regulation has become known, threatened regional governments with a range of sanctions if they did not comply. These included the withdrawal, in part or full, of education funding to regional governments; delays in the granting of new civil service teacher positions to regional governments; and delays in the provision of 'balancing funds' (*dana perimbangan*) to regional governments.

This regulation has had little effect at the regional level: as various commentators have noted, regional governments have taken little action in response (Ilfiyah et al., 2015; Republika, 2014). This does not appear to have been because of a lack of technical capacity at the local level to manage teacher redistribution; in general, local educational agencies appear to have the required data and analytical capacity to redistribute teachers in a more efficient and effective way.[5] Rather, the lack of action appears to have been in part because regional governments have not seen the threats contained in the regulation as credible and in part, because they have baulked at the political challenges that teacher redistribution entails. As noted above, teacher redistribution represents an attack on the interests of political and bureaucratic elites and teachers, both of whom have had significant capacity to push back against unwanted change. In the case of political and bureaucratic elites, this is because they have controlled the local state apparatus and its policy-making and implementation powers. In the case of teachers, it is because their electoral strength and political and social networks have given them the ability to effectively lobby local politicians, especially members of the DPRD and regional executives (i.e. the *bupati* or mayor). They have also, on occasion, been able to access the courts.

2   The Political Economy of Teacher Redistribution in Four Districts

Despite the serious political obstacles to teacher management reform, a small number of district/municipal governments have nevertheless introduced programs of teacher redistribution (Ilfiyah et al., 2015; USAID Prioritas, 2014). The introduction of these programs has not necessarily been a response to the Five Ministerial Decree nor motivated by technocratic/donor concerns. Where these programs have embodied such concerns, it has been because donors have been active within the region and played a crucial role in putting ideas on the table. The experiences of our four focus districts, all of which faced significant teacher distribution challenges (see Table 3.1), illustrate the dynamics at work and the different outcomes that have prevailed at the regional level. I have disguised the identities of the districts/municipalities at the request of the funders of the research and to protect informants. The results reported are based on fieldwork carried out between May and August 2015.

TABLE 3.1   Case studies

District Name	Need for redistribution				Redistribution?
	TSR SD < 26	TSR SMP <20	prpnsdist (median = 0.096)	jspnsdist (median = 0.189)	
	2010	2010	2010	2010	
District A	Yes	No	0.114	0.168	Some TR
District B	Yes	Yes	0.115	0.229	Yes
Municipality A	Yes	Yes	0.041	0.149	No
Municipality B	Yes	Yes	0.079	0.153	Recently some TR

Notes: (i) TSR = teacher student ratio; (ii) TR = teacher redistribution; (iii) prpnsdist and jspnsdist are measures of the extent to which civil servant teachers can be redistributed in a region at the primary and junior secondary levels respectively.
SOURCE: WORLD BANK, JAKARTA

2.1 *Municipality A*

Municipality A is a major city and, as such, lacks remote and rural areas. But it still has significant distribution problems (see Table 3.1). Several informants noted that the city has schools with too many teachers and others with too few, particularly with regards to subject teachers.[6] Yet the city government has so far done little to address teacher distribution problems, notwithstanding the fact that under its mayor, who was elected in 2013, 'redistribution of quality' (*pemerataan mutu*) within the school system is a key plank of the local government's education policy agenda. The mayor has put in place some measures—such as the reintroduction of school catchment areas and caps on senior secondary school fees—aimed at achieving this objective. But he has so far failed to implement teacher redistribution.

The city government's initial response to the Five Ministerial Decree—made under the previous mayor—was to kick the problem downstairs. In a Circulating Letter (*Surat Edaran*) issued in July 2012, the then head of the local education agency instructed school principals to deal with the problem by coordinating among themselves.[7] His replacement as head, who was appointed by the current mayor, appears to have more ownership of the problem. He has tried to produce local regulations providing for redistribution. But these have so far been held up in the legal section (*bagian hukum*) of the education agency. The problem, according to informed sources, has been that mid-level officials within the agency have been effectively sabotaging moves to rotate or redistribute teachers reflecting their interest in maintaining the patronage and political networks that link them to schools and, in particular, principals and teachers in 'favourite' schools most likely to lose from redistribution.[8]

2.2 Municipality B

Like Municipality A, Municipality B has significant teacher distribution problems despite lacking remote and rural areas (see Table 3.1). Again, like Municipality A, these appear to center on the distribution of subject teachers.[9] Between 2008 and 2013, the regional government did little to address this problem, the mayor and his regional secretary taking the view that redistribution was unnecessary since the city had too many teachers.[10] The city Education Board, an advisory body including a range of local education stakeholders, made a recommendation to the education agency at the time that it carry out a mapping of teacher needs and allocate teachers to schools accordingly. But this was never taken up.[11] One branch head (*kepala bagian*) in the education agency official explained that the issue of teacher redistribution had been discussed extensively within the education agency but that there had so far been little willingness to tackle the problem in any systematic or serious way. Indeed, they had floated the idea of kicking the problem downstairs to community-level education agency branches (UPTD). He stated that the key obstacle was the political challenges involved in teacher redistribution.[12]

Since 2013, it appears that the city education agency has, however, started to change direction on the issue. 2013 saw two important developments. The first was the election of a new mayor although, because of a Constitutional Court challenge to the election result, he did not take up the job until late 2014. His choice as head of the local education agency told us that teacher redistribution is one of his top priorities indicating that the agency may be more active in this area in future.[13] Having only been in the job for four months at the time of interview, however, he had not yet had the chance to make much progress so far.

The second development was the introduction of new and more demanding technical guidelines (*juknis*) for the professional allowance associated with the certification program. According to the head of the junior and senior secondary education branch in the education agency, the tighter requirements imposed by these guidelines raised the risk of a negative State Financial Audit Agency (BPK) or State Finance and Development Supervision Agency (BPKP)[14] audit finding if city claims regarding the number of teachers who are eligible for the professional allowance could not be fully substantiated. This in turn could trigger cuts to central government transfers to the city government. Beginning in 2013–2014, he has consequently carried out a detailed mapping of teacher needs in junior and senior secondary schools and been careful to ensure that teacher transfers were done in accordance with schools' genuine need for teachers. In contrast to the 5 Ministerial Decree, then, it would appear that, at least for this official, the new technical guidelines for the professional allowance combined with BPK/BPKP audit processes posed a credible threat to the city government even if the introduction of the new guidelines may not have been directly intended to affect teacher distribution.

2.3 District A

District A is a large district that includes urban and rural areas, some of which are remote. Like Municipality A and Municipality B, it has had significant teacher distribution problems, particularly at both primary and junior secondary level (Table 3.1). In contrast to these municipalities, however, it has been relatively active in redistributing teachers as well as changing their type, level and/or function (*jenis, jenjang, fungsi*)[15] for several years.

The local education agency began planning for teacher redistribution shortly after the central government issued Government Regulation 74/2008 on Teachers. This regulation established eligibility requirements for a professional allowance due to teachers through a new certification program, including that they teach face-to-face for at least 24 hours per week. The education agency carried out mapping (*pemetaan*) to establish areas of teacher shortage and excess from 2009 but it was not until 2012 that it actually began to redistribute teachers. Education agency figures show that, of 12,000 PNS teachers working in District A around this time, 454 were moved in 2012, 249 in 2013, 60 in 2014 and 129 in 2015. But the 2012 figure includes 251 who moved at their own initiative between 2009 and 2011, so the real 2012 figure should be 203.[16] The increase between 2014 and 2015 was made necessary by the introduction of a new national curriculum in 2013 which eliminated some subjects from the curriculum. In the wake of the new curriculum, the education agency carried out a remapping of teacher supply and need to determine areas of shortage and excess. It then reassigned teachers to new types or levels and in some cases new schools so that they could meet the 24-hour requirement.[17]

The key driving force of change in District A with regards to teacher redistribution has been a concern to help teachers meet the 24 hour and linearity[18] requirements for receiving the professional allowance attached to the certification program rather than concerns related to budgetary efficiency or educational quality (although the latter have been recognized as potential payoffs).[19] Change has not been donor-driven. USAID's Prioritas program, which operates in the district, only became operational there in 2013, well after the district government began to move on redistribution, although it has provided some legitimacy to the reforms by garnering international donor, education ministry and media attention (see, for instance, Jawa Pos 2014).[20]

The politics of redistributing teachers in District A had three discrete phases:
– *The first phase* entailed school supervisors (education agency officials who oversee school affairs) working out that many teachers in District A would be ineligible for the professional allowance unless the local government redistributed them to places and roles that enabled them to meet the requirements of *Government Regulation No. 74 of 2008*. They did this through discussions with school principals and teachers as part of their supervisory responsibilities, hearing complaints from teachers about being short of hours. They then made a recommendation for teacher redistribution to the head of the education agency's Civil Service sub-section (*Kasubag Kepegawaian*) through the School Supervisor Working Deliberative Group, a body bringing together the district's school supervisors.[21]
– *The second phase* entailed the head of the education agency's Civil Service sub-section working in conjunction with the head of the Civil Service Rotation Section (*Kabid Mutasi Kepagawaian*) at the Regional Civil Service and Training Agency (BKDD) to persuade the head of the education agency, the district head (*bupati*), the vice-*bupati* and other senior officials to sign off on a redistribution program. Parallel processes seem to have been going on in the local health agency with regards to civil servant health workers (and perhaps other agencies), so it is likely that officials in these agencies were involved as well.[22] The result was the issuance of *bupati* regulation providing the legal foundation for teacher redistribution within District A as well as redistribution of other civil servants.
– *The third phase* entailed the local government engaging in change management—that is, ensuring that teacher redistribution occurred without

provoking a destabilizing or politically damaging backlash from affected teachers. The key elements in this phase were threefold:

i   extensive and early socialization of the policy among teachers. This was carried out through school principals, the PGRI, and direct visits to schools by the then education agency head. In the latter case, the focus was on the opportunities presented by the certification program but the need for redistribution to enable teachers to meet certification requirements was also flagged.

ii early engagement of the regional parliament (DPRD), particularly the commission responsible for education matters (Komisi 4), to ensure that it was on board.

iii neutralization of protests by teachers who reacted negatively to proposed moves. It appears that a small number of teachers made individual protests about proposed moves through direct approaches to the education agency or the local parliament. One, a teacher with *preman* (street thug)-like tendencies, reportedly placed a gun on the table in his meeting with education agency officials, a clear form of intimidation. Education agency officials say that they successfully neutralized most protests by pointing out the benefits from proposed moves in terms of improving their eligibility for the certification program. If teachers continued to object, they were allowed to stay in their existing positions (although in these cases they did not receive the professional allowance if their teaching load remained below 24 hours or they did not meet the linearity requirements).[23]

The fact that teacher redistribution was so closely linked to the requirements of the certification program suggests that the principal motivations of the supervisors and the mid-level education agency officials who were so crucial in pushing the process forward and the senior officials who ultimately approved teacher redistribution were related to the dynamics of local patronage and political networks. As patrons within the system, they had a concern to ensure their clients at the school level received their due entitlements in order to consolidate political and patronage networks. As rent-seekers within the system, they also had a concern to maximize amount of the money within the school system that is available for potential appropriation.

2.4   *District B*

Like District A, District B is a large district that straddles urban and rural areas, some of which are remote; has had significant teacher distribution problems (see Table 3.1); and has been relatively active in redistributing teachers. Indeed, of our four regional cases, it has been by far the most aggressive reformer in this respect. Since 2007–2008, the regional government has redistributed almost 3,000 civil servant teachers, accounting for a very large proportion of the teaching labor force. The numbers redistributed were: 644 in 2008, 0 in 2009, 344 in 2010, 360 in 2011, 552 in 2012, 502 in 2013, 166 in 2014, and 331 in 2015. Some teachers who were transferred were moved to isolated parts of the district.

Importantly for our purposes, the first round of redistribution (2007–2008) happened just before the central government issued Government Regulation 74/2008 which made it compulsory for teachers to teach 24 hours face-to-face to be eligible for the professional allowance. In contrast to District A, then, redistribution does not appear to have been conceived from the outset as a way of ensuring that teachers receive the professional allowance. Rather technocratic concerns seem to have had a more significant influence reflecting two factors. The first relates to the personal capacities of the district's *bupati* from 2005 to 2015. Several informants described the *bupati* as 'educated' and 'capable of thinking'. The second factor is his apparent political strategy of seeking legitimacy for his education policies by securing the support of international donors. Under his rule, District B became home to a wide range of donor education projects including Bermutu, Prodep, and a UNICEF project on school-based management. As I note below, this meant that local education officials had access to technocratic ideas and policy solutions concerning teacher distribution at a crucial moment.

The politics of teacher redistribution proceeded in eight main stages.

- First, the *bupati* was elected in 2005 on the basis of promises to transform District B into a 'Clever District' (*Kabupaten Cerdas*). Teacher redistribution was not explicitly part of this agenda at this point. His five-year development plan for 2005–2010 identified education as a priority sector but made no mention of teacher redistribution.[24]
- Second, the government of District B applied for and was selected to be part of a World Bank-MoEC pilot study on teacher management. This study dealt with, among other things, issues of teacher distribution (see World Bank and Department of National Education 2010). This introduced the regional government, in particular the education agency, to relevant technocratic ideas.[25]
- Third, recognizing that the *bupati* was open to ideas for reform—indeed, in all likelihood demanding them—education agency officials carried out a mapping of teacher distribution within the district and presented the results to him.[26]

- Fourth, education agency officials began to 'socialize' teacher redistribution among parliamentary representatives through working group meetings (*rapat kerja*) with members of the DPRD committee (Komisi 2) responsible for education.[27]
- Fifth, teacher redistribution was carried out in 2007–2008. This precipitated a lot of complaints, many of which were directed to the DPRD. According to the DPRD representative that we interviewed, the DPRD held firm, having agreed to the policy.[28] The Bermutu project started in 2008—District B was one of the project's pilot regions. This project focused mainly on teacher training but also had a component related to the development of a teacher database.
- Sixth, teacher redistribution was subject to challenge in the local state administrative court (PTUN) around 2008–2009 (the dates are a little unclear). Only a small number of teachers were involved in the PTUN case (between 1 and 3 depending on the source of information). The case was expensive: for instance, it entailed flying in experts from Gadjah Mada University and elsewhere and hiring lawyers. This suggests that the teachers had financial support from other sources. Who backed the dissident teachers is unknown. However, several informants suggested that their motivation was to damage the *bupati* in the run-up to the 2010 district head and 2011 gubernatorial elections, so the backer may have been a rival politician or one of his supporters. In any event, they lost the PTUN case: the court found in favor of the government of District B.
- Seventh, the district government introduced an isolated areas allowance (*tunjangan daerah terpencil*) figuring that this would reduce resistance in the future.
- Eighth, the district government passed a regional regulation (*perda*) and series of *bupati* regulations (*perbup*) to provide a regulatory framework for teacher management and constrain future governments.

2.5 Summary

In sum, then, the four cases above illustrate that teacher redistribution has posed significant political challenges for regional governments, explaining why—in the context of no credible threat of sanctions from above—most regional governments have baulked at addressing teacher distribution problems. At the same time, however, they also illustrate that redistribution has been possible where:
- as in District A, mid-level government officials, especially ones at the local education agency, have judged that reform initiatives can be exploited for

patronage purposes; secured support from above; and devised effective strategies for managing the politics of reform (by, for instance, securing the support of the DPRD and buying off the losers from reform);
- as in District B, reform-minded district leaders have been elected providing an imperative for education agency officials to design reform programs and they have had access to relevant ideas and policy advice or
- as recently in Municipality B, the central government has devised and implemented policy instruments that, accidently or otherwise, provide regional governments with an incentive to carry out teacher redistribution;

3 Conclusion

Indonesia faces serious problems with regards to teacher distribution. This chapter has sought, using a political economy framework, to explain the origins of this problem, identify the political obstacles to reform, and specify the political conditions under which the country has made progress in promoting such reform. In policy terms, the implication of the analysis is that promoting a more equitable distribution of teachers in Indonesia will require not only new policy frameworks and programs that are appropriate in a technical sense but also effective in addressing the political challenges involved. Broadly speaking, the findings suggest that there are two prospective strategies. The first is to reduce the ability of political and bureaucratic elites and the patronage and political networks they control, particularly ones at the regional level, to resist teacher redistribution by transferring authority over the implementation of teacher management policy to the central government. The second, which might come into play if recentralisation is politically impossible and considered unlikely to work for other reasons, involves a combination of three elements: (i) a *disciplinary* component that seeks to alter the incentives faced by political and bureaucratic elites at the regional level with regards to teacher distribution by presenting regional governments with a credible threat that they will be punished if they do not implement teacher management reforms and/or a credible commitment that they will be rewarded if they do; (ii) a *working with the grain* component that seeks to promote teacher distribution by exploiting opportunities presented by the certification program, in particular, the financial incentive it has created for teachers to move schools in order to meet certification requirements, to replace school principals, and carry out school mergers; and (iii) a *facilitative* component that seeks to support redistribution in regions where the political preconditions for reform are already in place because the local leadership is supportive of reform.

Acknowledgement

The research on which this chapter is based was funded by Australia's Department of Foreign Affairs and Trade and the World Bank. An earlier version of the chapter was initially published in working paper form as part of Andrew Rosser and M. Fahmi (2016), *The Political Economy of Teacher Management in Decentralised Indonesia*, World Bank Policy Research Working Paper, 7913. The usual caveat applies.

Notes

1   On these results, see Pisani (2013).
2   A notable exception is Heyward et al. (2017).
3   This section draws heavily on Rosser and Fahmi (2018).
4   The term 'regional governments' refers here to provincial as well as district governments.
5   Interviews with district and provincial education officials in the four districts discussed later in the chapter, May–August 2015.
6   Interviews with the head of the Municipality A Education Agency, May 2015, and FAGI/FGII activist, May 2015.
7   Title of the regulation withheld because it identifies the municipality.
8   Interviews, Municipality A, May 2015.
9   Interviews with the head of Municipality B Education Agency, and the Branch head for SMP, SMA and SMK Municipality B, August 2015.
10 Interviews with former mayor of Municipality B and former head of the city education agency and currently (August 2015) Regional Secretary, Municipality B, August 2015.
11 Interview with the head of the Education Board, Municipality B, August 2015.
12 Interview, Municipality B, August 2015.
13 Interview, Municipality B, August 2015.
14 These agencies are respectively the state external and internal auditors.
15 Change in type = e.g. maths teacher becoming a science teacher; change in level = e.g. SMA maths teacher becoming an SMP maths teacher; change in function = e.g. teacher moving into an administrative position.
16 Interviews with senior education agency officials, District A, June 2015.
17 Interviews with senior education agency officials, District A, June 2015.
18 To receive the professional allowance, teachers have to teach subjects that are related to their academic qualifications and field of certification—i.e. teachers with maths qualifications should be teaching maths. This is referred to as linearity (*linearitas*).

19 This came through particularly strongly in interviews with key actors within the education agency at the time. Their respective positions and roles are discussed in the main text.
20 For a more general analysis of the way in which local elites exploit donor programs for political advantage, see Choi and Fukuoka (2014).
21 Interview with a school supervisor and education agency official, District A, June 2015.
22 Interview with senior education agency officials, District A, June 2015.
23 Interviews with senior education agency officials and a former head of the education agency, District A, June 2015.
24 Interviews with the current head of education agency in District B who was the head of the Basic Education branch in the mid-2000s, District B, July 2015; and the former rector of the local state university (former IKIP). District B, August 2015.
25 I wish to thank Susi Iskandar for her advice on this point.
26 Interview with the head of education agency in District B, July 2015.
27 Interview with a member of Komisi 2, District B, July 2015.
28 Interview with a member of Komisi 2, District B, July 2015.

References

Al-Samarrai, S., Sukriyah, D., & Setiawan, I. (2012). *Making better use of teachers: Strengthening teacher management to improve the efficiency and equity of public spending.* World Bank.

Bjork, C. (2003). Local responses to decentralisation policy in Indonesia. *Comparative Education Review, 47*(2), 184–216.

Choi, I., & Fukuoka, Y. (2014). Co-opting good governance reform: The rise of not-so-reformist leader in Kebumen, Central Java. *Asian Journal of Political Science, 23*(1), 83–101.

Heyward, M., Hadiwijaya, A., & Mahargianto, P. E. (2017). Reforming teacher deployment in Indonesia. *Journal of Development Effectiveness, 9*(2), 245–262.

Ilfiyah, A., Hendri, F., Rasiki, R., & Yudhistira, R. (2015). *Kegagalan pemerataan guru: Evaluasi SKB 5 menteri tahun 2011 tentang penataan dan pemerataan Guru PNS di Indonesia* [Failure in teacher equity: Evaluating the Joint 2011 Ministerial Decree by 5 Ministries on the equitable distribution and management of civil servant teachers in Indonesia]. Indonesia Corruption Watch.

Irawan, A., Eriyanto, L. D., & Sunaryanto, A. (2004) *Mendagangkan sekolah* [Commercialising schools]. Indonesia Corruption Watch.

Jalal, F., & Musthafa, B. (Eds.). (2001). *Education reform in the context of regional autonomy: The case of Indonesia.* Ministry of National Education, Ministry of National Development Planning, and World Bank.

King, D. (1995). Bureaucracy and implementation of complex tasks in rapidly developing states: Evidence from Indonesia. *Studies in Comparative International Development, 30*(4), 78–92.

Kompas. (1970, July 11). PGRI Bernaung Dibawah Sekber Golkar [PGRI finds shelter under Golkar Party Joint Secretary]. *Kompas.*

Kompas. (2010, June 9). SKB redistribusi guru disiapkan [Preparing a Joint Ministerial Decree for teacher distribution]. *Kompas.* Retrieved September 14, 2015, from http://edukasi.kompas.com/read/2010/06/09/20065384/SKB.Redistribusi.Guru.Disiapkan

McLeod, R. (2000). Soeharto's Indonesia: A better class of corruption. *Agenda, 7*(2), 99–112.

Mulkeen, A. (2010). *Teachers in anglophone Africa: Issues in teacher supply, training, and management.* World Bank.

Pisani, E. (2013, October–December). A nation of dunces? *Inside Indonesia, 114.*

Prawiro, R. (1998). *Indonesia's struggle for economic development: Pragmatism in action.* Oxford University Press.

Reeve, D. (1985). *Golkar of Indonesia: An alternative to the party system.* Oxford University Press.

Republika. (2014, October 20). Ini kabupaten yang berhasil melakukan pemerataan guru [Districts that have succeeded in equitable distribution of teachers]. *Republika.* Retrieved from http://www.republika.co.id/berita/nasional/umum/14/10/20/ndpeob-ini-kabupaten-yang-berhasil-melakukan-pemerataan-guru

Rosser, A., & Fahmi, M. (2018). The political economy of teacher management reform in Indonesia. *International Journal of Educational Development, 61*, 72–81.

Rosser, A., & Joshi, A. (2013). From user fees to fee-free: The politics of realising universal free basic education in Indonesia. *Journal of Development Studies, 49*(2), 175–189.

Schiller, J. (1999, May). *The 1997 Indonesian elections: 'Festival of democracy' or 'costly fiction'?* (Occasional Paper No 22). University of Victoria.

The Economist. (2014, December 13). School's in. *The Economist.* Retrieved from https://www.economist.com/asia/2014/12/11/schools-in?zid=306&ah=1b164dbd43b0cb27ba0d4c3b12a5e227

USAID Prioritas. (2015). *Policy brief: Teacher deployment in Indonesia.* USAID Prioritas.

Warta Ekonomi. (2018, July 18). Mendikbud berdalih sistem zonasi demi pemerataan guru, setuju? [Minister of Education and Culture argues school zoning policy leads to teacher equity, agree?]. *Warta Ekonomi.* Retrieved from https://www.wartaekonomi.co.id/read187867/mendikbud-berdalih-sistem-zonasi-demi-pemerataan-guru-setuju.html

World Bank. (1998). *Education in Indonesia: From crisis to recovery*. World Bank.

World Bank. (2013). *Spending more or spending better: Improving education financing in Indonesia*. World Bank.

World Bank & Ministry of National Education. (2010). *Implementation completion report: Pilot study: Teacher employment and deployment*. Ministry of National Education.

CHAPTER 4

The Role of Religious Beliefs in Teacher Education Students' Career Aspirations

Anne Suryani

Abstract

This chapter discusses the extent of religious beliefs in influencing students' motivations for entering teacher education and becoming a teacher, and their perceptions about teaching and career aspirations. The study applies the Factors Influencing Teaching Choice framework (FIT-Choice) (Watt & Richardson, 2007), which was psychometrically validated in the Indonesian context (Suryani, Watt, & Richardson, 2016). Students' *religious beliefs* and *practices* were assessed using the Religious Commitment Inventory (RCI-10) (Worthington et al., 2003). Over 800 final-year undergraduate teacher education students participated in the study. Connections between religion and career aspirations were confirmed by differences identified between religious groups. Muslim participants experienced the strongest religious influence to enter teacher education and tended to be more "devout" than Protestant and Catholic participants. Highly religious participants were likely to view teaching as a profession with a high social status and therefore exert more effort into teaching and persist in their careers. Perceptions of teaching as a highly skilled and professional occupation would predict students' intentions and efforts to improve their knowledge and skills. Current teacher education policies should consider factors influencing teacher education students' career aspirations, including religious beliefs, perceptions of teaching as requiring high expertise and knowledge, and satisfaction with their choice of profession.

Keywords

teacher education students – teaching motivation – career aspirations – religious beliefs – perception of teaching – education policy

1 Teachers and Teaching In Indonesia: Under Scrutiny and Criticised, Yet a Line up of Candidates

Headlines following the announcement of Indonesia's latest PISA 2018 results released in late 2019 highlight low teacher quality as the major contributing factors to low proficiencies in basic literacies, including reading and mathematics (for example, Khidhir, 2019; Syakriah, 2019). Many attribute the inefficiencies of the education system to ineffective teaching. Despite a proportion of these teachers being inadequately academically qualified nor certified, with others also unable to display minimum subject matter and pedagogical competencies, these are the teachers responsible for educating future generations.

There remains a pessimistic Indonesian teacher archetype who lacks a substantial understanding of content knowledge (for example, Kurniawati, Suryadarma, Bima, & Yusrina, 2018; De Ree, 2016) and a curricular vision (for example, Gunawan, 2017; Retnawati, Munadi, Arlinwibowo, Wulandari, & Sulistyaningsih, 2017). However, teaching is still a highly respected occupation in Indonesia and the interest in entering the profession among the young population has been sustained, to the point of significantly exceeding the demand for new teachers.

There are more students entering teacher education programs than positions available as teachers. Current statistics indicate that nearly 300,000 students are graduating from teacher education programs every year, while the need for the teacher workforce is around 40,000 annually (Ministry of Research, Technology and Higher Education [MoRTHE], 2018a). This suggests a high capacity of teacher education institutions to attract incoming students and produce teacher candidates annually. However, the reason why so many students still choose to enter the teaching profession in light of the few job opportunities and a critical perception of teachers' success has not yet been fully investigated.

In 2017, the teacher certification process in Indonesia was replaced by the Teacher Professional Education program (Pendidikan Profesi Guru/PPG) to improve teacher education standards (MoRTHE, 2018b). This one-year program includes a series of courses for aspiring teachers who have completed a 4-year university degree. The PPG also serves in-service teachers, including civil servants and non-civil servant teachers, who have some teaching experience (MoRTHE, 2018c). Overall, it aims to deepen their pedagogical knowledge and skills as well as their expertise on specific subjects.

There is relatively limited research on what factors motivate Indonesian youth to enter teacher education and become teachers. Responding to this knowledge gap, it is crucial to explore the sociocultural contexts shaping the teacher workforce in a country where religion plays an extremely important role in society. It is hoped that this information will assist Indonesian policy makers and teacher education institutions to attract and recruit the best students into teaching, and therefore increase the quality of Indonesian future teachers.

Heeding to a major insight of a study of youth aspirations in Indonesia, that a strong commitment to religious faith and plans for a future family are highly influential in young people's career choices (Nilan, Parker, Bennett, & Robinson, 2011), this chapter examines the extent to which religious beliefs influence students' motivations for entering teacher education and becoming a teacher. It also explores whether religious beliefs and perceptions about teaching influence teaching career aspirations. More specifically, this chapter aims to address the following empirical questions: Are there differences in motivations to become teachers across religious groups? And are there differences in perceptions about teaching and career aspirations across religious groups?

The study revealed that across the three religious groups included in the data, those who identified as Muslims rated *religious influences*—one among the 17 motivation factors hypothesised to contribute to students' decisions to become teachers—significantly higher than those who identified as Catholics and Protestants. Further, with regard to perceptions on teaching itself, there were significant differences among the three religious groups related to their perception on teacher expertise, social status, and satisfaction with choice. The study also found that those who were rated as highly religious were likely to view teaching as a profession with a high social status and, therefore, would exert more effort into teaching and persist in their careers.

The following section discusses the role of religion in the lives of Indonesian youth. The section also contextualises this inquiry within the literature and research on religious factors shaping aspirations to become a teacher and perceptions on teaching. The subsequent sections then describe the methodological and analytical approaches employed, the data, and present a discussion of the main findings. The chapter concludes with a reflection of possible future directions contributing to developing a better understanding of motivations behind entering the teaching profession in Indonesia.

2   Religion and Teaching in Indonesia

Most Indonesians perceive themselves as religious (Hassan, Corkindale, & Sutherland, 2008) and agree that a belief in God is essential for having good values (Pew Research Center, 2014). They believe that religion is a very important aspect in life and children should learn religious faith at home (World Values Survey Association, 2005–2009). This is intimately related to the state of the Indonesian republic as officially a secular state, but where religion plays an extremely important role in society. Not only are all Indonesians legally required to choose one of six religions acknowledged by the state: Islam, Catholicism, Protestantism, Hinduism, Buddhism, and Confucianism,[1] but religious education is also a compulsory subject from primary to tertiary study. Since childhood, people are often expected to participate in group worships and to belong to a religious institution. The extent of one's identity, aspiration, and internal value or moral system is deeply shaped by their religious beliefs, as they are reinforced through religious practices.

Indonesian youth are also recognised as deeply religious (Parker & Nilan, 2013). Indonesian Muslim youth consider religious involvement as related to social competence and are more likely to connect with others who have similar religiosity which affect their behaviour, values and religious practices (French, Purwono, & Triwahyuni, 2011). A previous study of Muslim university students in Indonesia revealed that many had a strong religious commitment and desire to spread Islam across societies, commonly known as *dakwah* or *Islamic missionising* (Parker, 2011). Some students chose certain professions such as teaching, lecturing or preaching to align with their religious commitment. Integrating faith and religious practices in a seemingly secular line of career may take the form of working in the field of Islamic banking.

Religion plays a large impact in people's behaviour (Salili, 2005). The expectancy-value theory put forth by Dowson (2005) suggests that "religious beliefs provide for high value, high expectancy and high motivation" (p. 13). Further, valued outcomes are at the core of every religion, which can be divided into after death (distal) outcomes, and before death (proximal) outcomes (Dowson, 2005). Regarding motivations for teaching from an Islamic perspective, the decision to become a teacher is reflective of Allah's will. This can be considered as a proximal outcome as Islam views teaching as a noble profession, and "paradise" serves as a distal outcome for Muslims. Because the valued outcome cannot be achieved instantly, religious values extend individuals' future-time perspective (Dowson, 2005). When there are similarities in religious beliefs and traditions across countries, differences in experiences with the same religion may manifest within distinct cultures (Sasaki & Kim, 2011). This aligns with the notion of *calling*, when an individual embarks on a particular vocation to fulfil a certain purpose, express a sense of meaning, and "to promote the greater good" (Dik, Duffy, & Tix, 2012, p. 113).

Religion shapes not only motivations, but also perceptions on work in Indonesia by associating particular occupations as "good" and "bad". For instance, politics is often perceived as an occupation closely related to corruption, while teaching is a noble and respectable profession. In Bahasa Indonesia teacher is translated as *guru*, someone with knowledge and expertise and serves as a positive role model for the society.

Past studies have identified pre-service teachers' reasons for becoming teachers, which include spiritual or religious-related reasons, such as a *sense of calling* and *to make a world a better place* (Marshall, 2009), *to answer a calling from God* (Low, Lim, Ch'ng, & Goh, 2011), *called by God* and *led by the Lord* (Smith & Pantana, 2010). Developing a deeper and more nuanced understanding on this issue is particularly needed in light of the sustained high interest among Indonesian youth to enter the teaching profession, despite the complex social positioning of teachers and teaching in Indonesia briefly elaborated in the introductory section. Furthermore, there is a need to investigate teacher education students' effort and persistence in teaching as well as their professional development and leadership aspirations.

3 The Research: Data and Methods

This study investigates the extent to which religious beliefs influence teacher education students' motivations for entering teaching and becoming a teacher, as well as their perceptions about teaching and career aspirations. More specifically, the inquiry is guided by the following questions: *Are there any different motivations to become teachers based on religious influences across religious groups? Are there any differences in perceptions about teaching and career aspirations across religious groups? What is the role of religious beliefs in students' teaching career aspirations?*

3.1 *Participants*

The study participants were final-year undergraduate teacher education students at two public and two private universities in Jakarta and Yogyakarta. These students were selected because they most likely had strong leanings towards entering the teaching profession. The four universities have reputable teacher education programs for over 50 years. In total, 854 students filled out paper-based questionnaires with response rates above 95%. Responses with substantial missing responses were excluded in the analyses, resulting in 802 responses retained from the following participants: Public university one ($n = 328$), Public university two ($n = 223$), Private university one ($n = 67$) and Private university two ($n = 184$). The sample consists of women ($n = 668$, 83.30%) and men ($n = 134$, 16.70%), with mean age 21.61 years. These students were studying science education (i.e. mathematics, chemistry, physics, biology, $n = 261$), English language education ($n = 128$), primary education ($n = 293$), early childhood ($n = 65$), special education ($n = 30$), and guidance and counselling ($n = 20$), with 5 participants did not answer their programs of study. Regarding participants' religion, 543 (67.71%) were Muslim, 192 (23.94%) Catholic, 56 (6.98%) Protestant, 4 (0.50%) Buddhist, 4 (0.50%) Hindu and 3 (0.37%) did not answer. These proportions were not representative of the Indonesian population.

3.2 Measures

Survey questions were developed in English then back-translated in Bahasa Indonesia. The study refers to the Factors Influencing Teaching Choice (FIT-Choice) (Watt & Richardson, 2007) framework which was initially developed and validated in Australia. This chapter focuses only on the religious beliefs as a motivational factor that influence participants' choice to become teachers. General findings regarding participants' motivations and perceptions towards teaching as a career have been published elsewhere (see Suryani, Watt, & Richardson, 2016; Suryani, 2017).

Students' *religious beliefs* and *practices* were assessed using the Religious Commitment Inventory (RCI-10; Worthington et al., 2003). It is anticipated that highly religious people would evaluate their world through religious representations and integrate their religion into their lives. *Religious commitment* is defined as "the degree to which a person adheres to his or her religious values, beliefs, and practices and uses them in daily living" (Worthington et al., 2003, p. 85). The religious commitment factors consist of intrapersonal religious commitment or *religious beliefs* (e.g. my religious beliefs lie behind my whole approach to life) and interpersonal religious commitment or *religious practices* (e.g. I make financial contributions to my religious organisation). All items were rated on a scale from 1 (*not at all true of me*) to 7 (*totally true of me*).

The FIT-Choice framework applied in this study is founded on the expectancy-value theory of achievement motivation (Wigfield & Eccles, 2000). The framework suggests that individuals' choices and behaviours are influenced by their expectancies and values (Figure 4.1). The original FIT-Choice framework (Watt & Richardson, 2007) consists of 12 motivational factors: *perceived teaching ability* (e.g. teaching is a career suited to my abilities), *intrinsic career value* (e.g. I am interested in teaching), *fallback career* (e.g. I was not accepted into my first choice career), *job security* (e.g. teaching will be a secure job), *time for family* (e.g. teaching hours will fit with the responsibilities of having a family), *job transferability* (e.g. a teaching job will allow me to choose where I wish to live), *shape future of children/adolescents* (e.g. teaching will allow me to shape child/adolescent values), *enhance social equity* (e.g. teaching will allow me to benefit the socially disadvantaged), *make social contribution* (e.g. teachers make a worthwhile social contribution), *work with children/adolescents* (e.g. I want to help children/adolescents learn), *prior teaching and learning experiences* (e.g. I have had good teachers as role-models), *social influences* (e.g. my family think I should become a teacher). In this Indonesian study, items in motivational factors began with *"I chose teacher education because..."*. Response options were rated from 1 (not at all important) to 7 (extremely important).

Five factors for perceptions about the teaching profession were also investigated. These include *expertise* (e.g. Do you think teaching requires high levels of expert knowledge?), *difficulty* (e.g. Do you think teaching is a stressful job?), *social status* (e.g. Do you believe teaching is a well-respected career?), *salary* (e.g. Do you think teaching is well paid?), *social dissuasion* (e.g. Did others influence you to consider careers other than teaching?) and one *career choice satisfaction* factor (e.g. How satisfied are you with the choice of teaching as a career?). Response options for perception factors were rated from 1 (not at all) to 7 (extremely).

In this study, there were five motivation factors added to include the Indonesian cultural context: *religious influences* (e.g. my religion suggests that being a teacher is a noble profession), *second job* (e.g. as a teacher I can do casual work after school hours), *tuition fee for teacher education* (e.g. tuition fees for teacher education are affordable compared to other programs), *admission into teacher education* (e.g. entry into teacher education is less competitive than other programs), *time for teacher education studies* (e.g. number of years in teacher education is shorter compared to other programs), and one perception factor: *media dissuasion* (e.g. the influence from mass media about poor working conditions in school that may discourage participants from teaching).

Students' plan for their future careers were measured by the Professional Engagement and Career Development Aspirations scale (Watt & Richardson, 2008). These outcome variables comprised of *planned effort* (e.g. the amount of effort participants would work at being a good teacher), *planned persistence* (e.g. the level of certainty that the participants will remain in teaching), *professional development aspirations* (e.g. participants' intention to undertake professional development), and *leadership aspirations* (e.g. participants' plan to take up a leadership role in schools). Items for these factors were rated from 1 (*not at all*) to 7 (*extremely*).

FIGURE 4.1   Theoretical framework: Indonesian teacher education students' motivations for choosing a teaching career (adapted from Watt & Richardson, 2007, p. 176; Suryani, Watt, & Richardson, 2016)

a   Professional Engagement and Career Development Aspiration (PECDA) Scale, by Watt and Richardson (2008, p. 415).
b   Factors developed in the current study to include relevant cultural dimensions in the Indonesian context.
c   Factors adapted from The Religious Commitment Inventory-10 by Worthington et al. (2003).

3.3 Data Analyses

This chapter reports findings from one-way multivariate analyses of variance (MANOVA) to compare all factors based on religious groups. Prior to conducting MANOVAs, a series of Pearson correlations was conducted between all independent variables to check for compliance with the MANOVA requirement that the dependent variables should be correlated in the moderate range (Meyers, Gamst, & Guarino, 2006). Only significant differences are presented in the results section. Several boxplots are presented to provide details regarding significant differences across subgroups (i.e. gender and religious groups). Lastly, a SEM model was estimated, modelling structural paths between factors with observed correlation $r \geq .50$ to test the extent to which perceptions about teaching and religious beliefs influenced professional engagement and career development aspirations.

4 Results[2]

Most participants ($n = 657$, 81.92%) planned to become teachers after study completion, 11.72% ($n = 94$) planned to teach for one to five years then switch to another career, 4.86% ($n = 39$) intended to pursue non-teaching occupations, and 1.50% ($n = 12$) did not respond. Along with those who did not plan to teach, the "career switcher" participants preferred to work as a private sector employee, business owner, lecturer, writer, volunteer, civil servant, artist/musician and housewife. Due to the limited number of Hindu and Buddhist participants, MANOVAs compared all factors for Muslim ($n = 543$), Catholic ($n = 192$) and Protestant ($n = 56$) participants.

Cronbach's alpha reliability coefficients indicated good internal consistencies for most of the factors (Suryani, Watt & Richardson, 2016). Cronbach's alphas for motivational factors range between .82 to .87, except for *job transferability* ($\alpha = .69$), *fallback career* ($\alpha = .73$) and *time for teacher education studies* ($\alpha = .74$). Perception factors have Cronbach's alpha values from .72 to .87. Cronbach alphas for professional engagement and career aspirations factors vary between .90 to .95, with α *religious practices* $= .81$ and α *religious beliefs* $= .89$.

4.1 Religious Beliefs and Practices

Participants rated their *religious beliefs* higher ($M = 5.96$, $SD = 1.09$) than their *religious practices* ($M = 4.65$, $SD = 1.39$). A significant multivariate difference was found between *religious beliefs* and *practices*, $F(4, 1532) = 9.30$, $p < .001$; Pillai's Trace $= .047$; partial $\eta^2 = .024$. Univariate tests using Bonferroni adjustment ($p < .025$) indicated significant differences occurred for *religious beliefs*. Tukey HSD post hoc tests ($p < .050$) revealed that Muslim participants' *religious beliefs* were significantly higher than for Protestants and Catholics. Furthermore, female participants across the three religious groups perceived themselves as more religious than male participants (Figure 4.2).

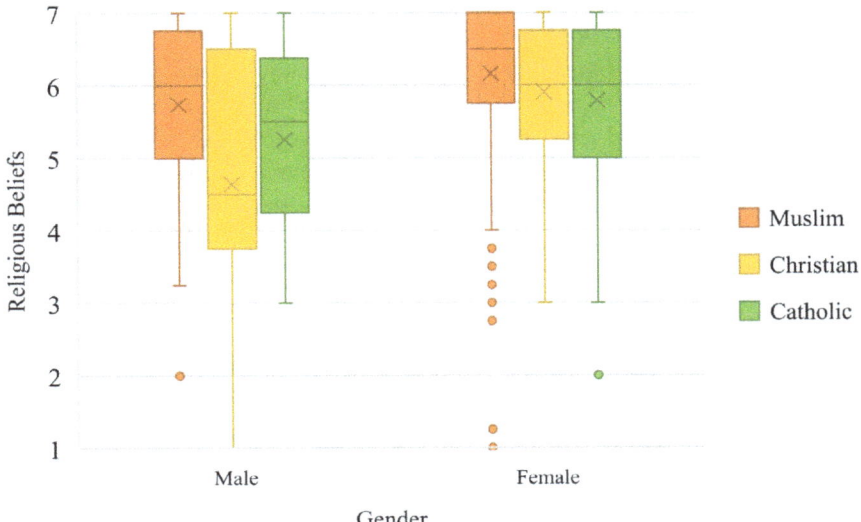

FIGURE 4.2   Different religious beliefs based on gender and religious groups
Note: Response options: 1 = not at all true of me, 7 = totally true of me.
Male Muslim n = 79, M = 5.74; male Christian n = 11, M = 4.64; male Catholic n = 37, M = 5.25; female Muslim n = 451, M = 6.16; female Christian n = 43, M = 5.90; female Catholic n = 154, M = 5.79; N = 775 participants

In terms of motivations, most participants chose to become teachers because they had a desire to contribute to the society, had positive learning and teaching experiences, wanted to work with children and adolescents, and had high intrinsic career values such as enjoyment they gained from working as a teacher. The next highest ranked motivations were the influence from their religious teaching, which was relatively equal with their motivations to attain a secure job, having opportunity to work a second job, as well as their perceived teaching ability (see Suryani, Watt, & Richardson, 2016). There were significant correlations across motivational factors, with religious influences significantly and positively correlating with all social utility values which include students' intentions to enhance social equity, make social contribution, and work with children/adolescents (Suryani, Watt, & Richardson, 2016). The findings are not surprising because all religious teachings encourage people to serve the society and becoming a teacher will support these values.

4.2 Were There Any Different Motivations to Become Teachers Based on Religious Influences across Groups?

Across three groups, only one motivational factor has significant difference: the influence from religious beliefs; $F(32, 1028) = 2.76$, $p < .001$; Pillai's Trace = .158; partial $\eta^2 = .079$. Univariate tests using Bonferroni adjustment ($p < .003$) indicated significant differences for *religious influences* and Tukey HSD post hoc tests ($p < .050$) showed that Muslims rated *religious influences* higher than Protestant and Catholic participants.[3] Female and male participants in each group experienced similar influences from their religion for becoming teachers (Figure 4.3).

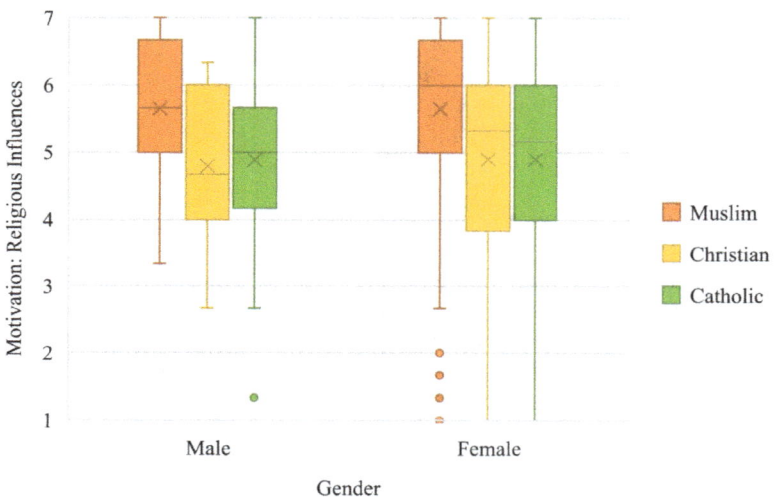

FIGURE 4.3 Different religious influences on motivation to become teachers based on gender and religious groups
Note. Response options: 1 = not at all important, 7 = extremely important. Male Muslim $n = 81$, $M = 5.66$; male Christian $n = 11$, $M = 4.79$; male Catholic $n = 37$, $M = 4.89$; female Muslim $n = 453$, $M = 5.65$; female Christian $n = 45$, $M = 4.90$; female Catholic $n = 152$, $M = 4.89$; $N = 779$ participants

4.3 Were There Any Differences in Perceptions about Teaching and Career Aspirations across Groups?

There were statistically significant multivariate differences among the three religious groups on perceptions about teaching, $F(14, 1426) = 3.36$, $p < .001$;

Pillai's Trace = .064; partial η² = .032. Univariate tests using Bonferroni adjustment ($p < .007$) indicated significant differences occurred for *expertise, social status* and *satisfaction with choice*. There were no significant differences found for participants' perception regarding teacher salary, the discouragement they experienced from family, friends, and mass media to become a teacher, and their perception that teaching is a difficult profession.

Results of the Tukey HSD post hoc tests revealed the following significant differences ($p < .050$): Protestant participants' perception that teaching has higher *expertise* was lower than the other groups; Muslim participants were likely to perceive that teaching has high *social status*. They also more satisfied with their choice for becoming a teacher than Protestant and Catholic participants.[4]

Female participants across three groups were more likely to perceive that teaching requires high expertise (Figure 4.4) and has high social status (Figure 4.5) compared to male participants. Female participants were also more satisfied with their plan to become a teacher (Figure 4.6).

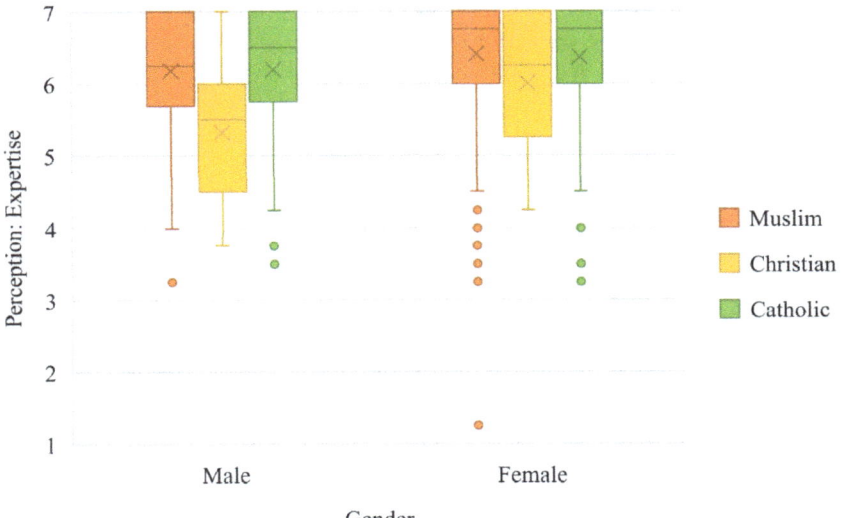

FIGURE 4.4 Perception that teaching requires high expertise based on gender and religious groups
Note: Response options: 1 = not at all, 7 = extremely.
Male Muslim n = 82, M = 6.18; male Christian n = 11, M = 5.32; male Catholic n = 37, M = 6.19; female Muslim n = 457, M = 6.41; female Christian n = 45, M = 6.05; female Catholic n = 154, M = 6.37; N = 786 participants

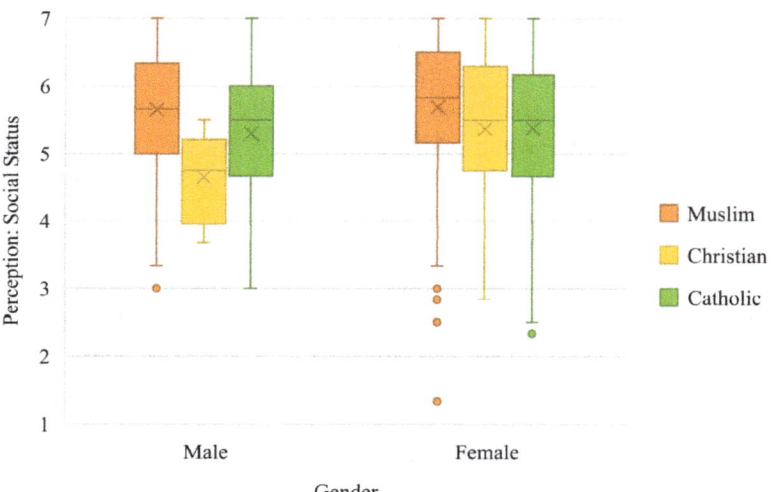

FIGURE 4.5   Perception that teaching has high social status based on gender and religious groups
Note: Response options: 1 = not at all, 7 = extremely.
Male Muslim n = 79, M = 5.66; male Christian n = 10, M = 4.65; male Catholic n = 36, M = 5.30; female Muslim n = 438, M = 5.69; female Christian n = 44, M = 5.37; female Catholic n = 151, M = 5.38; N = 758 participants

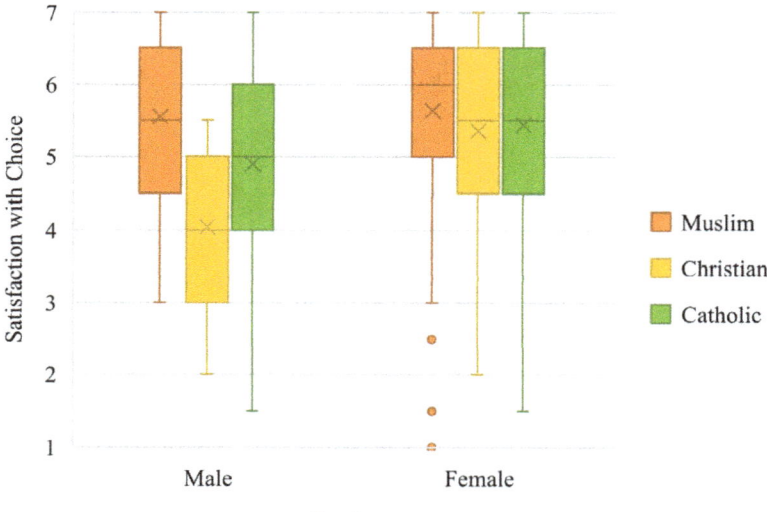

FIGURE 4.6   Satisfaction with choice of becoming a teacher based on gender and religious groups
Note: Response options: 1 = not at all, 7 = extremely.
Male Muslim n = 81, M = 5.56; male Christian n = 11, M = 4.04; male Catholic n = 35, M = 4.90; female Muslim n = 454, M = 5.64; female Christian n = 45, M = 5.36; female Catholic n = 154, M = 5.44; N = 780 participants

4.4 What Was the Role of Religious Beliefs in Students' Teaching Career Aspirations?

There were statistically significant multivariate differences among the three religious groups, F (8, 1522) = 3.17, $p < .001$; Pillai's Trace = .033; partial $\eta^2 = .016$. Univariate tests using Bonferroni adjustment ($p < .012$) indicated significant differences occurred for *planned effort, planned persistence* and *professional development aspirations* (Figure 4.7). Tukey HSD post hoc tests showed significant differences ($p < .050$): Muslim participants would put more effort into teaching, persist further in the profession, and have higher professional development and leadership aspirations compared with Protestant and Catholic participants. A series of boxplots indicated that female participants across all religious groups tended to allocate more effort into teaching and were more likely to persist in teaching compared to male participants (Figures 4.8 and 4.9). Interestingly, female and male participants from Muslim and Catholic groups tended to have similar professional development aspirations, but female Christian participants were more likely to undertake professional development courses compare to male participants in the same religious group (Figure 4.10).

Based on prior correlation results, two of seven perception factors with strong and significant correlations ($r \geq .50$) were included as predictors (*expertise* and *social status*) as well as *satisfaction with choice* and *religious beliefs* (for details of correlations see Suryani, Watt & Richardson, 2016). The study confirms that

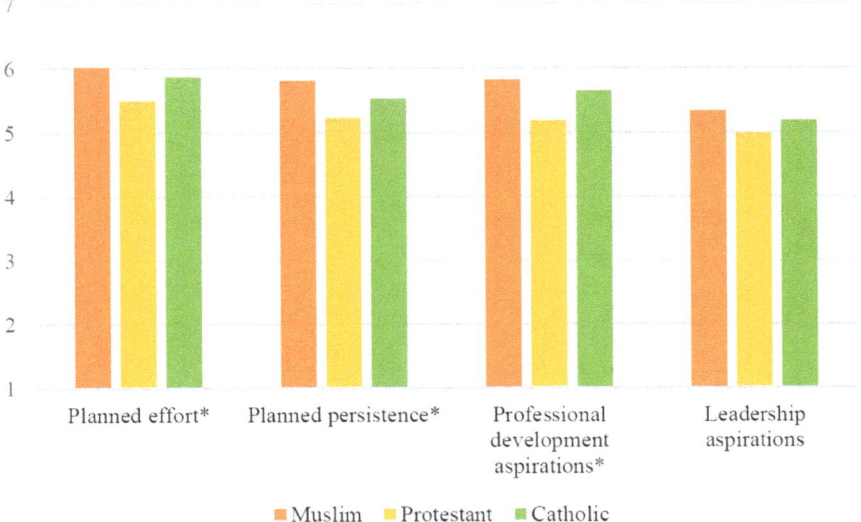

FIGURE 4.7　Different aspirations based on religious groups
　　　　　　Note: Response options: 1 = not at all, 7 = extremely.

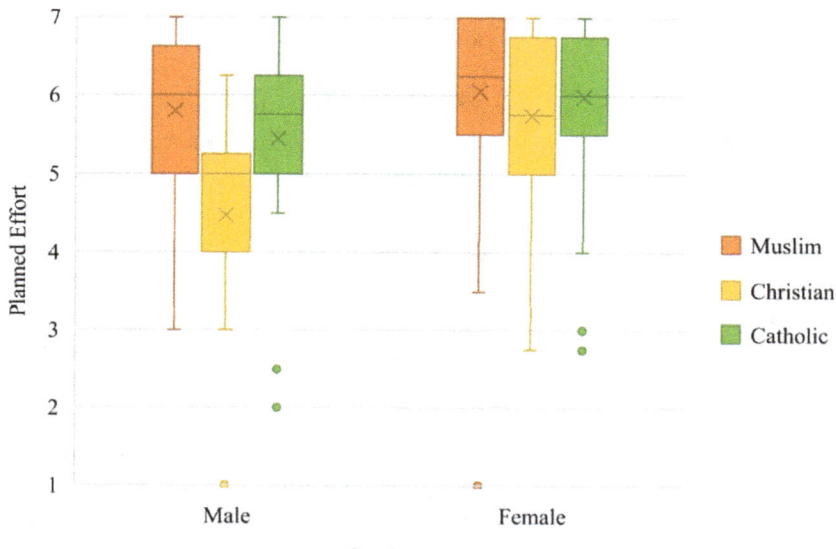

FIGURE 4.8   Planned effort based on gender and religious groups
Note: Response options: 1 = not at all, 7 = extremely.
Male Muslim n = 77, M = 5.79; male Christian n = 11, M = 4.48; male Catholic n = 37, M = 5.44; female Muslim n = 456, M = 6.05; female Christian n = 45, M = 5.74; female Catholic n = 155, M = 5.98; N = 781 participants

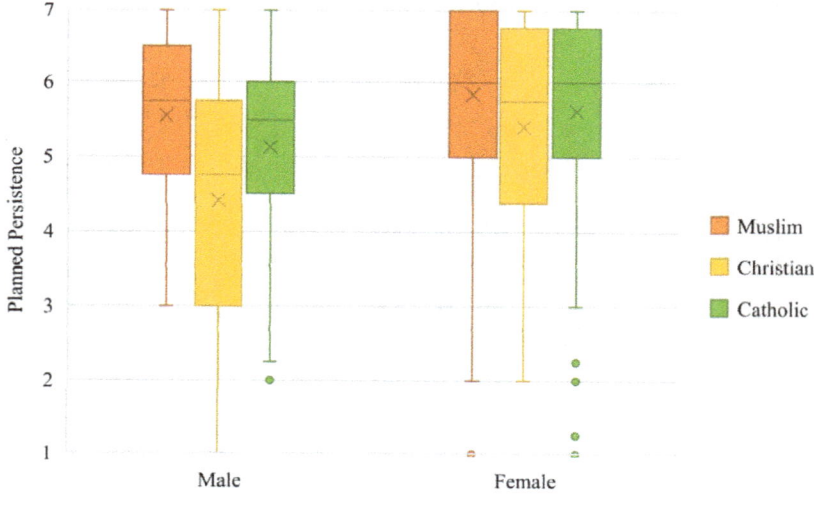

FIGURE 4.9   Planned persistence based on gender and religious groups
Note: Response options: 1 = not at all, 7 = extremely.
Male Muslim n = 78, M = 5.56; male Christian n = 11, M = 4.41; male Catholic n = 37, M = 5.13; female Muslim n = 454, M = 5.84; female Christian n = 45, M = 5.41; female Catholic n = 155, M = 5.62; N = 780 participants

THE ROLE OF RELIGIOUS BELIEFS IN STUDENTS' CAREER ASPIRATIONS   81

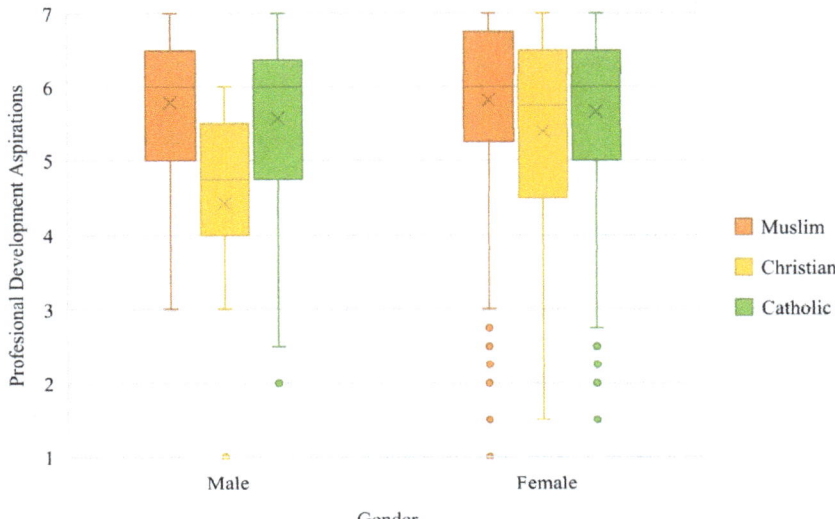

FIGURE 4.10   Professional development aspirations based on gender and religious groups
Note: Response options: 1 = not at all, 7 = extremely.
Male Muslim n = 79, M = 5.79; male Christian n = 11, M = 4.43; male Catholic
n = 37, M = 5.57; female Muslim n = 454, M = 5.82; female Christian n = 43,
M = 5.39; female Catholic n = 152, M = 5.67; N = 776 participants

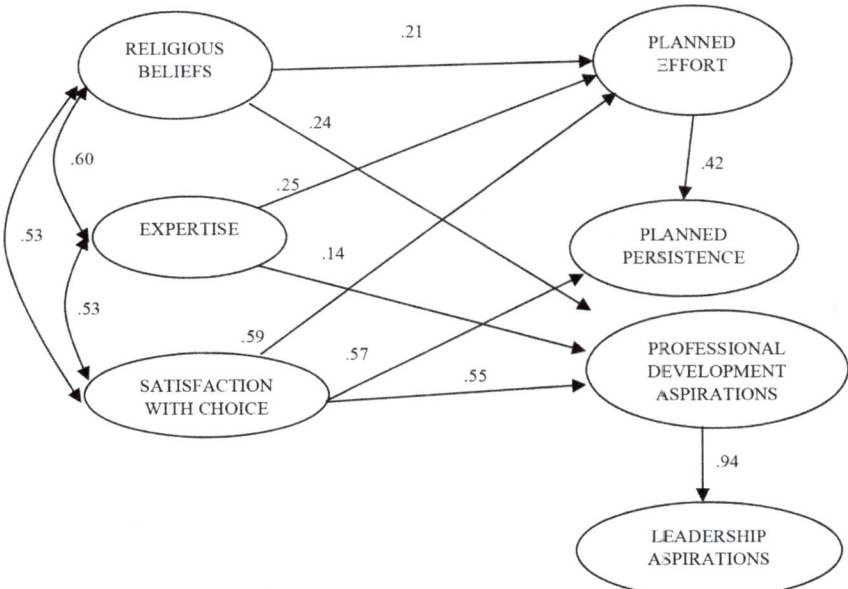

FIGURE 4.11   Structural model for perceptions, religious beliefs and PECDA factors
Note: Only significant structural paths are shown.

participants who were highly religious perceived teaching as an occupation with high social status. Therefore, they would put in more effort and stay longer in the profession.

The amount of effort students planned to put into their teaching was predicted by their religious beliefs, perceptions that teaching requires high levels of expert knowledge and their level of satisfaction with teaching as a career choice. Consequently, the length of time they planned to stay in teaching was predicted by their *planned effort* and *satisfaction with choice*. Their *professional development aspirations,* interestingly, were predicted by *religious beliefs, expertise* and *satisfaction with choice. Leadership aspirations* were predicted by *professional development aspirations*. The model was analysed using full responses and data fitted it well, χ^2 (284, N = 668) = 3.489, TLI = .951, CFI = .957, RMSEA = .061, and SRMR = .042 (Figure 4.11).

5 Discussion

5.1 *Religious Beliefs and Motivations to Become Teachers*

The study confirms that religious beliefs and influences play an important role in students' decision to become teachers and their career aspirations. Most Indonesians recognise that religion and the existence of God are very important aspects in their lives regardless of their religious affiliations. It is predictable that students' personal work goals correspond to their life goals that include the strong influence of religion. They would have the opportunities to serve others while working in a decent and noble profession at the same time. Teachers, lecturers, religious leaders or priests are considered as noble professions because they dedicate themselves to benefit the society while having to live in a modest circumstances.

This study suggests that Muslim participants tended to be more religious than Protestant and Catholic participants. This is consistent with the motivational factors that Muslim participants valued religion as the strongest influence to enter teacher education. Results highlighted that the stronger their *religious beliefs*, the more they followed religious teachings. Because Muslim participants in this study lived in a Muslim-majority, collectivist country at the time of the study, the social influences and pressure exerted upon these participants were also strong, and hence likely to increase their *religious beliefs*. For instance, in Jakarta and Yogyakarta where data were collected, television channels typically interrupted their program five times a day in accordance with the Muslim prayers while showing verses from the Qur'an to remind viewers to pray. Similarly, every Friday afternoon a long lunch break would be common in workplaces to allow Muslims enough time to pray. These types of practices however might not be experienced by those from minority groups, such Catholic and Christian participants.

5.2 Perceptions about Teaching as a Career

Since Muslim participants were likely to be more religious, they perceived teaching as a noble and respected profession and were more satisfied with their choices, compared to participants from Protestant and Catholic religious groups. A study on the influence of religion on career choice suggests that those with strong religious commitments frequently consider themselves as having received a calling from their God to choose noble career pathways (Dik, Duffy, & Tix, 2012). As predicted, the cohort of participants who rated themselves as more religious (in this study, Muslims) were likely to regard the teaching profession highly, and consequently they planned to put more effort into their future teaching and intended to persist longer in their teaching careers.

5.3 Gender Differences

Interestingly, female participants across all three religious groups experienced stronger influences from their religion for becoming teachers. They had a stronger perception of teaching as requiring higher expertise, has higher social status and they were more satisfied with their plan to teach. This is reflected in the Indonesian teaching workforce, particularly in urban schools, where teaching is dominated by women (World Bank, 2010). Gender role socialisation influences people's self-perceptions, goals and values, so that men and women have different self-concepts, different expectations for success across diverse activities, and different values and goals (Eccles, 1994, p. 599). These socialised expectations influence women's and men's educational and occupational choices.

Gender roles also influence the definition of successful task participation. For instance, if women define success in parenting as consisting of high levels of participation in their children's lives, they will prioritise their parenting and spouse-support roles rather than professional career roles and reduce their commitment to their career goals (Eccles, 1994). In the Indonesian contexts, the teaching profession is seen as fitting to women's roles due to the nature of teaching that involves dealing with children and adolescents. Additionally, the fewer working hours involved with teaching means female teachers would be able to finish work early (the typical Indonesian school day concludes around 2 pm) and have enough time to complete their household duties. Therefore, female participants were likely to be satisfied with their choice of profession as it conforms to cultural expectations.

Additionally, female participants were also likely to perceive teaching as requiring high expertise as well as having a high social status as it is one of the few women-dominated professions in a patriarchal society where women have power to directly influence the next generation of Indonesians. Teachers are directly responsible for their students' education and development inside the classroom, which may even extend to those students' post-schooling life.

5.4 *The Role of Religious Beliefs in Students' Teaching Career Aspirations*

The differences shown between religious groups indicated relationships between religion and career aspirations. As previously mentioned, participants who were highly religious were also likely to view teaching as a profession with a high social status and therefore exert more effort into teaching and persist in their careers. The findings specify that not only are Muslim participants likely to be more religious, they also tend to put more effort into their teaching careers, stay longer in the profession, and undertake professional development courses. Their strong religious faith can be beneficial to encourage these future teachers to persist in their career whilst facing challenges in their teaching such as limited school funding and resources.

6 Future Direction

As indicated in this study, the perception of teaching as a highly skilled and professional occupation would predict students' intentions and efforts to improve their knowledge and skills. This would make teaching more attractive to talented senior secondary graduates, which will subsequently improve the competitiveness of the teacher selection process and therefore potentially enhance the quality of future teachers.

Current government policies aiming to improve the quality of teachers however are heavily focused on increasing teacher salary, which has been proven to be ineffective. Initially, certified teachers who receive double basic salary tended to have higher satisfaction with their career, less likely to have a second job and tended to have less financial stress (De Ree et al., 2016; Kusumawardhani, 2017). Nevertheless, it is predicted that after two and three years, doubling their salary would not impact their effort in teaching and have no further impact on student learning outcomes and teacher performance, as measured by student test scores, teacher test scores, and teacher attendance (Kusumawardhani, 2017).

In light of these findings, we need to improve upon current teacher education policies to better reflect the reality of what motivates teacher education students—that is, religious beliefs, perceptions of teaching as requiring high expertise and knowledge, and satisfaction with their choice of profession, not merely teacher salary. This may translate to initiatives by teacher educators that encourage teacher education students to continuously undergo professional growth, as improving on one's teaching knowledge and skills to better the lives of others are valued by most religions. Therefore, it is interesting to follow up on the journeys teacher education students undertake from university to the workplace to determine the role religion plays in their teaching career.

Acknowledgement

The author would like to thank Professor Paul W. Richardson (Monash University) and Professor Helen M.G. Watt (The University of Sydney) for supporting this research project.

Notes

1. The majority of the population are Muslims (87.18%), followed by Protestants (6.96%), Catholics (2.91%), Hindus (1.69%), Buddhist (0.72%) and others (0.54%) (Statistics Indonesia, 2010). In this chapter, "Christian" refers to "Protestant".
2. This chapter reports partial findings from the first FIT-Choice study conducted in Indonesia. For details of psychometric validation in the Indonesian context, see Suryani, Watt and Richardson (2016).
3. See Suryani (2017) for findings on all motivational factors.
4. See Suryani (2017) for findings on all perception factors.

References

De Ree, J. (2016). *Teacher certification and beyond: An empirical evaluation of the teacher certification program and education quality improvements in Indonesia.* World Bank.

De Ree, J., Muralidharan, K., Pradhan, M., & Rogers, H. (2016). *Double for nothing? Experimental evidence on the impact of an unconditional teacher salary increase on student performance in Indonesia* (NBER Working Paper No. 21806). The National Bureau of Economic Research.

Dik, B. J., Duffy, R. D., & Tix, A. P. (2012). Religion, spirituality and a sense of calling in the workplace. In P. C. Hill, B. K. Dik, & B. J. Dik (Eds.), *Psychology of religion and workplace spirituality* (pp. 113–133). Information Age Publishing.

Dowson, M. (2005). Metaphysical motivation: An expectancy value perspective on why religious beliefs motivate. In M. L. Maehr & S. A. Karabenick (Eds.), *Motivation and religion* (Vol. 14, pp. 1–34). Elsevier.

Eccles, J. S. (1994). Understanding women's educational and occupational choices. *Psychology of Women Quarterly, 18*, 585–609.

French, D. C., Purwono, U., & Triwahyuni, A. (2011). Friendship and the religiosity of Indonesian Muslim adolescents. *Youth Adolescence, 40*, 1623–1633.

Gunawan, I. (2017). Instructional management in Indonesia: A case study. *Researchers World, 8*(1), 99.

Hassan, R., Corkindale, C., & Sutherland, J. (2008). The reality of religious labels: A study of Muslim religiosity. *Journal for the Academic Study of Religion, 21*(2), 188–199.

Khidhir, S. (2019). Why did Indonesia fare badly in PISA 2018? *The ASEAN Post*. Retrieved from https://theaseanpost.com/article/why-did-indonesia-fare-badly-pisa-2018

Kurniawati, S., Suryadarma, D., Bima, L., & Yusrina, A. (2018). Education in Indonesia: A White elephant? *Journal of Southeast Asian Economies, 35*(2), 185–199.

Kusumawardhani, P. N. (2017). Does teacher certification program lead to better quality teachers? Evidence from Indonesia. *Education Economics, 25*(6), 590–618.

Low, E. L., Lim, S. K., Ch'ng, A., & Goh, K. C. (2011). Pre-service teachers' reasons for choosing teaching as a career in Singapore. *Asia Pacific Journal of Education, 31*(2), 195–210.

Marshall, J. M. (2009). Describing the elephant: Preservice teachers talk about spiritual reasons for becoming a teacher. *Teacher Education Quarterly, 36*(2), 25–44.

Meyers, L. S., Gamst, G., & Guarino, A. J. (2006). *Applied multivariate research*. Sage.

Ministry of Research, Technology and Higher Education (MoRTHE). (2018a). *Menyoal pendidikan calon guru (About pre-service teacher quality)*. Retrieved from http://sumberdaya.ristekdikti.go.id/index.php/2017/07/11/menyoal-pendidikan-calon-guru/

Ministry of Research, Technology and Higher Education (MoRTHE). (2018b). *Teacher professional education [Pendidikan Profesi Guru]*. Retrieved from https://belmawa.ristekdikti.go.id/pendidikan-profesi-guru/

Ministry of Research, Technology and Higher Education (MoRTHE). (2018c). *Guidelines for managing teacher professional education program*. Directorate General of Learning and Student Affairs.

Nilan, P., Parker, L., Bennett, L., & Robinson, K. (2011). Indonesian youth looking towards the future. *Journal of Youth Studies, 14*, 709–728.

Parker, L. (2011). Where are the women in multiculturalism? *Australian Feminist Studies, 26*, 433–452.

Parker, L., & Nilan, P. (2013). *Adolescents in contemporary Indonesia*. Routledge.

Retnawati, H., Munadi, S., Arlinwibowo, J., Wulandari, N., & Sulistyaningsih, E. (2017). Teachers' difficulties in implementing thematic teaching and learning in elementary schools. *The New Educational Review, 48*(2), 201–212.

Salili, F. (2005). A psychological analysis of religious motivation with a focus on Islam and the Middle East. In M. L. Maehr & S. A. Karabenick (Eds.), *Motivation and religion* (Vol. 14, pp. 373–401). Elsevier.

Sasaki, J. Y., & Kim, H. S. (2010). At the intersection of culture and religion: A cultural analysis of religion's implications for secondary control and social affiliation. *Journal of Personality & Social Psychology, 101*(2), 401–414.

Smith, S. J., & Pantana, J. J. (2010). Preservice second-career teachers in a blended online-residential preparation program: Profiling characteristics and motivations (TEJ). *Faculty Publications and Presentations*, Paper 143. Retrieved from http://digitalcommons.liberty.edu/cgi/viewcontent.cgi?article=1162&context=educ_fac_pubs

Statistics Indonesia [Badan Pusat Statistik]. (2010). *Population census*. Author.

Suryani, A., Watt, H. M. G., & Richardson, P. W. (2016). Students' motivations to become teachers: FIT-Choice findings from Indonesia. *International Journal of Quantitative Research in Education, 3*(3), 179–203.

Suryani, A. (2017). Motivations and aspirations of teacher education students in Indonesia. In H. M. G. Watt, P. W. Richardson, & K. Smith (Eds.), *Global perspectives on teacher motivation* (pp. 248–296). Cambridge University Press.

Syakriah, A. (2019). Spotlight on teachers as Indonesian student competence worsens. *The Jakarta Post*. Retrieved from https://www.thejakartapost.com/news/2019/12/05/spotlight-on-teachers-as-indonesian-student-competence-worsens.html

Watt, H. M. G., & Richardson, P. W. (2007). Motivational factors influencing teaching as a career choice: Development and validation of the FIT-Choice Scale. *Journal of Experimental Education, 75*(3), 167–202.

Watt, H. M. G., & Richardson, P. W. (2008). Motivations, perceptions, and aspirations concerning teaching as a career for different types of beginning teachers. *Learning and Instruction, 18*, 408–428.

Wigfield, A., & Eccles, J. S. (2000). Expectancy–value theory of achievement motivation. *Contemporary Educational Psychology, 25*(1), 68–81.

World Bank. (2010). *Transforming Indonesia's teaching force* (Vol. II). World Bank, Ministry of National Education, Kingdom of Netherlands.

World Values Survey Association. (2005–2009). *World values survey wave 5*. Retrieved September 8, 2019, from http://www.worldvalues survey.org/WVS Online.jsp

Worthington Jr., E. L., Wade, N. G., Hight, T. L., McCullough, M. E., Berry, J. T., Ripley, J. S., Berry, J. W., Schmitt, M. M., Bursley, K. H., & O'Connor, L. (2003). The religious commitment inventory-10: Development, refinement, and validation of a brief scale for research and counseling. *Journal of Counseling Psychology, 50*, 84–96.

CHAPTER 5

The Boundary Crossing of Indonesian Out-of-Field Teachers

Esti Rahayu and Shuki Osman

Abstract

This chapter presents a study on teacher learning based on a case of four initially out-of-field teachers in Indonesia as they develop to become master or accomplished teachers. Employing the conceptual framework of "boundary crossing" and the notion of "boundary objects" (Akkerman & Bakker, 2011), the study investigates how teacher learning occurs where boundaries serve as not only sources of potential difficulties, but also opportunities for innovation and renewal related to perception of professional identity and practice. A component of the learning includes a move from "non-teaching space" into "teaching space". In-depth interviews with teachers and the analysis identifies four dialogical learning mechanisms: identification, coordination, reflection, and transformation. Findings show that as teachers cross boundaries, they identify discontinuities between different teaching spaces, while finding sufficient boundary objects which establish recognizable actions and interactions in the out-of-field space. The discussion includes the role of teacher reflection within a professional learning community to build on their experiences and ease boundary crossing. This study informs both the educational realities faced by many Indonesian youths in under-resourced communities where teachers commonly teach out-of-field; as well as of youths who are in teacher education programs to prepare themselves to be adaptable, capable, and informed.

Keywords

boundary crossing – identification, coordination, reflection, transformation – teacher learning

1 Introduction

In the Indonesian language, a teacher is called *guru*. In Javanese, a guru is someone who must be *digugu* (obeyed) and *ditiru* (as a role-model). Traditionally, teachers have been required to earn a degree in education and gain student-teaching experience before becoming a teacher (Shuls & Trivitt, 2015). Alternatively, people with any bachelor's degree are hired to teach for many reasons, including substituting for absent teachers for a short, medium, or long term; to resolve teaching load allocation issues in cases where there no teachers are available, or for various other reasons (Hobbs, 2013). These teachers are known as out-of-field teachers because they do not have a teaching qualification. The learning journey out-of-field novices take to become accomplished teachers can be viewed as a process termed "boundary-crossing". This chapter draws on the learning experiences of four accomplished teachers who were at one point in their career out-of-field novices. The discrepancies between what they learn at the university and their current job as teachers are conceptualised as boundaries, and the interactions and transitions from one site to another is known as a boundary-crossing. This chapter discusses the out-of-field teaching phenomenon in Indonesia and utilises a framework of boundary-crossing as a language to describe different learning phases. It presents a series of snapshots of the experiences of four out-of-field teachers and highlights key points of their learning framed through the concept of the mechanism of learning (Akkerman and Bakker, 2011).

2 The Out-of-Field Phenomenon

"Out-of-field" teachers are those who do not possess a teaching qualification or certification (Ingersoll, 2002), or who do, but teach a year level, subject, or field beyond their expertise (Du Plessis, 2017). Du Plessis argues that the origin of out-of-field teaching lies not in the level of education teachers have, but in the conflict between teachers' placements and their field of training (p. 15). Other terms to denote out-of-field are non-linear, mismatch, and misassignment. In Indonesia, this out-of-field teaching phenomenon exists and has been one of education's undiscussed epidemics.

A series of studies conducted by Richard Ingersoll (1999, 2002, 2003, 2005, and 2006) argued that out-of-field teaching should be understood as an organisational issue and a common practice in schools. The issue applies to all subject areas, year or school levels, and all types of schools (public, private, or independent). It is also known to be an international phenomenon (Du Plesis,

2017). This common practice causes poor quality of teaching effectiveness as teachers do not have the required knowledge in order to teach competently, such as subject matter knowledge, pedagogical knowledge and pedagogical content knowledge (Hisrch, 2006; Darling-Hammond, 2010; Du Plessis et al., 2015). These teachers do not have sound knowledge for teaching because they are either not trained teachers or they do not teach the subject matter or year level they are trained for. As a result, out-of-field teachers tend to be anxious and less confident about their teaching, which may lead them to burn out and leave the teaching profession.

While studies have found the negative impacts of being out-of-field teachers (Ingersoll, 2003; Du Plessis, 2014), Hobbs (2013) found that some teachers see out-of-field teaching as an opportunity. While some out-of-field teachers feel like they are "just filling in" and hope that it is short-term, other attempts to "make the most of it" regardless of subject matter, and some others end up "pursuing an interest", subsequently choosing to teach the subject permanently despite being out-of-field. These teachers stay in teaching because they feel supported, there is a culture of collaboration amongst staff, and the teachers put themselves as learners that lead into what Hobbs calls "identity expansion" (p. 27).

Lieberman and Pointer Mace (2009) defined accomplished teachers in two categories: (1) the number of years they have taught and (2) their ability to reflect on their experiences and become fluent about the complexity of their teaching. A study conducted in Australia showed that out-of-field teachers who stayed teaching for more than five years in the same field might not be officially qualified for it, but they developed significant expertise that made them competent and effective teachers (Du Plessis, 2017, p. 17). This aligned with Huberman's (1989) five professional life phases of teachers: survival and discovery (0–3 years), stabilisation (4–6 years), experimentation and reassessment (7–18), serenity and conservatism (9–30), and disengagement (31+). In the first phase, teachers find both supports and challenges, while in the second phase their identity and efficacy in the classroom are formed. In the third phase, teachers manage changes in role and identity, and in the fourth phase, teachers find work-life tensions and challenges to sustaining motivation. Lastly, in the fifth phase, they either sustain or experience declining motivation. While teachers do not necessarily "earn their stripes" by having taught a number of years, gaining years of experience means having better skills, expertise and the know-how of one's profession. Besides the years of practice, an accomplished teacher can be identified as "a member of a professional community who is ready, willing, and able to teach and to learn from his or her teaching experiences" (Shulman, 2004, p. 259).

2.1 Out-of-Field Phenomenon in Indonesia: School's Rationale for Out-of-Field Teacher Hiring Practices

Indonesia has one of the largest school education systems in the world, teaching over 50 million students across 34 provinces with 2.7 million teachers in general education and another 0.7 million in the religious education system (De Ree et al., 2015). The Teacher Law was enacted in 2005 as an attempt to improve student learning outcomes by focusing on teacher quality and to improve teacher qualifications by mandating that all teachers must have a university degree and teacher certification. According to a World Bank (2018) report, approximately 53% of the teachers in Indonesia have been certified, 17% are eligible for certification, and 30% are not eligible for certification. Although the out-of-field phenomenon has never been officially addressed by the Indonesian Ministry of Education and Culture, the World Bank report (2018) indicated that 47% of teachers were out-of-field.

The issue of out-of-field teaching is particularly rampant among one type of schools. According to the Ministry of Education and Culture Regulation no. 30/2014, the Indonesian government recognises three types of schools: (1) embassy schools, (2) national schools, and (3) joint cooperation schools (*Satuan Pendidikan Kerjasama*, or SPK). Embassy schools are intended for the children of expatriates who work in Indonesia, while national schools are regular schools serving all Indonesian students, which include both public and private schools. They implement the national curriculum. The third type of schools, SPK, is also meant to serve Indonesian students. However, they are distinct from national schools in their use of a foreign language—commonly English—as a medium of instruction, and implementation of an international curriculum (e.g. International Baccalaureate, Cambridge, Abeka, etc). Similar to national schools, they have to teach Indonesian language, civic, and religion, as well as to conduct the national examination.

Due to the enactment of this Regulation, starting 1 December 2014, all schools labelled "international" had to omit the word from the schools' names. These schools then had the option to be officially recognised as national or as SPK schools. Reregistration was required to become SPK schools. Based on the data from the Ministry of Education and Culture, by the end of 2014, 384 schools from kindergarten to senior secondary registered as SPKs. This number has grown to 537 schools by the end of 2017.

SPKs use English as the medium for instructions, and as such teachers are required to speak English fluently and be able to effectively deliver their teaching instructions in English. SPK schools commonly perform three types of teacher recruitment. The first is the recruitment of English teachers, whether from the US, Canada, UK, Australia, or New Zealand, who are certified to teach English. This was to fulfil the Ministry regulation. The rest of the subjects can be taught by Indonesian or national teachers. The recruitment of these local teachers belongs to the second type of SPK teacher recruitment. And this has led to the recruitment of out-of-field teachers as the priority is to fill up all teaching positions.

The out-of-field teaching phenomenon tends to be prevalent among SPK schools due to teacher shortage, particularly for subject matter teachers who are able to teach in English. The out-of-field phenomenon is a reality of the profession for both teachers and school leaders in many countries. It is neither an aberration nor restricted to only a few subject matters (Du Plessis, 2017). Hiring out-of-field teachers have become a solution to the teacher shortage problem, as well as the teacher practice problem. However, out-of-field teachers who stay in the job and perform as well as others for more than 10 years would eventually no longer be considered out-of-field. As previously mentioned, Du Plessis (2017) argued that after three to five years in a specific subject, teachers consider themselves specialists in their subject areas. They might not have the official qualifications, but they have developed significant expertise that makes them competent and effective teachers. The process involving overcoming challenges in their praxis and expanding their repertoire of teaching skill may be understood from the perspective of boundary-crossing. This conceptual framework is briefly described in the proceeding segment.

3   Boundary Crossing: A Framework

Boundary crossing refers to a person's transition as well as interactions from one site or community of practice to another. It is the distinctions between what is known and what is not yet known (Akkerman & Baker, 2011). The person who is crossing the boundary is called a boundary crosser or a broker. The broker enters into "a territory with which [they] are unfamiliar and, to some significant extent, therefore unqualified" (Suchman, 1994, p. 25). Guile and Griffiths (2001) added that boundary crossers will not only take advantages of construction from other contexts but also experience new knowledge construction and transformation of identities and skills. Boundary crossing offers opportunities for learning and can even be used as a tool for promoting learning (Tuomi-Grohn et al., 2003).

Akkerman and Bakker (2011) revealed four learning mechanisms and processes in crossing boundaries. The learning mechanisms include identification, coordination, reflection and transformation. *Identification* is the most crucial to all forms of learning and development because it is the practice of thinking (Guile & Griffiths, 2001). It refers to learning that involves determining relationships between the practices of each site, focussing on encountering and reconstructing the boundary. *Coordination* refers to overcoming the boundary in order to facilitate future and effortless movement between sites (Akkerman & Bakker 2011, p. 13). *Reflection* refers to "realising and explicating differences between practices and thus to learn something new about [our] own and others' practices" (Akkerman & Bakker, 2011, pp. 144–145). *Transformation* often involves some confrontation that arises as a result of the intersection of social worlds. This confrontation can lead to a reconsideration of practice. Akkerman and Bakker (2011) stated that "boundaries and crossing of boundaries mediate a deliberate target of change" (p. 17).

In supporting boundary crossing, boundary objects are needed. Wenger (1998) defines boundary objects as entities that can link communities together as they allow different groups to collaborate on a common task. Boundary objects serve as a bridge between fields of knowledge or practice.

Using the framework of learning mechanism described above, the study seeks to describe and explain the process with which teachers transition from their novice and out-of-field status to becoming experienced, if not accomplished or experts.

4 Methodology

This research was carried out in joint cooperation schools/SPK in Jakarta, Bandung, and Tangerang, Indonesia between May to August 2018. The purposefully selected participants include four local SPK teachers who are Indonesian nationals, who have been teaching in SPK for more than 10 years and three additional school leaders. The data are based on interviews with the teachers on their learning journey from out-of-field novices to accomplished teachers, and interviews with leaders on their reasons for hiring out-of-field teachers as well as the support they provided to these teachers. The interviews were digitally recorded and transcribed. A thematic analysis (van Manen, 1990) of the interview data was used to identify themes within the overall inquiry on the reasons for out-of-teacher hiring practices and the teachers' learning mechanisms.

5 Results

5.1 *School Perspectives on Recruitment of Out-of-Field Teachers*
All of the school leaders stated their concerns about having difficulties when finding Indonesian teachers who speak English fluently and can deliver the subjects in English effectively. They have at least two options for hiring local

teachers. The first option is to hire English Education graduates. English education graduates are prepared to teach English at both junior and senior secondary levels. If the schools hired them, they would get qualified teachers who are able to teach in English. However, these teachers could also be hired to teach English at the pre-school or primary education level, or teach various non-STEM subjects at the secondary level and teach those classes in English. The second option is to hire anyone with a Bachelor's degree regardless of areas of expertise, who exhibit a passion for teaching and speak English fluently.

Both hiring options have consequences. The first group consists of teachers who know how to teach English at the secondary level, but may have to teach subjects for which they lack content knowledge or at levels that are different from their training. These English education graduates would need to develop their content- and pedagogical content knowledge for other subjects or to teach students below secondary levels. In the second group, teachers who hold Bachelor's degrees come from various backgrounds, such as natural sciences, engineering, economics, law, and others. These teachers are not trained to teach, and as such the schools would have to develop their what Lee Shulman (1986) terms as "content knowledge", "pedagogical knowledge", and "pedagogical content knowledge".

All of the school leader interviewees were aware of this and admitted to having allocated a significant amount of money for teachers' professional development from the moment they joined the school. This included solid induction and sharing sessions done by more experienced teachers, teamwork planning, as well as ongoing professional learning. Lastly, when the schools cannot find the appropriate teachers, their last resort is hiring teachers from neighbouring Asian countries like Malaysia, the Philippines, and Singapore.

5.2   Out-of-Field Teachers

The results of the interview and discussion below address the schools' support for out-of-field teachers and the teachers' learning process. Table 5.1 provides a brief overview of the four teachers in terms of their qualifications, subjects they taught throughout their teaching career, and their current teaching field/subject. Illustrative excerpts from the interview with each of the teachers are included in the discussion below.

Teacher 1: Ani.   Ani started her teaching journey as a learning support assistant (LSA). She initially applied for a librarian position, but during the interview, the principal offered her an LSA position and she took it. The challenges started as soon as the induction began, because the presenters in the induction used technical terms with which she was unfamiliar, such as "scaffolding" and "holistic". Because the school set a mentor-mentee system, she was able to

TABLE 5.1 Participants' qualification and teaching experience

Name	Qualifications	Years of teaching	Subjects and levels they have taught	Current subject and level
Ani	Bachelor of communication (Journalism)	13	Nursery, toddler, preschool	Preschool
Nita	Bachelor of English education	15	Nursery, toddler, preschool, primary school teaching Bahasa Indonesia, and arts	Primary school teacher (teach mostly all subjects)
Adri	Bachelor of chemical engineering	13	Mathematics and science in junior and senior high school	Secondary School teaching mathematics
Eko	Bachelor of economics (Management)	14	All subjects in primary schools	Technology integrator for all levels.

ask her mentor and learn from other resources including books and the internet. She felt enriched during her first few years as she was provided with a substantial amount of training, such as first aid training, sessions on topics such as children development and multiple intelligences, and on developing teaching materials using everyday materials. Throughout her teaching career, she has taught students at multiple levels, both as an LSA and a classroom teacher.

Teacher 2: Nita. Nita graduated from English Education and planned to be an English teacher in a junior or senior high school. During micro-teaching in her 7th semester, she taught English at a senior high school and found that she does not enjoy teaching senior high school students. Instead, she enjoyed teaching English to younger children which she did part-time. After graduation, she worked for a newly established bilingual pre-school and started as a nursery classroom teacher. She then moved up to toddler class. During her first years, she learnt a lot about early childhood education. Then, she moved to a primary school and had to teach various subjects.

Teacher 3: Adri. Adri graduated from Chemical Engineering and worked as a process engineer for 6 months. During his probation, he realised he did not enjoy working with machinery. He wanted to work with people. After leaving the factory, he was more selective in applying for jobs. He still wanted to work in the field of engineering but would prefer to work with people. While waiting for the next job, he worked part-time in a tuition centre teaching mathematics and science. He enjoyed teaching but never thought of making it as a career. Seeing his enthusiasm in teaching, his father suggested him to apply to become a teacher. He refused, but his father was persistent in persuading him to give it a try. And he did. The only teaching experience he had was teaching at the tuition centre. The school invested a lot of resources when training him to improve his pedagogical knowledge. He realised that he wasn't very successful during his first year, so he extended the contract for another year, as he wanted to view his own development. He took up multiple roles in addition to teaching. On the third year, he became the Head of the Mathematics Department for the junior high school he was working in. He has developed and used various teaching materials to teach mathematics, and he now supervises other mathematics teachers.

Teacher 4: Eko. Eko graduated with a degree in economics and lectured in his alma mater for two years after his graduation. He did not enjoy teaching at the university. When there was a vacancy to teach in a primary school, he applied for the position. During the induction, he learnt about multiple intelligences. It was eye-opening for him as he learnt that every child is different and require different approaches to learn. Besides teaching at the primary level, he held various roles at the school that enabled him to learn about management, for example, how to organise school activities, communicate with parents, and so on. His interest kept growing and during his fourth year of teaching, he developed an interest in using technology in his classroom. He then found a school which allowed him to explore his ideas of integrating technology into the classroom. He ended up working as a technology integrator at one of the most established SPKs in Jakarta. He continued presenting in international conferences regarding technology integration in teaching for various subjects. As a technology integrator, he assists teachers in using technology to create materials, manage classrooms, present information, facilitate in-class work, and help students use technology to create and learn.

All of the teachers above are boundary crossers with different experiences. Even though they come from different professional paths, all are currently accomplished teachers. Nita, a high school English teacher who ended up teaching at the primary level; Ani, a journalism graduate; Adri, an engineer; and Eko, an economics graduate became out-of-field as they did not have the official required qualification. Their learning experiences are described below through Akkerman and Bakker's (2011) four learning mechanisms.

5.2.1 Identification

Identification is about knowing what the diverse practices are about in relation to one another (Baker & Akkerman, 2017). During the induction, Ani recognised the boundaries of her previous knowledge as she struggled, stating,

> I didn't understand the terms they used during induction like "scaffolding"—I thought it was a kind of activity that requires craft and creativity—then "holistic"—I was wondering whether this kind of school offers religion to students. The more training sessions I joined, the more confused I became. But I asked a lot during the induction and learned more from other resources after the induction.

Not yet crossing the boundaries of her knowledge, here she recollected her confusion.

Adri realised that at the beginning of his teaching career, he did not know how to manage his class,

> On my first few months, I was unsure how to handle the 7th and 8th graders, so after they finished the exercise I gave them, I let them go to the library to do something else, as long as they didn't disturb their classmates.

Here, Adri identified his lack of knowledge in classroom management.

Although Nita was equipped with knowledge on how to teach, teaching primary school students required a lot of effort from her.

> Teaching mostly all subjects were never easy. I had to teach arts, I had to teach mathematics with an inquiry.

Nita who had trained to be a high school English teacher identified her knowledge boundaries, and practices beyond her expertise which in this case was teaching primary children and various subjects.

Eko learned about multiple intelligence that taught him every child is different. This new knowledge provided him with a way to think about what children do and what they are interested in doing and how to support each child given their uniqueness. This is an identification process where, as Akkerman and Bakker framed it, "the learning potential resides in a renewed sense-making of different practices and related identities" (p. 144). It also represents "a focus on a renewed sense of practices and reconstruction of current identity" (p. 147).

5.2.2 Coordination

It is a process when boundary objects play their roles in providing bridges between fields. Coordination is about "creating cooperative and routinized exchanges between practices" (p. 150).

The school leaders interviewed provided opportunities for the out-of-field teacher novices to learn on the job. They provided a safe environment for the teachers to grow through hands-on professional developments, as well as through learning from colleagues who were ready to answer questions whenever the teachers needed help. Resources that helped them achieve their classrooms' learning outcomes were also made available. All participants in this study admitted that they had school leaders who gave them a chance to grow. Ani recalled,

> I was fortunate when I applied because I was offered to be a learning support assistant. I didn't apply for that position because I knew I had no teaching background and experience. During the interview, the school leader offered me that position with all the training needed.

Nita also remembered,

> During the teaching demo, I was asked to do storytelling. I had to make animal sounds, but instead of "woof woof" for dogs, I said "guk guk [Indonesian term used to refer to barking]". The school leader later corrected me after the demo. After that, she [the school leader] sent me for early childhood education training to equip me with everything I needed to teach young children.

Eko reminisced,

> When I moved to this school as a technology integrator, my school leader allowed me to make decisions related to the use of technology. You name it: books, training. Now I have Maker Space (technology-related laboratory) as a participatory learning environment.

Here, the training served as boundary objects that facilitated learning, and the teachers engaged in coordinating their interaction with these objects to eventually become boundary crossers.

In a different example, Adri recollected,

> The school has invested a lot of money to send me to a variety of professional developments. Also, the mentor-mentee system in this school enabled me to learn from my mentor without borders. My mentor answered all of my questions, even the stupid ones.

In this excerpt, in addition to professional development sessions, what served as a boundary object for Adri was a mentor. Thus, individual people, resources such as books, and experiences such as professional development training are boundary objects that are involved in the process of coordination where, through routinisation, new practices become part of a set of automatised or operational practice. These boundary objects are a part of the support mechanism in boundary-crossing.

5.2.3 Reflection

Reflection is a more profound effect of boundary-crossing. It results in an expanded set of perspectives and thus a new construction of identity that informs future practice. This learning mechanism emphasises the potential of boundaries to enhance the reflection of practice (Hobbs, 2013 p. 23). In the examples below, each teacher reflected on the process of shifting the boundaries of their competencies or knowledge—from previously out-of-field to, then, in-field—as well as the benefits of reflecting.

Ani presented her reflection journal. It was mostly filled with doodles of important quotes she received from colleagues, from her school leaders and professional development presenters that always motivated her to teach better every day. She also kept some digital pictures of what she has done in the classroom, with notes of what worked and what didn't. She stated that she referred to her journals to help new teachers find their own teaching styles.

Nita used her daily reflection journal to reflect before taking the next role. For example, as the school approaches a new academic year, the school leader would map the allocation of teachers for the upcoming year. The school leader would either place her at the same level or move her to a different level. Nita would use her reflection journal to provide reasons for why she should move or stay.

It took four years for Adri to be sure that teaching is for him. Every November, his school leader asked whether he would like to get his contract extended. He was given two months to consider the offer. During that period, he would consider many aspects before deciding to extend. And every year, because he was not satisfied with what he has achieved, he would ask for a contract extension. He said it was his way to challenge himself to be better. When Eko took on a new position as a technology integrator, he saw how his past roles and experiences in previous schools had prepared him for this job.

As illustrated above, all teacher participants learned about themselves and their practice through the teaching journey. They moved out of their comfort zone because not only did they think it was possible to do so, but they also realised the benefits to be gained from it. Bakker and Akkerman (2016) argue that this mechanism is a step further than identification as people became aware of their own roles as well as learned to appreciate them through the eyes of others.

5.2.4 Transformation

Transformation leads to profound changes as the teachers in this study are no longer out-of-field teachers. They are not only experienced or accomplished teachers but also certified teachers now. As out-of-field novices, they were not trained teachers prior to the assignment. They received on-the-job training for their professional development.

In order to transform, the teachers experienced "confrontation" (p. 146) and "hybridization" (p. 148). Confrontation is a "disruption in the current flow of work" (p. 147). These confrontations were shown in Ani's experience of not understanding the technical terms the trainers used during the inductions as well as Nita's experiences of moving from one level to another to determine which levels she worked best with, and she finally found her world in primary education. Adri's previous experience working within his field of training or expertise did not bring him happiness, as he did not interact with people. This caused him to confront his own belief that teaching might bring him joy, despite at first not wanting to make teaching as his main job. Eko's experience in following his passion in the technology involved clashing with his colleagues who disagreed with him regarding the use of technology in the classroom. If such a conflict did not occur, transformation cannot be expected.

Confrontation might happen multiple times, shaping them to become the teachers they are and, in the future, better teachers. The knowledge and practices that brought frustration or confusion became their new routines. Akkerman and Bakker (2011) noted that in a way transformation is the opposite of coordination mechanism, stating that coordination,

> … reflects a smooth, effortless, and routine process of people or objects moving back and forth between practices, whereas [transformation] involves confrontations and continuous joint work. (p. 151)

> … [This] *continuous joint work at the boundary* is required to preserve the productivity of boundary-crossing. (p. 149)

This study found that this transformation of practices and identity also represent a career change for all of the teachers.

6   Conclusion

All four teachers in the study experienced learning during their boundary-crossing. They came from different fields of expertise such as economics, journalism, and engineering, but they all chose to become teachers. They found discrepancies between their academic qualification and their current occupations. Most of them were not prepared to teach, at least not at the level and in the subject matter they found themselves teaching.

While they faced obstacles, they did not take the teaching role itself as an obstacle. With the help of boundary objects like individuals such as their leaders and colleagues and resources such as books and professional development training, they were offered the opportunities to learn and underwent boundary-crossing to finally become accomplished teachers with more than 10 years of teaching experiences. The teachers in this study shared some similarities in terms of their motivation to learn, support network, ongoing reflection and willingness to change. They were redefining the out-of-field teaching situation as an opportunity for learning. Furthermore, the enactment of Teacher Law in 2005 allowed these teachers to gain recognition as having acquired official teaching qualifications through certification. Certification officially acknowledged the professional development they had participated in and the teaching hours they have completed.

The study is limited to the learning journey of four out-of-field teachers and their path in learning how to teach using the lens of boundary-crossing learning mechanisms. Their motivation to stay in the job in relation to monetary reasons is overlooked, a possible area for future research. This study is also limited to teacher participants in big cities like Jakarta, Tangerang, and Bandung. Since the sample of participants of the study was a purposeful sample, the study aims neither to display consistency across situations and time periods nor to develop generalisability of the findings. This study is, however, capable of highlighting insights with regard to opportunities in growth and learning among novice teachers in SPKs and elsewhere, who are willing to teach and are proficient in the English language. Through the learning they may do in the workplace, out-of-field novices can transform to become accomplished teachers.

There are a number of interesting opportunities for future research related to this study. First, as the focus of this study was on the learning mechanisms of out-of-field novices to become accomplished teachers, other studies may explore the impact of out-of-field teachers on students' achievements. Secondly, other studies may further contribute to the understanding of the complexity of the out-of-field teaching phenomenon in Indonesia. Data emerging from this study can also be further analysed and used to refine future studies on out-of-field teaching phenomenon in Indonesia.

References

Akkerman, S. F., & Bakker, A. (2011). Boundary crossing and boundary object. *Review of Educational Research, 81*(2), 132–169. doi:10.3102/0034654311404435

Bakker, A., & Akkerman, S. (2017). The learning potential of boundary crossing in the vocational curriculum. In *The Wiley handbook of vocational education and training.* Wiley Blackwell.

Darling-Hammond, L. (2010). Teacher education and the American future. *Journal of Teacher Education, 61*(1–2), 35–47.

De Ree, J., Muralidharan, K., Pradhan, M., & Rogers, H. (2015). *Double for nothing? Experimental evidence on the impact of an unconditional teacher salary increase on student performance in Indonesia* (No. w21806). National Bureau of Economic Research.

Du Plessis, A. E. (2017). *Out-of-field teaching practices: What educational leaders need to know.* Sense Publisher.

Du Plessis, A. E., Carroll, A., & Gillies, R. M. (2015). Understanding the lived experiences of novice out-of-field teachers in relation to school leadership practices. *Asia-Pacific Journal of Teacher Education, 43*(1), 4–21

Du Plessis, A. E., Gillies, R. M., & Carroll, A. (2014). Out-of-field teaching and professional development: A transnational investigation across Australia and South Africa. *International Journal of Educational Research, 66*, 90–102.

Guile, D., & Griffiths, T. (2001). Learning through work experience. *Journal of Education and Work, 14*, 113–131.

Hirsch Jr., E. (2006). *The knowledge deficit: Closing the shocking gap for American children.* Houghton Mifflin Company.

Hobbs, L. (2013). Teaching 'out-of-field' as a boundary-crossing event: Factors shaping teacher identity. *International Journal of Science and Mathematics Education, 11*(2), 271–297. doi:10.1007/s10763-012-9333-4

Huberman, M. (1989). The professional life cycle of teachers. *Teachers College Record, 91*(1), 31–57.

Ingersoll, R. (1999). The problem of underqualified teachers in American secondary schools. *Educational Researcher, 28*(2), 26–37.

Ingersoll, R. (2002). The teacher shortage: A case of wrong diagnosis and wrong prescription. *NASSP bulletin, 86*(631), 16–31.

Ingersoll, R. (2003). *Out-of-field teaching and the limits of teacher policy*. Retrieved from http://repository.upenn.edu/gse_pubs/143

Ingersoll, R. (2005). The problem of underqualified teachers: A sociological perspective. *Sociology of Education, 78*(2), 175–178.

Ingersoll, R. (2006). *Understanding supply and demand among mathematics and science teachers*. Retrieved from http://repository.upenn.edu/gse_pubs/136

Lieberman, A., & Pointer Mace, D. H. (2009). The role of 'accomplished teachers' in professional learning communities: Uncovering practice and enabling leadership. *Teachers and Teaching: Theory and Practice, 15*(4), 459–470.

Shulman, L. S. (1986). Those who understand: Knowledge growth in teaching. *Educational Researcher, 15*(2), 4–14.

Shulman, L. S., & Shulman, J. H. (2004). How and what teachers learn: A shifting perspective. *Journal of Curriculum Studies, 36*(2), 257–271.

Shuls, J. V., & Trivitt, J. R. (2015). Teacher effectiveness: An analysis of licensure screens. *Educational Policy, 29*(4), 645–675.

Suchman, L. (1994). Working relations of technology production and use. *Computer Supported Cooperative Work, 2*, 21–39.

Tuomi-Gröhn, T., & Engeström, Y. (Eds.). (2003). *Between school and work: New perspectives on transfer and boundary-crossing*. Pergamon.

van Manen, M. (1990). *Researching lived experience: Human science for an action sensitive pedagogy*. State University of New York Press.

World Bank. (2018). *Indonesia economic quarterly, June 2018: Learning more, growing faster*. Retrieved from https://openknowledge.worldbank.org/handle/10986/29921

PART 2

School and Institutional Practices

CHAPTER 6

The Implementation of Character Education Programs in Indonesian Schools

Wahyu Nurhayati

Abstract

This chapter explores approaches to schools' implementation of character education, focusing on the strategies employed in assessing character change in the student. Using the "7 E's" (Explain it, Examine it, Exhibit it, Expect it, Experience it, Encourage it, and Evaluate it), a framework of teaching character trait introduced by Thomas Lickona (2004), the study analyses the differences, similarities, as well as affordances and limitations of each approach as practiced by six primary and secondary schools in Jakarta, Indonesia. Qualitative data were based on focus group discussions with select groups of teachers and principals captured. The main finding of this study emphasises the importance of a clear and effective assessment guide for teachers to observe character changes in students. The assessment guide includes the behavioural indicators of each trait fostered in school, based on understandings of the developmental stages of children and adolescents. Implications of this study include the need for more studies to examine various other frameworks to guide the development of assessment models for the implementation of character education in Indonesia.

Keywords

character education – values education – moral development – evaluation criteria – education assessment

1 Introduction

According to the Indonesian Education Law (20/2003), the purpose of education in Indonesia is not only to provide academic development but also to encourage students to develop positive character through classroom learning and various co-curricular and extracurricular activities. Subsequently, the Ministry of Education and Culture of Indonesia have officially implemented character education in the national curriculum of elementary and secondary schools. Through the Presidential Regulation 87/2017 on Strengthening the Character Education (*Penguatan Pendidikan Karakter*, or PPK), the government further explicitly lays out a set of educational goals of building good character, accepting and respecting differences based on culture, race and religion. PPK aims to foster good values, such as honesty, responsibility, respect for others, and to develop a good moral compass among younger generations. Currently, character education programs have been implemented in various primary and secondary schools, focusing on character building through school-based activities.

The government considers implementing character education as beneficial to shaping a student's personality and helps them become good human beings and citizens. To embody these intentions, the Ministry of Education and Culture has established 5 core values to be fostered in schools: integrity, religiosity, nationality, independence, and mutual cooperation. The values are a manifestation of the educational philosophy expressed by Ki Hajar Dewantara, a historical education philosopher and practitioner in Indonesia. He stated that education aims to educate the heart (feeling), the head (knowledge), and the hand (skill). This is in line with Thomas Lickona (2001), who stated that character is comprehensively defined to include thinking, feeling, and behaviour. According to Lickona (2001), character education is a deliberate effort to help people understand, care about, and act upon core values. For example, to possess the value of integrity, someone must understand integrity, care about integrity, and practice integrity. The result of character education is the actual changes in a student's character. For this purpose, a comprehensive collaboration is needed between students, teachers, and the curriculum through every phase of school life.

The Ministry of Education and Culture has provided guidance regarding the implementation of character education, however, schools are given the flexibility to develop methods of enacting it through school policies and classroom practices, including assessing the outcomes and effectiveness of character education. As a result, various strategies of assessment to evaluate character change in the student has been applied by schools. This chapter discusses how three schools interpret, implement, and assess their mandate and goals of developing good characters among their students. A focus group discussion with six teachers from two primary schools and one high school was conducted to identify particular strategies and methods of how schools conduct character education, including the assessment methods implemented by schools. The analysis and discussion are presented using a framework on teaching character traits offered by Lickona (2004), namely, the 7 E's (Explain it, Examine it, Exhibit it, Expect it, Experience it, Encourage it, and Evaluate it) elaborated on in later sections.

2   Character Education in Indonesia

2.1   *What Is Character Education?*

Before we address the discussion on character education, we need to consider what "character" means in this chapter. The word "character" originated from Greek, which meant "to engrave" (O'Sullivan, 2004). Therefore, the character is an engraved trait which causes a person to behave in certain ways. According to Lickona (2001), a character is "knowing the good, desiring the good, and doing the good". Furthermore, Lickona and Davidson (2005) distribute character into performance character and moral character that cannot be separated from one another. Performance character refers to one's characteristics that support the school and work achievement, including effort, perseverance, diligence and attitude. On the other hand, moral character denotes one's characteristics relating to ethical or moral functioning which supports successful interpersonal relationships, such as honesty, respect, caring, and fairness. Nucci, Krettenauer, and Narváez (2014) acknowledged that character education was wider than behaviour control, discipline, training, or indoctrination. It involves long-term learning and development to reinforce the individual as a whole. It can be concluded that character education is a long-term process of building good behaviour cognitively, emotionally, and behaviourally that is in harmony with the moral law.

Although families have a responsibility for building children's character, schools play an important role in supporting families to foster or promote good character in children because they spend most of their time in school. The solid connection between schools and families can give a better result for character building. Schools can provide the curriculum, school culture, and programs to instil good values personally and socially.

Character education is not a new idea for Indonesian schools; it has been a part of their mission long before the PPK was. However, it was implemented unofficially through the curriculum and instruction, or through the school culture and regulations, classroom rules and norms, and daily interactions between teachers and students. Not all schools have made their character education agenda explicit and the teaching of values as well as student character development goals intentional. Indonesian teachers have taught values based on traditional and religious teachings, such as greetings, respect for older people, politeness to others, obedience to parents, and worship to the Almighty God. Normally, teachers become role models who inspire and encourage their students to become a good person. Most private schools in Indonesia are established by faith-based institutions and some are particularly more mature in their consideration and articulation of their character education programs. This is the rationale behind selecting three private schools as part of the study.

2.2 The Importance of Character Education

The younger generation is a crucial human resource for developing a nation in the future. It is important to maintain the quality of the younger generation physically and intellectually, including their thoughts and feelings that influence their daily behaviour. Juvenile delinquency, such as drug abuse, student brawls, bullying, and various crime has become the government's attention (Subdirektorat Statistik Politik dan Keamanan, 2018). This societal crisis signifies the decline in the quality of character of the younger generation. Some frame this as a consequence of an education that emphasises the development of intellectual abilities, while ignoring the spiritual and behavioural aspect of the lives of children and youth.

In recent years, the Indonesian government has put more emphasis on the importance of building national character, without ignoring the cognitive and competencies development aspect of the nation. Character education provides an important role in counteracting the moral decadence of the younger generation in an attempt to prepare high-quality human resources.

Although inculcating values and morals are often seen as a family's obligation, schools also play a significant role in developing and promoting good character to their students; the objective of education is developing competence and encouraging students to become good people. However, teaching someone to be smart is much easier than educating them to be wise. According to Lickona, Schaps, and Lewis (2007), the focus of character education is developing the core ethical values, such as honesty, respect for others, and responsibility, which are needed to become a good human being. Students in school learn and develop good values by discussing, observing behavioural models and repeatedly practicing it in their daily lives. To support this character-building process, the Ministry of Education of Indonesia has implemented a character education curriculum beginning from the primary school level.

2.3 The Policy Context

As previously mentioned, the Presidential Regulation No. 87/2017 on Strengthening Character Education (*PPK*) defines character education as an education movement conducted by schools to strengthen students' character through harmonising their heart, thought, and body, with the involvement and cooperation between schools, family, and society. The movement is framed as a crucial part of the "National Movement for Mental Revolution", a campaign promoted by President Joko Widodo. The purpose of this program is to build good character among all students: religious piety, honesty, tolerance, discipline, hard work, nationalism, love of peace, care for the environment, and an aptitude to work towards bringing about social changes for the future. The regulation puts character education as the soul of the national education system. Its implementation invites public support and involvement through formal, non-formal and informal education, and takes into account Indonesia's multiple diversities.

The Ministry of Education and Culture has implemented the PPK in primary and secondary schools. It specifies five main characters to be fostered in schools, including religiosity, nationalism, independence, integrity, and mutual cooperation. The teaching of these values and character building is done through learning activities integrated into and supported by the 2013 curriculum, using three main approaches: class-based character education, school culture-based character education and community-based character education. This study finds that schools employ various types of methods in conducting the PPK program or enacting character education due to differences in their understanding of character building itself.

2.4   The 7 E's Framework

Generally speaking, Indonesian schools do not have a model on which to plan, implement, and evaluate character education programs, therefore, the purpose of the chapter is to increase the understanding of this topic. The following 7 E's Framework provides a response to the lack of the model that can fulfil the gap in implementing efficacious character programs.

In this chapter, the 7 E's framework guides the discussion regarding assessing behavioural change in students. Lickona and Davidson (2005) established the 7 E's of teaching a character trait are as follows: `

1. "Explain it": defining and describing to teachers and students what the character looks like and discussing its importance.
2. "Examine it": verifying the character in literature, history, and current events.
3. "Exhibit it": teachers showing the character through personal example.
4. "Expect it": schools creating an environment to communicate their expectations of students in building and exhibiting that particular character, such as through mutually understood rules and consequences.

5. "Experience it": providing spaces and opportunities for students to experience the character through everyday interactions, relationships, and activities.
6. "Encourage it": promoting the character through goal-setting and daily practice.
7. "Evaluate it": assessing the character through feedback.

3 Methodology

This chapter illustrates how the 7 E's Framework can be applied to describe and explain well thought out character education programs. Likewise, this framework can be used by schools whose administrators and teachers want to examine their character education programs for possible improvement. The study explores school practices in the implementation of character education programs. We applied qualitative data collected in a focus group discussion conducted by the Centre for Educational Assessment, Ministry of Education and Culture of Indonesia in March 2018. This qualitative method was used to support the exploration of various practices of character education implemented by schools at varying levels. A multiple case design was used to understand the differences and similarities between the case (Baxter & Jack, 2008). Six teachers from three private schools in Jakarta, the capital city of Indonesia, participated in focus group discussions to identify the actual assessment practice used by schools. Schools were randomly selected from a list of ten schools that had implemented character education long before the government established the PPK. The implementation of character education programs in most private schools in Indonesia are established by faith-based institutions and some are particularly more mature in the consideration and articulation of their character education programs. This is the rationale behind selecting three private schools as a part of the study.

4 Findings

Two primary schools and one senior secondary school participated in the focus group discussions. The findings from these discussions are presented below. The section lays out teachers' description of the components of character education enacted within their schools. The following section further analyses the ways each school enact different components or practical principles of teaching character, utilising the framework of the 7 E's of teaching character traits.

4.1 School A

School A was a private Christian primary school. The character education program in this school was called "BEST" and was based on Christianity. Values represented by BEST are:

B = Be Tough
E = Excel Worldwide
S = Share with Society
T = Trust in God

One of the teachers expressed their experience regarding students' character before they involved in the BEST character program:

> Our teachers not only provided academic lessons but also built the student's character since the first day they attended school. Our students in first grade were diverse in their characters, as influenced by parenting styles. There were parents who excessively pampered their children. As a result, children tended to be disrespectful of others and were dependent on others. (T2)

She further reported on the implementation of character education in her school:

> Character education in our school started since children entered first grade on the first day of starting school. For example, first-grade students were welcomed by teachers and guided to greet friends, teachers, and school employees by saying "good morning" to them. We introduced students to respect for their friends, teachers and everyone they met at school. Anyone who visits our school, such as parents or guests, were amazed because students welcomed their arrival in a friendly and respectful manner. (T2)

Each year, the school selects one particular character trait from the Bible, such as faithfulness, love, and patience, as a theme of the character education. The teacher continued:

> Before the beginning of the new school year, we determined one value from the Bible as a theme for our BEST character program. For example, this year we selected "love" as the theme. This theme was divided into twelve subthemes which are applied every month during the academic year, such as "caring" for January's theme and so on. Each month the school determines one-character trait to be fostered by habituation,

which is supported by the curriculum and the teaching and learning process. Furthermore, we organised a meeting with students, teachers, parents, and school employees inform them of the program, its purpose and advantages, and illustrated the design and activities involved of the program. (T1)

The school developed activities during the teaching and learning process which allowed teachers to observe students' behaviour and recorded their observation in an assessment sheet. Rewards and punishments were applied to motivate students to commit to good behaviour and strengthen their character building. Teachers rewarded student attitudes and behaviour in the classroom by giving BEST Character stickers or pins. The total number of stickers or pins students obtained for one month would be counted to determine the student with the most BEST Character awards, who would be awarded the BEST Character student of the month certificate. Moreover, the students' photo would be displayed in front of their classroom for a month. This program received great support from other students and parents because it influenced students' behaviour at school and at home.

Teachers evaluated the character change using behaviour rubrics developed by a team of teachers at the school. The behaviour rubrics contained indicators used to guide teachers when observing students' behaviour every month. Teachers stated that this method made assessing behaviour change simpler and easier because the behaviour indicators were clear. A teacher of School A stated:

> Selecting the BEST character student was one of the most awaited events every month. With curiosity students asked me: "Mam, when would I be chosen as a BEST character student?" Every student wanted their photo to be displayed in their classroom. I encouraged them to be more eager to do good to everyone, such as friends, teachers, and parents, not only to be the BEST character but also for their future life.

4.2 School B

School B was a private Islamic Primary School. This school valued inquiry-based learning, evidence-based practice, and aimed to nurture critical thinking through their practices in implementing K-12 education. One of the teachers expressed the following:

> Our school is an Islamic public school that upholds aspects of diversity and love for Indonesia, so that the identity of students as Indonesians

and Indonesian-speaking people can be maintained and developed in accordance with their character and interests. According to the theory of child development, primary school is an exploratory stage. At this age, a child has high curiosity and has energetic behaviour, so there needs to be habituation in learning to instil good characters, independence, and creativity of children. (T4)

Character education in this school was organised on the basis of six core values selected from Islamic religious teachings, including honesty, respect, courage, love, humility, and nationalism. The motto of the school was "Faith, Independent, Creative, and Nationalism". One teacher stated:

The majority of our students came from wealthy families, therefore, many of them were dependent, less able to share and respect others. Character education in our school was implemented since first grade. The character-building process is implemented through intra-curricular, co-curricular, and extracurricular activities. Various school activities aimed to build students' responsibility, nationality, and religiosity were applied in addition to academic lessons. For example, to maintain a sense of responsibility, students in each grade in daily rotation cleaned their classroom by sweeping and throwing garbage into the trash. This responsibility aimed to encourage students to care for their environment. Students must attend the flag ceremony every Monday to increase their sense of nationalism. The school organises daily collective prayer to strengthen students' faith and religious piety. (T3)

Since the first day of attending school in the first grade, students were trained to greet others, smile, say thank you, help others, and apologise, which aligned with the school's goal to teach the six core values mentioned above. In every school activity, students were motivated to display good behaviour through a motto: "Yes, I can". This motto encouraged students to change their bad character into a good character. For example, not all students were willing to apologise if they were guilty. Several students were ignorant or shy. The teacher motivated and encouraged ignorant and shy students to apologise, with a motto: "Yes, I can!", so that they obtained the courage to apologise.

A multi-rater assessment, a method to collect appraisals from multiple observers, was conducted by the classroom teacher, a subject teacher, and the school counsellor. Each teacher recorded their assessment of students' behaviour through anecdotal notes. At the end of the semester, the school organised an assembly to appreciate students' achievements in terms of academic and non-academic areas. Various performances such as singing and dancing were also presented by students. Additionally, School B provided awards to high achieving students, including those who achieved the best assessment in character education. Awarding students with good behaviour aimed to encourage other students to promote and conduct good behaviour.

4.3 School C

The third school was a private Catholic senior secondary school and unique because 100% of its students were male. Character education in this school was based on five basic values (4C and 1 L) from the Ignatian Pedagogy (IP) that were highly respected by all teachers and students. The 4Cs and 1 L are Competence (intelligence), Compassion (caring for others), Conscience (spiritual), Commitment, and Leadership. The vision of this school was to place itself as the centre of character building in the field of education and to continue improving the competence of their students. The motto of this school was "Intelligence plus Character". For the school, it takes both attributes—intellect and sound character—to enable individuals to become good leaders that will bring a positive and good influence on others.

School C was popular for encouraging character development through disciplinary actions. The most crucial and valued character which all students, teachers and school employees must demonstrate in all their conduct was "honesty". A teacher commented:

> When we entered the front gate of the school, a large inscription that said, "BE HONEST" was displayed on the wall of the front school gate. The highest rule that must be adhered to by students, teachers and school employees was "No Cheating". Students who get caught cheating will be immediately expelled from the school without any prior warning. (T5)

There were two special programs intended to instil good values for students. The first program was "compassion week", a humanitarian social event to cultivate care for the environment and for others, and included activities like picking up garbage in the river and helping out in slum communities. The second was a "live-in" and "sit-in" program. The "live-in" program allowed students to live in a rural community with a poor family. A teacher explained:

> Various experiences were narrated by students who participated in the "live in" program. The majority of students stated that it was a thrilling and memorable experience because they have never visited a rural community that had limited living facilities and lived away from their family.

Nevertheless, at the end of the program, they claimed to be severely separated from the host family where they lived-in. (T6)

The "sit-in" program provided the students with an opportunity to be a student of a different school or boarding school for several days, including schools of different faiths, such as Islam. The purpose of this program was to foster student's tolerance, empathy, and manners. Students were given a book to report their experiences during the program. Each student was assessed by a peer and the host, and assessment results were written on an assessment sheet.

Assessment for students was conducted using student's journal book and their teachers' evaluation book. Students' journal books contained reflections of their experiences in various school activities and their assessment of their friends' behaviour. The teachers' evaluation book reported their appraisal to students' behaviour. At the end of the semester, an appreciation day was organised to reward students' achievements.

4.3.1 Summary of Findings

This study represented the implementation of character education in three private schools in Jakarta, Indonesia, based on the 7 E's framework. Table 6.1 presents a summary of the findings.

5 Discussion

Lickona and Davidson (2005) distributed character into two categories: Performance character and Moral character, which can be translated into a number of cognition and emotion values. The evidence from our study suggests that all schools implemented both categories. The participants reported that they have fostered Performance character, such as being tough (School A), creative (School B), and competent (School C), and Moral character which related to ethics such as respect (School A), caring (School B), and honesty (School C). All of these values cannot be separated from religious values since the major sources of character education in the three participating schools originated from religious values (Moslem (Islam?), Christianity, and Catholicism).

The first principle in 7 E's framework of character education is "Explain it", which involves schools establishing a plan for character education, including through identifying specific themes. The findings show that schools determined the themes of their character education programs from their respective religious philosophies. School A implemented BEST (Be tough, Excel worldwide, Share with society, and Trust in God) character program, which

TABLE 6.1 Summary of findings

The 7 E's framework	School A	School B	School C
Explain it	BEST character: B = Be Tough, E = Excel Worldwide, S = Share with Society, T = Trust in God.	School Motto: Faith, Independent, Creative, and Nationalism.	4C: Competence (intelligence), Compassion (caring for others), Conscience (commitment), and Commitment (commitment).
Examine it	The Bible	The Holy Quran	The Bible
Exhibit it	Teachers as role model.	Teachers as role model.	Principal leadership, and Teachers as role model.
Expect it	Expected through reward and punishment.	Expected through a motto: "Yes, I can".	Expected through rules and consequences.
Experience it	School learning activities and relationship.	Intra-curricular, co-curricular, and extracurricular programs.	External and internal school activities and special events, such as compassion week, Live in and Sit in programs.
Encourage it	Through daily practice	Through daily practice	Through goal settings
Evaluate it	Teacher's anecdotal notes.	Multi-rater assessment.	Teacher evaluation, student reflections, peer appraisals.

was inspired by Christian values. School B, developed *Faith, Independent, Creative, and Nationalism* for the themes of their character education program. Although this theme was not purely from the values of the Moslem faith, it was implemented with nuances from it. School C selected the 4C (Competence, Compassion, Conscience, Commitment) and 1 L (Leadership) themes from the Ignatian Pedagogy.

The three schools established characters and values based on the results of religious studies coordinated by each Educational Institution. For example, school A defined "tolerance" as "to accept others and their differences". School A further classified the value into several behaviour indicators originating from the Bible, such as accepting "differences of opinion", "cultural diversity", "religious differences", and "cooperation with others". One teacher narrated his experience in the following comments:

> Our school is leading to its high discipline based on character education. As a Catholic school, we adopted the Ignatian pedagogy and spirituality which focused on 4C pillars, consisting of Competence, Compassion, Conscience, and Commitment. These themes inspired the teaching and learning activities, such as compassion week and live-in programs, and has become the basis for developing school regulations, such as "No cheating". Students and teachers understood these regulations and their consequences. (T5)

The second principle is "Examine it". It focuses on identifying and defining character values. Expressing religion as the basis and inspiration shaping character education in Indonesia, schools corroborated values from the Bible (Schools A and C) and the Holy Quran (School B). Moral characters such as honesty, caring, and respect others are based on religious values. Therefore, all religions (Christian, Islam, and Catholic) preach it in their scripture. A teacher in this study expressed her experience regarding this:

> Our Primary School is a Christian school that is committed to Christian values. These values become the source, identity, and provision for our community. We educate our students to be a good Christian who internalise the BEST character including Be tough, Excel worldwide, Share with society, and Trust in God. (T2)

Recently, in a religiously diverse society like Indonesia, there is more emphasis on schools to foster religious tolerance. Hence, respect for others is also a very important character in maintaining national unity and societal harmony.

The third principle is "Exhibit it". In character education, teachers are role for learning good values and teachers guide students towards developing good characters. Schools A and B used teacher modelling while asking students to imitate the behaviours displayed by teachers as one method to instil good values. School C positioned all school personnel, including teachers, principal, and staff members as role models and motivators for students. This provided a good example of ways other schools can optimise the "Exhibit it" principle by implementing a comprehensive approach involving the entire school community to model for students, allowing students to adopt good characters and imitate sound behaviours. Additionally, it provides a conducive environment for students to develop good character through the teaching and learning process as well as school activities. One teacher reported:

> The role of the teacher was very important in our BEST character program. Every morning all the teachers welcomed students in the schoolyard. Meeting and greeting students and their parents and training students to greet their teachers and friends. Students imitated what their teachers did. After several meetings, they would become accustomed. In the extracurricular programs, such as music, sports or dance, teachers provided examples of behaviours and guided students to cooperate and respect their friends as a team. (T1)

The fourth principle is "Expect it". Schools need to reinforce the character traits students are expected to build. A reward-and-punishment system is commonly used for this process. Giving rewards may result in reinforcing the expected behaviour, while punishment is expected to discourage unexpected behaviour. The findings suggested that all schools implemented a method to communicate the expectations and promote the development of good characters and behaviour. School A used stickers or pins for their reward-and-punishment system, to recognise d affirm positive behaviours and character traits, as well as recognise violations or to discourage bad characters. School B motivated their student to perform good character with a motto: "Yes, I can", while School C implemented rules (No cheating) and consequences (expulsion) to foster good character to students. One teacher commented informed us:

> The most crucial and important thing in our school is that all school rules and norms must be obeyed, and their violation will result in only one consequence: expulsion from the school, especially if students, teachers, or school employees are found to be dishonest. It motivated us to always obey the applicable rules and norms. (T6)

The fifth principle is "Experience it". The findings showed that character education was integrated into the daily lessons and school activities (intra-curricular, co-curricular, and extracurricular programs). This integration allowed students to experience the character trait in their everyday school activities and relationships. School A established monthly themes and integrated them into behaviour indicators to explain the themes. For example, on January the theme of the character education was "Tolerance" and "Love". School A consolidated the theme into behaviour indicators to guide the lessons. Similarly, school B prepared various activities, such as intra-curricular, co-curricular, and extracurricular activities, which invites all students to experience the character, through scouting, boarding school, traditional art, and sport. School C conducted several internal and external school events in collaboration with other schools and communities to educate their students through special events such as Compassion Week, Live-in, and Sit-in programs. One teacher remarked:

> Several students reported that our Live-in and Sit-in programs were very useful for mingling with people from various backgrounds. They would always remember the experience during the programs. Some students even still had good relations with the people they met in those programs. (T6)

The sixth principle is "Encourage it". The findings indicated that primary schools in this study implement routines with the aim of promoting character-building and familiarising good values. For example, students greet teachers every morning and pray before and after lessons. Repeated practices through routines combined with a reward and punishment system are considered suitable for a primary school setting. For high school students (in School C), the school utilises a goal-setting approach for students to encourage character development among students, such as setting a goal to interact with new friends and develop a new community, or to display tolerance towards individuals of other religions. While older high-school-age students can be expected to adjust and manage their behaviours, it is considered easier for younger primary school-aged students to learn values through a reward and punishment system.

The final or the seventh component of 7 E's principle of character education is "Evaluate it". In practice, the school's implementing the 7 Es will evaluate their students by examining their students' behaviour over the course of the program. Evaluation is conducted as an effort to compare students' behaviours against the standard or character development goals set by the school. At the end of the program, it is the school's hope that students may embody one or a set of character traits deemed important by the school for students to develop. The findings revealed that all schools used teachers' anecdotal notes to assess students' behavioural changes. Teachers recorded student behaviour during school activities using observation forms and took anecdotal notes to assess their behaviours against rubrics. In practice, School C's teacher assessment is complimented by a student self-evaluation and a peer evaluation, while School B implemented a multi-rater assessment to ensure evaluations remain objective. Teachers reported students' character development in semester report cards that are shared with parents.

It can be summarised that the three schools participating in this study exhibited differing methods to implement the 7 E's of teaching a character trait (Lickona, 2004). The cases presented here illustrate the ways this set of principles can guide schools to more effectively apply character education, as well as better organise activities to build a student's character. The schools we examined implemented character education and means of evaluating students through the development and use of behaviour rubrics, anecdotal reports, daily journals, and peer evaluation.

6 The Implication of the Study

The findings above will inform principals and school administrators that there are various methods and approaches to implementing different components of character education and eventually assessing character change in students. The study illustrated the usefulness of the 7 E principles of teaching character traits in determining the design of character education programs. It also demonstrated how assessing the effectiveness of character education may help schools improve their educational practices. It is hoped that the outcomes of character education programs include improved characters and behaviours among students, by reflecting on whether the school is effectively utilising the 7 E principle character traits and any additional traits that the school seeks students to develop.

This study addressed assessments on character education in a small geographic region of Indonesia. It provided a baseline for future research in terms of assessing character education. In order to obtain a broader and in-depth understanding of character education in the Indonesian context, future research should also involve public schools, communities and policymakers in all of the 34 provinces of Indonesia.

7 Conclusion

This study analysed how three private schools in one region of the province of Jakarta in Indonesia implemented character education. The findings revealed that schools implemented character education programs based on religious values (Christian, Moslem, and Catholic) and generated themes for these programs. The primary schools conducted a self-familiarising method, while the high school applied a goal-setting method. Furthermore, to evaluate the results of the character education programs, teachers used self-evaluation, peer evaluation, and anecdotal notes. The assessments were usually performed for one semester.

This study was conducted in one region of the province of Jakarta in Indonesia. While the findings of this study cannot be generalised to the wider school settings in the whole of Indonesia, qualitative insights from the participating schools contribute to an understanding of school practices enacting the visions of character education. Future studies can expand the data points and insights on innovative and effective implementation of character education by comparatively investigating practices in public schools, Islamic schools (*madrasahs*), and other types of schools such as boarding schools.

Acknowledgements

The research reported in this chapter is based on a project supported through the Ministry of Education and Culture of Indonesia funding scheme and conducted by a team and colleagues (Moch. Abduh, Asrijanty, Mira Josy Moestadi, Rumondang Purwati, Rahmawati). The views represented in this chapter are those of the author and do not represent the views of the team.

References

Baxter, P., & Jack, S. (2008). Qualitative case study methodology: Study design and implementation for novice researchers. *The Qualitative Report, 13*(4), 544–559.

Lickona, T. (2001). *What is effective character education*. Retrieved September 16, 2015, from https://athenaeum.edu/pdf/What%20is%20Effective%20Character%20Education.pdf

Lickona, T., & Davidson, M. (2005). *Smart & good high schools: Integrating excellence and ethics for success in school, work, and beyond*. Center for the 4th and 5th Rs/Character Education Partnership.

Lickona, T., Schaps, E., & Lewis, C. (2007). *CEP's eleven principles of effective character education*. Character Education Partnership.

Nucci, L., Krettenauer, T., & Narváez, D. (2014). *Handbook of moral and character education*. Routledge.

O'Sullivan, S. (2004). Books to live by: Using children's literature for character education. *The Reading Teacher, 57*(7), 640–645.

Statistics Indonesia. (2018). *2018 criminal statistics*. Author.

CHAPTER 7

Fostering Quality Education and Global Engagement through Sister School Partnership: Perspectives of Teachers

Ahmad Bukhori Muslim

Abstract

Quality improvement and global benchmarking practices that have been implemented by a number of primary and secondary schools in Indonesia include sister-school partnerships. While sister-school partnerships between schools in Indonesia and Australia have been ongoing for some time, little is known on how these partnerships may support students' learning and development of institutional international partnership. Employing data based on questionnaires, interviews, and classroom observations, this descriptive qualitative study investigates teachers' perspectives and practices on the administration of sister school partnership among Indonesian and Australian schools, as well as the benefits of and challenges in sustaining and developing this program. The results show various benefits that the 20 teacher study participants in both Indonesia and Australia have acknowledged about sister school partnership, including learning autonomy and authenticity, fluency in both English and *Bahasa Indonesia*, as well as increased cross-cultural understanding. These qualities are necessary to support students' global engagement and partnership as future leaders. Despite these positive perspectives, the study also identifies a few challenges in the sustainability of sister school management.

Keywords

sister school – students' global engagement – learning autonomy and authenticity – cross-cultural understanding – international educational exchange

1   Introduction

Improving the quality of schooling to prepare more competitive, globally minded human resources is of paramount importance. In many developing countries such as Bangladesh (Hussain & Chishti, 2016) and Indonesia, the task of providing, running, and maintaining quality education has become a shared responsibility among different parties, where the public or private sector extends beyond the government's limited reach. Quality education is considered the best legacy that the younger generation, regardless of their economic and social backgrounds, should receive as future capital, given the strong international partnership among countries. Investment in quality education for the younger generation is especially crucial for developing countries in their efforts to develop a competitive edge and better their chances in maximising their potential for participation and contribution in a global market.

Many studies have contributed in understanding ways to improve the quality of education in developing countries like Indonesia, especially at the primary and secondary levels. One approach to quality improvement is through benchmarking with schools from developed countries (Ossiannilsson & Landgren, 2012). Similar to sister city partnerships conducted by government administrations, benchmarking in education may occur in the form of building sister school partnerships between schools in a developing country and those in a developed country. For example, schools in Indonesia, Afghanistan, Pakistan and Turkmenia may connect with counterparts from countries like Australia, the United Kingdom, the United States and other European countries (Nurenberg, 2010). One purpose of this practice of benchmarking is to facilitate mutual learning and share best practices in teaching and learning.

Many schools in Indonesia have been involved in regional and international benchmarking partnerships. At the regional level, since 1997, Indonesia has taken part in the sister school network project initiated by the Association of Southeast Asian Nations (ASEAN). The Southeast Asia Minister of Educational Organisation (SEAMEO) stated that two years after the initial establishment of this regional association, facilitated by the Indonesian Embassy in Bangkok, 20 schools from Indonesia—including five junior secondary schools, 10 senior secondary and five secondary vocational schools—have joined the partnership and were matched with Thai schools. Beyond the ASEAN network, Indonesia also holds similar partnership with other countries, including Australia. Starting in 2005, Ausindo Educational (AE), a non-profit and non–government organisation, mediated the visits of several Indonesian schools from Banten and West Java provinces to the state of Victoria. In addition to this, through the BRIDGE (Building Relationships through Intercultural Dialog and Growing

Engagement) Project which started in 2010, as many as 91 teachers from 47 Indonesian schools in seven provinces including Jakarta, South Sumatra, Bali, East Java, South Sulawesi, West Nusa Tenggara and West Kalimantan have visited Australia. The Project's goal was to forge an ongoing partnership among schools in both countries (Australian Department of Education, 2015).

For Indonesia, sister school partnerships are envisioned to help the government and schools improve their quality so that Indonesian students become more competitive globally. Through sister school partnerships, Australian teachers believe that such collaborations may help their students learn Bahasa Indonesia and engage in further international cooperation, which underlines the component of engagement among schools as equal and benefiting both parties. However, having been implemented for more than one decade with a large amount of financial support from both government and private sectors, there has not been a study which examines whether the school partnerships facilitated by the BRIDGE Project and AE have been effective in achieving its main goals. Therefore, this study focuses on teachers' understanding and perspectives on the practice of sister school partnerships, as well as the benefits and challenges they face when organising these partnerships. This focus is justifiable considering the central role of teachers in administering such partnerships. Findings on this study are expected to provide information on how to better organise this international engagement, maximise its benefits, as well as manage challenges in its implementation.

1.1 Sister School Partnerships Worldwide

Sister school partnerships are practiced worldwide and have a long history dating back to the 1920s (Pryor, 1992; Cucchiara, 2011). The existence of sister school partnerships has been documented during the Hitler era of Germany, which survived despite the main purpose of this partnership was to develop cross-cultural understanding. many difficult challenges in their implementation. At that time, This vision has prevailed up until today and expanded to include language learning, which is an integral part of learning another culture.

Sister school partnerships are similar to mentorship programs done within schools (Henry, 2009) at an individual level, which introduced the notion of "big brothers" and "big sisters". The sister partnership concept is also similar to practices in governance, with the development of sister cities or sister states in government administration. The term "sister school" (or "brother school") originally referred to relationships between two colleges or universities related to commerce (Pryor, 1992). In the educational context, especially at primary and secondary levels, sister schools are understood as the pairing of schools, commonly from two different countries, in order that they may work together to achieve a set of shared purposes, including improving students' learning of foreign languages and cultures from each respective country. Studies have found that sister school partnerships may contribute to the development of cross-cultural understanding and respect for cultural differences among students (for example, Marion, Rousseau, & Gollin, 2009). In the Indonesian context, along with the introduction of English language teaching at the primary years of education, Indonesian schools are usually paired with their counterparts in English inner circle countries (Kachru, 1992) such as Australia, England, and the United States. Such partnership is not only expected to enhance the quality of English learning but also develop their cross-cultural understanding for future global engagement.

Sister school partnerships have continued to evolve. More recently, the definition has been expanded to include various types of relationships between two schools, including those that share a strong historical connection, those who hold common social activities involving students from both schools, and two schools under the same management (Cambridge Advanced Dictionary). The term "sister school" adopted in this study is defined by the relationship or connection between two or more schools in different countries involving students and community members for the purpose of learning the language and culture of the countries involved, mediated by technology.

Many independent agencies worldwide organise sister school partnerships in different regions such as European countries, the United States and Australia. Some agencies are Sister School (The United States and Africa), Sister City (European countries) and Asia Education (Australia). While the aims of sister school partnerships vary from one region to another, in general they allow students to develop global perspectives and an understanding of the globalised world, and to develop or strengthen relationships between the schools involved. This is carried out in various ways, such as exchanging teaching and learning materials, language and culture learning, and other cross-cultural communication activities. To provide a comprehensive objective of sister schools, for instance, the Victorian Department of Education in Australia initiates sister school partnerships, with the purpose to

> ... strengthen the relationship between Victorian schools and overseas, broaden the knowledge and understanding of students by enabling them to gain an understanding, appreciation and respect for other cultures, support the teaching of that language in the Victorian school and English in the overseas school, develop ties of friendship through regular communication, develop opportunities for teachers to exchange course material, information on methods and practices and on educational matters in

general, provide opportunities for contact and interaction with the wider school community, promote Victorian education overseas, and facilitate visits of students and teachers to the sister school. (p. 3)

Based on this statement, it is interesting to identify how these aims of enhancing partnership, knowledge and understanding, and cultural appreciation and respect are implemented by participating Indonesian and Australian school sisters. Because the management of sister schools is the responsibility of all parties, the administration of sister school partnership in this study was mediated by different government-supported and private organisations such as BRIDGE Project and Ausindo Educational (AE). As the involvement of school principals and parents significantly influence students' learning (Cheng & Weng, 2017), all parties should work together to improve education quality. Therefore, it is necessary to examine how participating teachers and school principals perceive the administration of sister school partnerships.

1.2   Sister Schools for Authentic Learning, Technology, and Sustainable Development

Educators believe that language learning will become more effective when learners are involved in authentic and meaningful activities. Gilmore (2007) argues that authentic learning relates to many aspects such as learning material design, learners, learning social and cultural environments, and the communicative purpose of language learning. Teachers should be able to provide learners with real context when practicing the four language skills (listening, speaking, reading, and writing). Language learning is also considered powerful when it enables students to make meanings in their social life through authentic learning experience.

Authentic language learning has various definitions. Some scholars believe that authenticity relates to the language produced by native speakers, particularly in oral skills such as listening and speaking (Porter & Roberts 1981; Little, Devitt & Singleton 1989). Similarly, Benson and Voller (1997) argue that authenticity is the language produced by real speakers or writers to convey ideas to the real audience. Some scholars propose that authenticity also deals with natural activities or tasks given to the students (van Lier, 1996; Benson & Voller, 1997; Lewkowicz, 2000; Guariento & Morley, 2001). Additionally, authentic learning refers to the social situation in the classroom which is relevant with the real condition of language acquisition (Rost, 2002) and assessment (Bachman & Palmer, 1996; Lewkowicz, 2000), including the ability to behave and think as acceptable to the target language and culture (Kramsch, 1998).

Furthermore, language learning for millennials should make use of technology. With the help of technology, teachers can create a 'personal engagement' with students (van Lier, 1996, p. 128). To support this, English teachers could create blogs for teaching writing, organise a teleconference or email correspondence with native speakers, and utilise social media for authentic language learning. These activities are expected to support more effective language learning as students are engaged in technology-based activities. Thus, the main benefits that school sister partnerships may give are language learning and effective use of Information and Communication Technology software as utilised by the participating schools in this study.

Additionally, authenticity and technology also relate to learning motivation and achievement. This is especially more salient among technology savvy students living in the digital revolution age. Authentic technology-based learning materials, including those for English, can increase students' learning interests in classrooms (McGarry, 1995; Peacock,1997), as is the case with Malaysian students (Chena, Nurkhamida, Wang, Yang, Lue, & Chang, 2013). Meanwhile, most English language learners also like direct learning and games (Yamat, Fisher, & Rich, 2014). These scholars believe that authentic learning such as email correspondence and teleconferences encourage students to directly keep in touch with native speakers of English through oral activities including listening and speaking. These real and meaningful activities build students' confidence and consequently improve their motivation. In this case, students' learning achievements are influenced by teachers' use of digital media (Cheng & Weng, 2017).

The development of authentic learning materials and activities through information technology still faces challenges. For most schools in developing countries, information technology is still a luxury that not all students can afford. In the Indonesian context, not all schools have access to internet-connected computers and only students in large cities enjoy the luxury of information-technology supported learning activities. Additionally, a lack of skills in operating software poses further challenges. Even if schools have sufficient information-technology facilities, teachers' technological literacy may yield another problem. Many senior teachers who are digital immigrants feel insecure in using technology within their classrooms. In a study of teachers' readiness in using technology while teaching English, many older teachers were found unprepared to use the new technology in their classrooms (Cimermanova, 2013). To remedy this, these teachers needed to be supported by younger teachers who are technology savvy. They would also need the support of school principals, so teachers may develop more positive attitudes towards the use of technology in their classrooms. In fact, the attitudes of school principals have a great impact on teachers' use of digital teaching (Cheng & Weng, 2017).

Language learning for empowerment also relates to cross-cultural understanding, a knowledge necessary to develop a more harmonious global world. The early idea of establishing sister schools was developing the cross-cultural understanding of the participating young people so that they can become open minded global citizens (Pryor, 1992). It is argued that students who have early exposure to people of different cultures, religions, races and countries are more open and welcome to differences so that they can build stronger and more respectful international networks. This skill is invaluable when they become adults and serve as policy makers in their own countries. The result of a study by Marion, Rousseau and Gollin (2009) on sister school partnership in California and Afghanistan illustrates this notion. They found that a pen pal program administered during the program enables the participating students to develop the importance of mutual respect and understanding about different cultural values to which students in both schools adhere. In addition, studying the effect of exchange students between American and German high schools, Schenker (2013) found that the participants show increased interests in learning about the culture of their counterparts.

Finally, cross-cultural understanding also supports equality in education as part of sustainable development. In a global world, demand for equality in education and other social aspects (Haughton, 1999; Agyeman, Bullard, & Evans, 2002) and global agenda (Sachs, 1999), particularly between developed and underdeveloped nations, has become higher, considering the importance of quality education as the most basic human right that all governments should strive for their own citizens. It is the responsibility of the government to provide equal educational opportunities for more equal educational outcomes (Meyer, 2016). As part of their whole professional development approach (Chen & McCray, 2012), in-service teachers should show positive attitudes, comprehensive knowledge, and skilful practice of all activities, including sister school management. This practice enables teachers to learn curriculum, teaching methods and learning resources from their international counterparts as a means for building their school readiness for international engagement (Kuh, 2007). Such support for equity in education approach may be identified from the participating Indonesian and Australian teachers in this study.

2   Method

This section describes participants of the study, data collection, and data analysis.

2.1   *Participants*

Of the 20 participants in the research, 10 are Australian teachers of Bahasa Indonesia and the other 10 are Indonesian teachers of English. All the Australian teachers work at secondary colleges in Melbourne, Australia; the Indonesian teachers teach at Indonesian primary and secondary schools across the country. The 10 participating Australian teachers have qualifications in foreign language teaching, and extensive training in teaching Bahasa Indonesia; some of whom are Indonesian nationals with Australian permanent residency. These educators all participate regularly in the Victorian Indonesian Language Teachers Association (VILTA) conferences in Melbourne. Of the 10 Indonesian teachers; most have a background in English education, and a small percentage have non-English educational degrees.

To be a part of the research the teachers needed to meet the following criteria:

– They must be teachers of Bahasa Indonesia or English and have school partners within their respective countries, either under ERIDGE or Ausindo Educational.
– They have a strong commitment to initiating and maintaining partnerships with their counterpart schools.
– They need to be focal points in the management and maintenance of sister school partnership.

With these criteria, the selected teachers were also expected to maintain the partnership program as well as improve the enthusiasm of their students in learning either Indonesian or English through the partnership program. Additional detail of teachers' accounts is shown in the questionnaire result in Table 7.1.

Respondent teachers involved in the study have good professional experience. As point number 3 in Table 7.1 illustrates, most of them have been in the profession of teaching Bahasa Indonesia or English for more than five years. The Australian respondents were all experienced teachers with a strong ambition to improve the quality of Bahasa Indonesia teaching as well as to maintain its positive reputation among their students. Similarly, participating Indonesian teachers had good experience of English teaching. Most teachers, particularly at junior and senior high schools, are professional English teachers who have relevant study backgrounds and sufficient training programs in the area of English language teaching. Resonating Gilmore (2007) on authentic learning, these teachers believe that sister school practices provide students with authentic learning materials and asocial and cultural environment that they can use in authentic communication with their counterparts overseas.

TABLE 7.1　Teachers' accounts

1.	Venue of teaching English/Bahasa Indonesia	10 teachers at Australian schools
		10 teachers at Indonesian schools
2.	Number of partnership teachers	16 teachers have only 1 partner teacher
		4 teachers have 1–2 partner teachers
3.	Length of teaching experience	5 teachers have less than 5 years
		10 teachers have less than 10 years
		5 teachers have more than 10 years
4.	Number of students in partnership	3 teachers have less than 20 students
		13 teachers have 20–50 students
		4 teachers have more than 50 students
5.	Reasons to become English/Bahasa Indonesia teachers	12 teachers love teaching English/Bahasa Indonesia
		4 teachers like the salaries offered
		4 teachers have to teach Bahasa Indonesia/English because none wants to

2.2　*Data Collection*

This study is a qualitative descriptive in nature as it describes the practice of sister school partnership and its benefits and challenges among Indonesian and Australian schools as perceived by the participating teachers. Data were generated from questionnaires and interviews from teachers of Indonesian language partnerships at 10 Australian schools and their Indonesian school counterparts, including four former International Standards Pilot Schools (*Rintisan Sekolah Bertaraf Internasional*, RSBI) schools that were also involved in sister school partnerships. The questionnaires and interviews were distributed and conducted online and offline in 2015. The questionnaires asked teachers' perspectives on the implementation of sister school partnerships, its possible benefits, and possible challenges impeding future improvement. The study also employed classroom observations at schools in the two countries.

The first research question was addressed by classroom observations and questionnaires administered to the participating teachers on their understanding, perspectives and implementation of sister school partnership in their schools. The second question was answered through interviews with 10 respondent teachers from both countries on the benefits and challenges that they face when establishing the partnership. The first section of the questionnaire asks participants' demographic background and the implementation of sister school partnerships at their schools. The second section of the questionnaire investigated teachers' understandings and perspectives on sister school partnership, its benefits and challenges. The interview was administered to confirm the questionnaire results and explore the teachers' questionnaire responses in further detail. Both questionnaire and interview questions for Australian respondents were written in English whereas those for Indonesians were in Bahasa Indonesia.

Both Australian and Indonesian schools have different geographical locations. Most Australian schools involved in sister school partnerships are in sub-urban or regional areas of Victoria, including Bendigo, Somerville, and Weerona. Only a few schools are in urban areas, such as the Mac. Robertson Girls' High School in the city of Melbourne. Due to some political sentiments like the Bali bombing in 2002, students' interests in learning Bahasa Indonesia among urban Australia has decreased. On the other hand, most Indonesian schools involved in sister school partnership are in big cities such as Bandung, Tangerang, and Serang. Only a few schools are in small Indonesian towns such as Kuningan, West Java, and Lebak regency of Banten province. This occurs because most schools in big Indonesian cities have more access to information about sister school relations than those located in rural areas.

2.3   *Data Analysis*

The study draws upon three data sources; questionnaires, interviews, and observations. Interviews were transcribed on a thematic basis. Findings from both questionnaires and interviews were categorised into three main themes: understanding and perspectives of sister school partnerships, its benefits, and the challenges. Confirmed by observational results, these themed findings were then analysed by relevant theories of authentic and autonomous English learning to answer the two proposed research questions. Interviews identify teachers' perspectives on the administration of the sister school program at their schools.

Due to research ethics requirements, permission for participation, questionnaire distribution, interviews and classroom observations were sought from respondent teachers. To support validity and anonymity, interview transcription was also crosschecked with participating teachers for information accuracy. Since participation in this study was voluntary, a few teachers withdrew from the study.

2.4 *Ausindo Educational (AE) and* BRIDGE *as Agencies for Sister School Partnerships*

Sister school partnerships in this study are mediated by Ausindo Educational (AE) and BRIDGE. AE is a non-profit organisation that focuses on pairing schools in Indonesia and Australia as an alternative solution to broaden students and teachers' perspectives and give them an international touch for higher quality education. Since its establishment in 2005, the number of schools interested in partnerships under AE has increased significantly and this number is expected to grow.

In addition to AE, the government of Australia launched a partnership program called BRIDGE in 2008 (Building Relationships through Intercultural Dialog and Growing Engagement). This partnership connects Australian schools with their counterparts, particularly in Asian countries, including Indonesia. The main purpose of this partnership is to develop students' relationship with their counterparts in Asian countries through intercultural dialog and engagement. It is believed that students who have built good cross-cultural relationships and understanding will grow and become tolerant adults who are committed to intercultural and international cooperation. Under the BRIDGE project, by 2010, as many as 91 teachers from 47 Indonesian schools in seven provinces (Jakarta, South Sumatra, Bali, East Java, South Sulawesi, West Nusa Tenggara and West Kalimantan) had been involved the sister school partnership program and connected with their Australian school counterparts toward forging mutual relationships between schools in both countries.

Establishing international partnerships is among the approaches emphasised for school development in Indonesian schooling. Sister school partnership is supported by Indonesia's Education Law. Article 50 of the Education Law (20/2003) states that each district/municipality should groom at least one school (referring to the RSBIS) within the district to achieve an internationally recognised or standardised quality. One of the approaches or models for schools to gain an international standard is for them to partner with schools abroad, especially from developed countries or countries with high performance on international assessments (OECD, 2016). In 2013, Article 50 was abolished out of the Education Law, on the basis of issues and concerns of the Article's impact on widening educational disparity and inequity. The vision behind the Article, however, remains valid: to improve students' English competencies, to expand Indonesian students' opportunities to compete in international academic competition, and to learn good educational practices from schools in other countries.

3 Findings and Discussion

The finding of the study has two sections: the teachers' perspectives on sister school partnership, and the benefits and challenges in managing said partnership.

3.1 Teachers' Perspectives on the Sister School Partnership

As the questionnaires and interviews revealed, all participating teachers had positive perspectives on the establishment of sister school partnerships. Teachers tend to have more positive perspectives as indicated by the increasing request for sister school partnership along with the improvement of diplomatic relationships between Indonesia and Australia. One Australian teacher said,

> I think it is a good idea to have [a] sister school partnership with a school in Indonesia. I want to promote my Bahasa Indonesia program to my students. This partnership, you know, motivates my students to learn Bahasa Indonesia. Now, I have more than 20 students in my class of Bahasa Indonesia. They really love it to have partners from Indonesia to practice their language.

In terms of the process of establishing the sister school partnership, each of the participating schools are at different stages. In the Australian context, the partnerships are predominantly initiated and managed by teachers of Bahasa Indonesia language; school principals only serve in a support role to the partnerships. Meanwhile, in Indonesia, the school principals are more dominant in determining the sustainability of the partnership. Several schools in both countries have had active relationships and have signed Memorandums of Understanding, and undergone exchanges of teachers and principals. Most schools, however, are still in the initial stages of their partnership and need assistance in establishing joint activities and exchange program from various supporting agencies, such as AE and BRIDGE.

Another indicator of good perspectives is that language programs at both countries already have a good structure. Most respondent teachers in Australia have a strong Bahasa Indonesia program that is sufficiently supported by school principals, parents, and members of school councils. For this reason, the program can attract many students. At Australian primary schools, students from years 1–5 can sign up for Bahasa Indonesia as a LOTE (Language Other Than English) subject. Similarly, the teaching of English in Indonesian schools is also professionally managed. At the junior and senior high school level, English as a subject is mandatory and is a high priority. Borrowing from Vygotsky's social constructivism, these show the importance of social attitudes in supporting students' learning process, from teachers, parents, and particularly, school principals in running school activities (Cheng & Weng, 2017).

However, when considered as an elective subject, the teaching of English at Indonesian primary schools is not as professional at as those at the higher levels of secondary and tertiary education. Some English teachers have an academic background outside of English language education and have insufficient training experience in relevant areas. Low quality language teaching has been found in studies such as by Suherdi (2012), who observed teaching practices that are still grammar-based, not focused on interactive communication skills (Musthafa, 2001). Considering the high interest from students in learning this foreign language, English language teachers need more training for professional development.

All respondent teachers in both countries also show strong determination to maintain sister school partnerships. Most Australian teachers have strong ambitions to become better and more effective teachers of Bahasa Indonesia; they believe in the value of their profession and the importance of maintaining the existence of a Bahasa Indonesia program within their schools. One Australian teacher said,

> I am confirmed to be fully dedicated teacher of Bahasa Indonesia. I am glad that I have strong support from my school principal. This sister school partnership really helps me, you know, and my students to have a more quality Indonesian language program. I hope it will develop more.

Similarly, most Indonesian respondents, especially English teachers of primary schools who do not have relevant educational backgrounds, show strong aspirations to be more effective teachers by joining more professional development programs. Although English is not a compulsory subject, they strongly hold the belief that their students need English skills which will be beneficial for their future careers.

3.2   *Perceived Benefits of Sister School Partnership*

As projected, sister school partnerships come with benefits. First and foremost among them are opportunities for global engagement. As the interview and observation results show, all Australian respondents confirmed that the sister school partnership enabled them to relate to their counterparts in Indonesia and vice versa. Exchange programs to Indonesia enables Australian teachers to develop their knowledge of intercultural understanding as well as teaching experience and resources to improve their teaching professionalism. Teachers in both countries believe that it is important for students to know more about culture, traditions, and customs different from their own. Most teachers themselves feel more empowered to become open-minded global citizens and argue that students should be able to experience this sense of global engagement. Confirming Pryor's (1992) and Rousseau and Gollin's (2009) findings on impacts of exchange visits among sister schools, teachers in both countries found that various activities such as correspondence and exchange visits have fostered within students the importance of mutual respect and understanding about different cultural values essential for their global life. Another Indonesian teacher confirmed that a homestay program in Melbourne had opened up her students' perspectives on Australian culture, foods, drinks. This Indonesian teacher said,

> My students learned a lot when, you know, they visited Melbourne. Can you imagine? These young people have to live with their homestays for one week. They have to really experience different drinks, foods, and other customs.

Sister school partnerships are also beneficial for students' learning. Almost all respondent teachers believe that the partnership helps their students to become autonomous learners with learning facilitated by interactions with their counterparts from overseas. Australian students have displayed learning autonomy by engaging in email correspondence with their Indonesian peers. Through the use of communication technology, sister school partnerships become more beneficial for students (Chena et al., 2013). For example, teleconferences resolve challenges faced by students in classrooms in Indonesia and Australia posed by distance and financial limitations. One Australian teacher confirms,

> Most of my students show enthusiasm when they are engaged in teleconference with their Indonesian friends. They can practice some greetings in Indonesian language they have learned so far. I encourage them to use both teleconference and regular mail to practice both speaking and writing skills.

This phenomenon of students taking over their own learning trajectories with learning mediated through international school partnerships is also observed in other studies (McGarry, 1995; Benson & Voller, 1997). For Indonesian teachers, sister school partnerships can help their students' English learning. ICT-based communication activities such as email correspondence and conversation via teleconference as well as traditional communication and regular mail enable students to have a real and meaningful context of their English as they complete authentic learning tasks to develop their listening, speaking, and reading. During exchange visits, students can also autonomously use culture to provide context for their English learning (Little, Devitt, & Singleton, 1989; Van Lier, 1996). It seems that technology communication such as Skype and email correspondence can compensate for limited financial support most Indonesian teachers experience in maintaining the sustainability of sister school partnerships.

Overall, these Indonesian teachers believe that exchanges through the sister school partnership have helped provide authentic and meaningful learning experiences. Using ICT, email, online conversations, social media, and engaging in exchange visits encourage students' interests in learning about each other's respective cultures and languages. These findings are relevant with the findings of similar studies on authentic learning and international engagement (Schenker, 2013; Porter & Roberts, 1981; Rost, 2002; Guariento & Morley, 2001; Lewkowicz, 2000; McGarry, 1995; Peacock, 1997; Little, Devitt, & Singleton, 1989; Van Lier, 1996). In this context, increased motivation and interests in English will not only provide Indonesian students with an essential soft skill for better international engagement but also improve school reputation.

3.3 Challenges in Sister School Partnership Administration

Respondent teachers in both countries agreed that the administration of sister school partnerships also come with challenges. The first challenge mentioned by many respondents is an inadequate support for the actual partnership. For Australian respondents, the main challenge was the insufficient support from their school principal, parents, and school councils. Not all principals, parents, and members of school councils agree with the establishment of sister school partnerships. As many as five respondents were lucky enough to have supportive school principals and members of school council who believe in the importance of school activities that allow students to develop cross-cultural understanding. These individuals also believed that cross-cultural understanding can be developed by learning languages other than English like Bahasa Indonesia. With this understanding, they were willing supporters of activities that develop partnerships with Indonesian schools. Some other Australian teachers mentioned that their school principals are not really concerned with the sustainability of Indonesian language programs at their schools and may want to switch to other foreign languages.

Meanwhile, the main challenge for Indonesian teachers is insufficient financial support. A large amount of funding is required to implement activities under sister school partnerships, especially for exchange visits. Prior to

2012, the Indonesian government provided funding for RSBI, which are select schools that were prepared to become internationally standardised schools. This funding became the main source to facilitate school sister partnerships. However, limited funding meant that applicant schools had to convince policy makers that their sister school partnerships deserve funding. The challenge became harder when, as the result of a judicial review in 2012, the Indonesian government declared that the RSBI program was unconstitutional, ceasing its financial support. Consequently, many RSBI schools stopped their support for the administration of sister school partnerships, leading to the decreasing number of sister school partnership. It is fortunate that the termination of RSBI did not impact private schools, who managed to sustain their sister school partnership with Australian schools. A similar challenge for sustainability is also shown by schools under the BRIDGE project. Many schools ended their sister school partnership as Australian government also terminated their funding.

For Indonesian teachers, minimum support directly relates to limited school facilities and financial support from parents. Some teachers argued that teleconferences with students in Australia were sometimes not easy as they did not have a sufficient number of computers and proper internet connections. Meanwhile, not all parents can afford to send their children to take part in exchange programs to Melbourne. In the interest of sustaining the partnerships, efforts to gain financial support could be in the form of soliciting support from parents whose children are involved in the partnership. Resonating Meyer's (2016) finding, schools could also seek financial supports from other parties such as companies and non-binding sponsors.

Lastly, according to the respondents, particularly the Australian teachers, one factor that posed a challenge to the partnership is travel advisory due to fluctuating diplomatic relations between the two neighbouring countries. What makes Australian students interested in learning Bahasa Indonesia is their expectation to have a real communication with native speakers of the language. Most Australian respondents expressed strong disappointment when their government issued a travel advisory to Indonesia in light of escalating diplomatic tensions. In one instance, several Bahasa Indonesia teachers had previously initiated an exchange program, during which they would take their students to Indonesia for a two-week in-country training. They had already been granted permission by the regional Department of Education. However, due to the travel advisory, the teachers had to cancel the trip to Indonesia, causing students' disappointment. One teacher said,

> Last year, for in-country training, we could only take our students to Kuala Lumpur, Malaysia, not Jakarta, Indonesia. We didn't receive approval from the education office due to travel advisory. My students

were disappointed to find that the language spoken in KL was a bit different from what they have learned in the classroom. To reduce their disappointment, we had to invite some Indonesian speakers from Jakarta to come to Kuala Lumpur.

Travel advisories to Indonesia may reduce the motivation of Australian students to learn Bahasa Indonesia as they cannot practice the language they learn with Indonesian native speakers. Fortunately, the advisories are not permanent and could be lifted with improving bilateral relations between Indonesia and Australia.

Other challenges mentioned by both Indonesian and Australian respondents in managing sister school partnerships include identifying the person in charge, school level matching, and financial support. These challenges are also found in similar partnerships such as school-based mentoring (Brady, Dolan, & Canavan, 2014; Henry, 2009). If Brady et al. (2014) found teacher's excessive workload as a big challenge in organising school-based mentoring; similarly, it is not easy to find teachers with strong commitments to manage sister school partnerships and maintain its sustainability due to their high work volume. As for school partnering, matching participating schools from two different countries are not always an easy task. In this study, most Indonesian schools interested in a partnership were senior high level whereas more Australian primary schools show higher interests in the partnership. Henry (2009) also identified that a lack of financial support from parents posed additional challenges to school sister partnerships.

Despite these challenges, all respondent teachers in both Australia and Indonesia showed optimism that the sister school partnership program will survive and gain wider acceptance from schools in both countries in the future. This optimism is rooted in an understanding of the importance of maintaining a good geopolitical relationship between Indonesia and Australia. As neighbouring countries, we should have a better understanding of each other; this is achievable through language learning programs—especially of Bahasa Indonesia and English—which are strengthened by sister school partnerships.

4   Conclusions

This chapter concludes with the following points. Firstly, teachers in both countries had positive perceptions towards sister school partnership programs in their respective schools. The partnership programs in both countries received mostly positive support of all parties, including school principals, teachers, parents, school councils, and government. Secondly, all participating teachers found that the partnership was beneficial for students in their process of learning a foreign language—for Indonesian students learning English, and for Australian student learning Bahasa Indonesia. The Indonesian teachers found the partnerships helpful in improving their students' English skills and motivation to learn. Meanwhile, the Australian teachers believed that the partnerships improved their Indonesian language program and increased students' interests in learning Bahasa Indonesia. Thirdly, sister school partnerships have helped both Indonesian and Australian schools improve the quality of their students and teachers' experience as well as understanding of the two cultures. As these students will one day become future leaders, such school partnership enhances the bilateral cooperation between Indonesia and Australia.

As a form of global engagement among schools, sister school partnerships have become a means of sustainable development, particularly in education as a part of social equity, social harmony and peace education. For Indonesian students, sister school partnerships provide equal opportunities for students to receive quality education and learn cross-cultural understanding from their Australian counterparts as well as personal development as global citizens for more a more harmonious world. As part of readying schools for global engagement, Indonesian teachers should have sufficient exposure to relevant curriculum, effective teaching methods and learning resources.

Despite these positive perspectives and perceived benefits, the study also highlights some challenges the implementation of this partnership still faces, including financial and institutional support. Therefore, the Indonesian government should first provide support for sister school partnerships, particularly those administered by non-profit organisations like Ausindo Educational and those not funded by governmental institutions like the BRIDGE Program. Second, the government should maintain the political and social stability of the country so that the 'travel advisories' issued by the Australian government are lifted and Australian students can experience in-country training in Indonesia. Furthermore, for more comprehensive accounts of sister school partnerships, future study should also include students so that information regarding educational cross-cultural relations and its benefits become more reliable.

References

Agyeman, J., Bullard, R. D., & Evans, B. (72002). Exploring the nexus: Bringing together sustainability, environmental justice and equity. *Space & Polity, 6*(1), 77–90.

Benson, P., & Voller, P. (Eds.). (1997). *Autonomy and independence in language learning.* Longman.

Brady, B., Dolan, P., & Canavan, J. (2014). What added value does peer support bring? Insights from principals and teachers on the utility and challenges of a school-based mentoring programme. *Pastoral Care in Education, 32*(4), 241–250.

Chen, J. Q., & McCray, J. (2012). A conceptual framework for teacher professional development: The whole teacher approach. *NHSA Dialog: A Research-to-Practice Journal for the Early Childhood Field, 15*(1), 8–23.

Chena, G. D., Nurkhamida, B., Wang, C. Y., Yang, S. H., Lue, W. Y. & Chang, C. K. (2013). Digital learning playground: Supporting authentic learning experiences in the classroom. *Interactive Learning Environments, 21*(2), 172–183.

Cheng, Y. & Weng, C. (2017). Factors influence the digital media teaching of primary school teachers in a flipped class: A Taiwan case study. *South African Journal of Education, 37*(1), 1–12. doi:10.15700/saje.v37n1a

Chung, K. (2008). *Korean English fever in the U.S.: Temporary migrant parents' evolving beliefs about normal parenting practices and children's natural language learning* (Dissertation). University of Illinois at Urbana-Champaign, Amerika Serikat.

Cucchiara, M. (2011). *"Bitter times:" The poor school sisters of Notre Dame in Hitler's Germany, 1933–1945* (Doctoral thesis). University of Notre Dame, Indiana. Retrieved May 31, 2019, from https://curate.nd.edu/downloads/und:fi881j94n2s

Dello-Lacovo, B. (2009). Curriculum reform and 'Quality Education' in China: An overview. *International Journal of Educational Development, 29*(3), 241–249.

Guariento, W. & J. Morley (2001). Text and task authenticity in the EFL classroom. *ELT Journal, 55*(4), 347–353.

Haughton, G. (1999). Environmental justice and the sustainable city. In D. Satterthwaite (Ed.), *Sustainable cities.* Earthscan.

Henry, L. (2009). School-based mentoring: Big brothers big sisters. *The Education Digest, 74*(5), 45–46.

Hussain, A. & Chishti, S. H. (2016). Effectiveness of private sector participation in the delivery of quality education at secondary school level in Kurram agency. *Journal of Research and Reflections in Education, 10*(1), 80–92.

Kachru, B. (1992). *The other tongue: English across cultures.* University of Illinois Press.

Kramsch, C. (1993). *Context and culture in language teaching.* Oxford University Press.

Kuh, G. D. (2007). What student engagement data tell us about college readiness. *Peer Review, 9*(1), 4–8.

Lewkowicz, J. (2000). Authenticity in language testing: Some outstanding questions. *Language Testing, 17*(1), 43–64.

Little, D., Devitt, S., & Singleton, D. (1989). *Learning foreign languages from authentic texts: Theory and practice.* Authentik in association with CILT.

Marion, M., Rousseau, J., & Gollin, K. (2009). Connecting our villages: The Afghan sister schools project at the Carolina friends school. *Peace & Change, 34*(4), 548–570.

McGarry, D. (1995). *Learner autonomy 4: The role of authentic texts*. Authentik.

Meyer, K. (2016). Why should we demand equality of educational opportunity? *Theory and Research in Education, 14*(3), 333–347.

Musthafa, B. (2001). Communicative language teaching in Indonesia: Issues of theoretical assumptions and implications in classroom practices. *English Quarterly, 33*(1–2), 63–67.

Nurenberg, D. (2010). "It takes more than saying 'Honey' to make your mouth sweet": The necessity of multiparty cooperation to promote peace in a US–Turkmen student exchange partnership. *Multicultural Review, 19*(3), 17–25.

OECD. (2016). *PISA 2015 results in focus*. Retrieved March 9, 2017, from https://www.oecd.org/pisa/pisa-2015-results-in-focus.pdf https://www.oecd.org/pisa/pisa-2015-results-in-focus.pdf

Ossiannilsson, E., & Landgren, L. (2012). Quality in e-learning – A conceptual framework based on experiences from three international benchmarking projects. *Journal of Computer Assisted Learning, 28*, 42–51.

Peacock, M. (1997). The effect of authentic materials on the motivation of EFL learners. *ELT Journal, 51*(2), 144–156.

Porter, D., & Roberts, J. (1981). Authentic listening activities. *ELT Journal, 36*(1), 37–47.

Pryor, C. B. (1992). Building international relations for children through sister schools. *Phi Delta Kappan, 73*(5), 399–402.

Rost, M. (2002). *Teaching and researching listening*. Longman.

Sachs, W. (1999). *Planet dialectics: Exploring in environment & development*. Fernwood Publishing, Witwatersrand University Press, Zed Books.

Schenker, T. (2013). The effects of a virtual exchange on students' interest in learning about culture. *Foreign Language Annals, 46*(3), 491–507.

Suherdi, D. (2012). The use of quality pedagogic language in the teaching of English in Indonesian setting. *EDUCARE: International Journal for Educational Studies, 4*(2), 67–89.

Turner, D. (2008, February 21). Overseas parents place high premium lessons in English. *Financial Times*.

UNICEF. (2000). *Defining quality in education*. Paper presented at the International Working Group on Education meeting, Florence, Italy.

Van Lier, L. (1996). *Interaction in the language curriculum: Awareness, autonomy and authenticity*. Longman.

Voogt, J., & Knezek, G. (2016). Guest editorial: Technology enhanced quality education for all –Outcomes. EDUsummIT 2015. *Educational Technology & Society, 19*(3), 1–4.

Appendix A: Questionnaire Items

No.	Topics	Possible answer
1.	Where do you teach Bahasa Indonesia/English?	Respondents enter their school name and its address
2.	How many teachers are in your partnership?	a) Only 1 teacher b) About 2 teachers c) About 3 teachers
3.	How long have you been teaching at your current school?	a) Less than 5 years b) Less than 10 years c) More than 10 years
4.	How many students do you have in your partnership?	a) Less than 20 students b) 20 to 50 students c) More than 50 students
5.	How do you decide to become English/Indonesian teacher at this school?	a) I like teaching Bahasa Indonesia/English. b) The salary offered is interesting. c) None wants to teach the language at the school.

Appendix B: Interview Guide

1. As a teacher, what benefits do you get from sister school partnership at your school?
2. What about for your students? What do they get from this activity?
3. Do you have challenges in implementing the sister school partnership? If yes, what are they?
4. How do you get financial support for this sister school partnership?
5. How is the future of sister school partnership at your school?

CHAPTER 8

Politics of Gender and Gender Studies in Higher Education

Widjajanti M. Santoso and Nina Widyawati

Abstract

This chapter presents a comparative case study evaluating the politics and positioning of gender knowledge—or knowledge regarding the concept of gender and gender issues—in higher education (HE). The case study seeks to examine the social contexts shaping supportive and prohibitive institutional policies and practices regarding the place of gender studies and construction as well as dissemination of gender knowledge in HE institutions. The chapter also discusses the ways that gender knowledge and gender studies struggle to define and maintain its existence. The comparison is based on two different programmatic approaches of teaching about gender at the University of Indonesia, a flagship public university in Indonesia. This study is based on semi-structured interviews conducted with academics and faculty members in two programs within the University of Indonesia (UI), the flagship public university in Indonesia. The analysis shows that in the higher education context, while a ghettoisation approach to studying gender is productive and necessary—as exemplified in a dedicated graduate program focusing on gender studies, the approach lacks sustainability. A diffusion of gender knowledge through infusion or integration in other disciplinary studies—in this case through the Communications Studies Program—proves more sustainable for the endeavour.

Keywords

gender issues – gender studies – higher education – gender mainstreaming – college programs

1 Introduction

Indonesia has largely achieved gender parity in education participation. However, gender disparity and imbalance are still prevalent in economic and political participation, favouring the dominant participation of males. Within education, curricular content and materials taught in schools are still found to express traditional values regarding men and women, and project conservative gender norm and roles, and expectations of the division of labour based on sex. A United Nations Development Programme (UNDP) report (2009) noted that gender inequality awareness in Indonesia is minimal among educators and students, and the issue is rooted in "inadequate contextualisation of gender concepts in a way that makes sense within existing Indonesian socio-cultural and religious beliefs and traditions" (p. 77).

In light of this situation, the Government of Indonesia recognises gender inequality as a challenge and seeks to underline not only the importance of girls and women to receive an education but also of teaching all students about gender and gender issues. The Government implements gender mainstreaming policies with the stated aim of furthering gender equality. This chapter presents a comparative case study evaluating the politics and position of gender knowledge—or knowledge regarding the concept of gender, as well as gender issues—in higher education (HE). The case study seeks to examine the social contexts shaping supportive and prohibitive institutional policies and practices regarding the place of gender studies and construction as well as dissemination of gender knowledge in HE institutions. The chapter also discusses the ways that gender knowledge and gender studies struggle to define and maintain its existence.

The comparison is based on two different programmatic approaches of teaching about gender at the University of Indonesia, a flagship public university in Indonesia. This study is based on semi-structured interviews conducted with academics and faculty members in two programs within the University of Indonesia (UI), the flagship public university in Indonesia. The first is the Graduate Program of Gender Studies (GPGS) in the School for Strategic and Global Studies, and the second is the Communications Studies program (CSP) in the Faculty of Social and Political Sciences. The analyses point out the ways that the setup and structure of the former program illustrate the phenomenon of "ghettoisation" of gender knowledge, while the latter illustrates a diffusion of gender perspectives and knowledge via integration of gender topics within disciplinary studies, or the curriculum and program at large. While the GPGS is a graduate-level program, the CSP is offered at both undergraduate and graduate levels, leading to a Bachelor's, Master's, and Doctoral degree. The comparative analysis seeks to explore what mechanisms and components of the structural or programmatic positioning of the study of gender either support or pose problems to the teaching of gender. This positioning is in turn linked to institutional factors such as a restructuring of the university, academic (or faculty) hiring and structural norms, and financial support and sustainability of university units.

The analysis shows that in the higher education context, while a ghettoisation approach to studying gender is productive and necessary—as exemplified in a dedicated graduate program focusing on gender studies, the approach lacks sustainability, as GPGS itself struggles to maintain its operations. A diffusion of gender knowledge through infusion or integration in other disciplinary studies—in this case through the Communications Studies Program—proves more sustainable for the endeavour.

The chapter is organised as follows. The next section discusses the main conceptual framework used within the analysis, including ghettoisation and diffusion of gender knowledge. This discussion includes a brief historical context of the development of gender studies in HE in Indonesia as it pertains to the terminologies having emerged within the discourse during those times. It then proceeds with a short description of the two programs—the GPGS and the CSP—and the analysis.

2   The Evolution of Gender Studies: Ghettoisation and Diffusion as Approaches to Gender Knowledge Development

The two concepts used as approaches to construct and disseminate knowledge on gender are, firstly, ghettoisation, where studies and knowledge about women are constructed, disseminated, and taught as a separate body of knowledge, predominantly by women and for women; and secondly, the diffusion of gender knowledge, where gender knowledge, perspectives, and topics are integrated or infused into disciplinary studies and subjects.

2.1   *Ghettoisation*
Ghettoisation starts from a commitment that women's perspective matter. Education has historically represented patriarchal norms (Bernard, 1989; Chafetz, 1997; Delamonte, 2003; Smith, 1989, 1990, 1997), wherein academia male views and men have dominated the production, dissemination, and legitimisation of knowledge (Smith, 1989). Women were rarely written about or cited, and their expertise often ignored or devalued as evidenced by a dearth of citation of academics works done by women (Delamonte, 2003).

Evans (1982) shows that the rise of women studies was in response to this. Women studies within the academy became "a site of struggle" for social power (p. 73), as it supported women's movement and contributed to women empowerment. Professional feminists, as professional academics, positioned women studies as a critique of the patriarchal structure of the academy, but in the process were framed as radical feminists. As a corollary, women studies were positioned as subordinate to other discipline-based studies. This is the conceptual origin of ghettoisation. The study of women or the feminist perspective emerged as an isolated body of knowledge. It drew largely from Marxist perspectives to critique the hegemony of a male-dominated society, pushing back on mainstream Marxian and sociological theories, while in the process "ghettoising" themselves (Stacey & Thorne, 1985). The feminist knowledge grew but developed as a niche that seldom intersected with other disciplines.

The ghettoisation of women studies as a phenomenon shaped an approach of teaching gender knowledge where students are taught feminist theories and methodologies within a separate women or gender studies track. There were, however, drawbacks since women studies lacked connections into other disciplines. It led to resistance against feminism as a legitimate perspective.

2.2 *Diffusion of Gender Knowledge*

The concept of diffusion of gender knowledge began as a strategy of knowledge dissemination in international development processes and bureaucracy, expressed through policies and praxis. Highlighting the importance of gender equality, diffusion of gender knowledge is inherent in strategic policies targeting gender equality in society (True & Mistrom, 2001), social interventions (Moser &Moser, 2005), and research programs (Santoso, 2016). Diffusion of gender knowledge becomes a social practice highlighting the importance, for example, equal access to male and female within organisations. Within this perspective, gender analysis serves as a general tool supporting policymaking, development practice, and used in academia, departing from a sole focus on feminist perspectives and methodologies.

The term *gender* in gender studies historically emerged in response to the resistance to women's studies and seek to encourage acceptance to women's studies. It also represents a strategy of mainstreaming women's studies. Within this tradition, in education diffusion of gender knowledge has an aim of expanding gender awareness and is done through the integration or infusion of gender perspectives and topics within-subject or discipline-based studies.

3 Politics of Gender and Gender Studies in the University of Indonesia

3.1 *Gender and Women Studies in Indonesia*

Studies on gender and women studies in Indonesia are scattered and historically almost non-existent. There is a very small number of Indonesian historians that have focused on the subject of women or gender (Rahayu, 2007). Most recently, *Jurnal Perempuan* included an article on the growth of gender studies, which presented a discussion of the concept of feminist pedagogy.

Even fewer studies on gender studies in higher education in Indonesia exist. An AusAID report (2011) is among the few. It provides a comprehensive work summarising the state of gender studies and knowledge in Indonesia and included a focus on the Gender Studies Research Centre at the University of Indonesia. The report also noted an existing high demand for expertise on gender knowledge and gender specialists as they are few and far between within the bureaucracy and academia. While gender and women's movement progress, it has not flourished as a subject or area of study within HE institutions nor research institutes (Santoso & Djohan, 2014), such as University of Indonesia (UI) and the Indonesian Institute of Sciences. Gender knowledge has, as such, grown unevenly within the women's movement and in academia.

Contributing to our understanding of gender studies in Southeast Asia, Karim (1993) points out that the development of gender studies in countries such as Indonesia, Singapore, and Malaysia is facilitated by the support of the global network of feminist academics. Indigenous knowledge produced then contribute to exposing the differing issues related to women and gender within different country contexts, such as women and migration. Based on interviews data, it was discovered that the University of Indonesia Gender Studies Program's development also received support from Canadian feminist groups.

3.2 *Evolution of the University of Indonesia Gender Studies Program*

The University Rector's launched the idea to develop a program for women studies in the late 1980s. It was then called the Women Studies Program (*Program Studi Kajian Wanita*). From the start, it experienced a backlash of resistance with critical voices warning against following the feminist wave from the Western world. But the global dynamics of the women's movement propelled by the International Conference for Women in 1975 instilled the visions of the education and empowerment of women, including at University of Indonesia.

In 2012, the program changed its name to the Gender Studies Program (*Program Studi Kajian Gender*). The shift from women to gender communicates to the wider audience, including students, that the focus of the study is beyond women issues. This shift also expresses the shift in the wider discourse on women and gender issues and studies, exemplified in the use of Centre for Women Studies (*Pusat Studi Kajian Wanita*) during the New Order era (1966–1998) under President Soeharto, to Centre for Gender Studies (*Pusat Studi Kajian Gender*) in the Post-Reformation era (1998 onward).

In the so-called Post-Reformation era, universities in Indonesia underwent structural changes, a process which significantly impacts the sustainability of gender studies and the centre. Among the most significant change is the re-arrangement of faculty members as based within the different discipline-based schools or colleges, or *fakultas* in Indonesian. This move was biased favouring discipline-based studies and marginalising multi-disciplinary programs such as gender study (Magarey, 2014). As a compromise, gender studies at the University of Indonesia were then housed at the School of Strategic and Global Studies (*Sekolah Kajian Strategik dan Global*), where students can choose gender studies as a minor.

Since its early beginnings, the core subjects of the Graduate Program on Gender Studies (GPGS) had been feminist theories and methods, where students were taught to understand and represent women's issues and women's points of view. Lecturers and students engaged in gender-sensitising practices. Early phase lecturers were pioneers of women studies in Indonesia while the younger lecturers learned through their training and tutelage under their senior counterparts. They worked to further gender knowledge in their academic life, by building a network and creating a conducive environment to grow their expertise knowledge, in light of the significance and vulnerability of women studies in the university.

4   Programmatic Comparison of the Place and Study of Gender: Ghettoisation versus Diffusion

This section presents a brief overview of both programs, the Graduate Program of Gender Studies (GPGS) and the Communications Studies Program (CSP). It is followed by a comparison of the two programs, as an investigation of the place and pursuit of gender knowledge and studies within the programs. As mentioned, the two programs were selected for their illustrative representation of the two distinct approaches and positioning of gender knowledge and studies in higher education: ghettoisation and diffusion of gender knowledge. The analysis done compares and contrasts not only the curricular components of the programs, but also the organisational and supporting structures, which allows for the discussion of institutional and, arguably, political contexts of the two approaches.

4.1 The Graduate Program for Gender Studies

The GPGS from the beginning of their existent, focus on women's issues and experiences in a variety of social domain, including religion, health, environment, from the perspective of feminist theories and methodologies. The curriculum is updated every three years, following the idea that the contents have to critically reflect and address the contemporary phenomenon and changes or growth in society.

Students begin by going through phases of gender sensitisation, before then putting their gender knowledge into practice through an internship program in NGOs and other institutions of their choices. By doing so they have several advantages. Firstly, students have the opportunity to apply gender perspectives and further their gender sensitisation experiences, and secondly, they begin to work on their research or thesis, a requirement of program completion. All of the academic activities support the thesis writing. The importance of helping students finish their program on time is linked to the ability of GPGS to maintain a bargaining position within the university contributing to the university's performance and accreditation index. The gender program scores favourably by ensuring that students completed within a maximum of 4 semesters.

A former chairwoman notes of the quality and variety of student work, as well as the passion of students undertaking gender studies as exhibited in their thesis. She stated,

> I want to update a little bit about new theses topics from our new graduates, that consist of child marriage, position of women in *adat* (traditional) law, position of complexities of transgender, ageing women and health insurance, gender and politics of budgeting, woman in development, struggle of household helper, woman subjectivity in literature, sexism in corruption news coverage, feminist destruction in social media, *Laki-Laki Baru* (New Man—masculinity) and sexual division of labour. Every theses writer has a personal attachment to the topic. They are involved as a researcher in the field and they have their own standpoint related to their topics. Each has some kind of attachment to women and other marginalised groups.

Looking at the history of women study, financial aid is necessary to attract students, especially females, who have an interest in this subject. This support had been a part of what contributed to the development of a critical mass of women study researcher. This would also be an affirmative action policy in gender knowledge development and dissemination to produce a large number of gender specialists.

4.2 Gender Knowledge in Communications Studies Program

The diffusion of gender knowledge first started at the graduate level in the late 1990s. In a 2018 interview with the Program Chair, the person noted that a lecturer's involvement in several general-related research and activities facilitated the integration of gender topics in the courses in CSP. The lecturer had completed graduate study in the United States, during which she was involved in a project aimed to monitor the implementation of the Convention on the Elimination of all Forms of Discrimination Against Women (CEDAW). Her participation in the project expanded her knowledge on women's issues and developed a sensitivity on gender-based inequality including in her experiences growing up.

The CSP does not face challenges with regard to faculty hiring or staffing, and student intake. It is a popular program with many interests from students pursuing their Bachelor's, Master's, and Doctoral degrees. Prior to the standardisation of tuition fee, the CSP applied one of the highest fee structures. Their abundance of fiscal resources increased their capacities, for instance, to rent a whole building to house the program.

The CSP does not offer a stand-alone course on gender within the study of communications but infuses gender topics in its curriculum. A gender is an object of study in the context of communications studies. The interest to learn about gender issues in the subject of communications beginning in the mid-2000s became the rationale for lecturers and students to together work to integrate gender topics into the curriculum. The students had in fact also developed their interests in gender perspectives and issues having sat in courses offered in the GPGS. The CSP began offering "Media and Minority" as an elective course. The course offering, however, lasted for only five years due to departmental structural constrains, involving too many CSP elective courses being offered, and particular eligibility requirements limiting those who can enrol in these elective courses.

This stood in contrast to an increase in the interest of communications studies students to integrate gender topics within their research. In the last 10 years, there had been a 10% increase in the number of communications studies theses that focused on gender issues. Categorically, these theses explored contents of feminist theories and perspectives, such as feminist literature and metaphors, femininity, body politics, and patriarchal ideologies; and gender issues in society, such as masculinity, gender-based violence, androgyny, including through the analysis of social media such as the use of *Facebook,*

WhatsApp, Instagram, and online women's journal. Some of the theses also positioned women as the subject matter, and explored women's perception or use of communication methodologies, and also women's communication patterns in organisations and in the family.

4.2.1   Human Resources and Lecturers

The GPGS was developed under the leadership of the founding mothers and several young students who worked alongside each other on gender issues. There are now volunteers and individuals connected to the Program through the various activities and research, and also due to their historical attachments to the issue. All have a passion to both pursue and further gender knowledge. Program lecturers are housed in other colleges and teach courses within GPGS on a voluntary basis. The Program currently has only one permanent staff. All others are the non-permanent supporting staff. Previously, during the development stages of the Program, it was able to attract lecturers from other colleges and also external gender studies experts from various NGO, research institutes, or government institutions.

A focus on gender in the CSP was initiated and driven by female lecturers with interests in applying women's perspectives in studying communications, as well as the issues of women in communications. More recently, lecturers have integrated gender issues and topics into the discipline, and currently, gender is a thematic component of the graduate program for communications (offered at Master's and Doctoral levels). The lecturers have expertise in communications, as well as in gender issues within the context of communications.

Conditions of academic linearity which is still implemented in Indonesian higher education system—where lecturers must display multiple academic qualifications in the same area as the one which he/she teaches—is met. As such, the CSP currently faces no difficulties in assigning lecturers to teach about gender issues.

4.2.2   Impact of University Institutional Restructuring: New Hiring & Tuition Policies

The university implemented a new policy which prohibits the hiring of external individuals as lectures, with the exception of issue-specific experts assuming the role of theses-readers. The GPGS has but a few lecturers based in the program. Most are outside experts. As such, the Program currently faces limitations in not being able to bring in external lecturers. This has put more burden to existing lecturers. This situation produces a further gap between ideals of furthering the gender movement with the place of gender studies in an academic institution.

According to government regulation, as a program, the GPGS also needs to be supported by six "core" faculty members who hold doctoral degrees and are faculty members at the university. Due to academic linearity constraints, in the case those faculty members who are housed in various discipline-based programs become a core faculty member supporting the GPGS, that means while their work with GPSP adds to their existing workload, their contributions would not add to their cumulative scores supporting their career track progression.

The limitation is not experienced by the CSP. There are lecturers in the communications studies program with expertise on gender. They may have included gender issues in their thesis or discussion and are able to infuse gender topics into their communication courses. By doing so, they suffice the linearity requirement and will not face difficulties when applying to progress in their professorship status.

Another set of constraints faced by the GPGS is linked to new university policy on standardisation of tuition. Prior to the standardisation, GPGS offered one of the lowest tuition rates on campus, as a way to attract students to study gender. Many GPGS students come to the program with limited financial capacities. Many are women who have to allocate tuition from their *"uang perempuan"*, or literally women's money, which refers to the family budget they manage and is commonly limited because priorities are for their children's education and the general household spending. Many of them are single parent, who has to struggle to make ends meet. Financial aids are helpful but are rarely available.

For the sake of increasing revenue and attract students, the Program offer gender sensitisation workshops which later can be counted as course credits earned. Participants for these workshops are often staff from the Ministry of Religious Affairs, as well as the Ministry of Women Empowerment and Child Protection. At the time of this chapter's writing, this revenue scheme is not implemented, as Ministries have experienced budget cuts and reduced allocation for capacity building activities for staff surrounding gender awareness and knowledge.

The CSP does not experience budget constraints. As a popular subject and program of study, they are able to attract more students and prior to standardisation of tuition, the program had one of the highest tuition rates on campus. As mentioned before, they offer programs at the undergraduate and graduate levels. They also offer professional programs, offering evening courses for professionals. The professional program charges an even higher rate, as it targets individuals who already work in media or other communications-related fields.

5 Discussion: Ghettoisation of Gender Studies & Tensions Rooted in Higher Education Policies

As depicted above, the ghettoisation of gender knowledge as exemplified through the GPGS is rife with tension. Several policies, whether based on national HE policies or internally imposed by the University of Indonesia, pose as structural obstacles that disincentivise ghettoisation of gender knowledge. Two problematic policies are discussed here: a bias against multidisciplinary programs in higher education, and the prohibition of relying on external expertise within a program study, which for gender studies is a necessity.

5.1 Bias against Multidisciplinary Programs in HE in Indonesia

The academic linearity requirement is a part of a national policy for higher education. It requires faculty members who teach in one discipline to have done all their academic training—from Bachelor's to Doctorate programs—in the same discipline. As such, academics housed in a discipline-based program who happened to have graduate training (for instance at a Master's level) in gender, would not be able to use this record to contribute to their application for professorship status increase.

The impact for the GPGS is particularly devastating. Firstly, the Program loses some of their lecturer who chooses to "return" to their respective colleges, where they were hired. This, in turn, may secondly impact GPGS ability to attract potential students from the university. Thirdly, this prohibits gender studies and the Program to be able to build the critical mass to further the construction of gender knowledge, and train new producer of gender knowledge, further decreasing the number of expertise available on gender and gender issues.

The national policy requiring all postgraduate programs to be housed in their respective discipline-based college, as opposed to a separate unit of the Graduate School (*Pasca Sarjana*), is particularly problematic for gender studies. Gender studies are multidisciplinary by nature. Its core courses are on in psychology, law, social science and humanities, community health, environment, and others, and they are based in various colleges.

This institutional restructuring poses a problem impossible to resolve for the GPGS. It also forces faculty members who teach in the Program to have to choose between their passions for teaching gender studies courses and being accountable to teach in their respective colleges. This also disincentivises their participation in multidisciplinary programs, as their participation won't contribute to their tracked achievements for their career progression.

5.1.1 Internal Policy against Bringing in Outside Expertise

From its early beginnings, the GPSG founding mothers realised the importance of relying on networking and outside expertise. Women's studies have been supported by a mixture of academic experts who are passionate about gender knowledge, and NGO-based activists contributing to the women's movement (Santoso, 2012), which signals an awareness of the need to both be producing knowledge regarding gender, as well as be connected to social practices. And yet, the university's new management policies and agenda of increasing institutional efficiencies at all cost, have ignored this important characteristic of gender studies programs, and curbed the program's ability to rely on gender experts outside of the university. In this case, the university has shifted its role from supporting the growth of the nation-state to emphasising a market-based mechanism of standardisation, oblivious to the uniqueness of particular study areas such as gender studies.

Upon the policy's implementation, the GPGS lost lecturers who held temporary or non-employee status, disregarding their expertise nor their overseas training on feminism. Further, the centralisation of staff and placement of multidisciplinary graduate programs into discipline-based colleges have caused GPGS to lose their supporting staff, such as the librarian, the secretary, the finance officer, and general management staff.

These institutional policies have had the effect of undermining GPGS' position and the position of gender studies in general within higher education. This mirrors the condition at the national level, where gender studies are not included in the list of official programs of study recognised and approved by the government, according to the latest standing regulation issues in 2007 by the then Directorate General of Higher Education under the Ministry of Education and Culture (Decree 163/2017). This directorate general has since 2014 developed into the Ministry of Research, Technology, and Higher Education (Santoso & Djohan, 2014).

6 Conclusion & Implication

The chapter has focused on a comparative case study exemplifying the ways that institutional changes in HE have not appreciated the role of multidisciplinary programs within HE, undermining and contesting efforts of academics who have been building their career on multidiscipline areas of knowledge. The GPGS as exemplifying ghettoised gender knowledge holds a far more vulnerable position, than the diffusion of gender knowledge occurring through the CSP. While the diffusion of gender knowledge as a strategy for gender knowledge dissemination has worked well, ghettoised gender knowledge is in survival mode.

As the analysis has shown, institutional organisational changes can have a significant effect on gender studies. By implementing changes in hiring policies especially regarding hiring outside experts and restructuring programs to be housed in discipline-based colleges, the university has undermined the work and positioning of GPGS within academia and HE institution. This mirrors the current lack of recognition of gender study programs as an official academic program in higher education within national policy. This displays a disregard or lack of awareness of the government's commitments to gender mainstreaming policies, captured in the Presidential Decree 9/2000. Similarly, gender mainstreaming policies are out of the consideration of university institutional restructuring policies and bureaucratic reform.

Similar to what is occurring in Western academia, the changing role of the university affects women studies. The drive toward organisational efficiencies through standardisation breaks existing networks of human resources and modes of knowledge production. The social responsibility of the HE institution to provide more access to women and the study of women and gender become a lower priority, in the process obliviating the "herstory" of knowledge building and production.

The GPGS a knowledge producer has tasked itself with the indigenisation of feminism and gender studies in Indonesia and has actively been involved in both regional and international academic networks. In the face of these institutional changes, they face serious challenges. This highlights the need to question what the role of the global feminist network is in supporting each other in the process of knowledge production and whether the global network is slowing down in its academic pursuits.

References

AusAid. (2011). *Study of knowledge needs and supply constraints for gender research in Indonesia's knowledge sector* [Final Report]. AusAid & Universitas Indonesia Graduate Program in Gender Studies.

Bernard, J. (1989). The dissemination of feminist thought: 1960–1988. In R. A. Wallace (Ed.), *Feminism and sociological theory* (pp. 23–33). Sage.

Chafetz, J. S. (1997). Feminist theory and sociology: Underutilised contributions for mainstream theory. *Annual Review of Sociology, 23*(1), 97–120.

Delamont, S. (2003). *Feminist sociology.* Sage.

Evans, M. (1982). In praise of theory: The case for women's studies. *Feminist Review, 10*(1), 61–74. Retrieved from http://www.jstor.org/stabel/1394780

Gerung, R. (2016). Feminist pedagogy: A political position. *Jurnal Perempuan, 21*(3), 265–271.

Karim, W. J. (1993). Gender studies in southeast Asia. *Southeast Asian Journal of Social Science, 21*(1), 98–113.

Magarey, S. (2014). *Dangerous ideas: Women's liberation – Women's studies – Around the world*. University of Adelaide Press.

Moser, C., & Moser, A. (2005). Gender mainstreaming since Beijing: A review of success and limitations in international institutions. *Gender & Development, 13*(2), 11–22.

Rahayu, R. I. (2007). *Konstruksi historiography feminisme Indonesia dari tutur perempuan*. Retrieved from https://www.academia.edu/3256748/Historiografi_Feminisme_Indonesia

Santoso, W. M. (2012). Dorothy Smith tokoh feminis sosiologi. In W. M. Santoso & A. Windarsih (Eds), *Perspektif perempuan & pembangunan: Refleksi 80 tahun Melly G. Tan*. Gading Inti Prima.

Santoso, W. M. (2016). *Penelitian dan pengarusutamaan gender: Sebuah pengantar [Research and gender mainstreaming: An overview]*. LIPI.

Santoso, W. M., & Djohan, E. B. (2016). Kajian Gender dan Tantangannya bagi Perkembangan Multidisiplin di Indonesia. In W. M. Santoso (Ed.), *Ilmu Sosial di Indonesia: Perkembangan dan Tantangan* (p. 87). Yayasan Pustaka Obor Indonesia.

Smith, D. E. (1989). *The everyday world as problematic: A feminist sociology*. Northeastern University Press.

Smith, D. E. (1990). *The conceptual practices of power: A feminist sociology of knowledge*. Northeastern University Press.

Smith, D. E. (1997). Consciousness, meaning, and ruling relations: From women's standpoint. In *Millenial milestone. The heritage and future of sociology in the North American Region. Proceedings of the ISA Regional Conference for North America* (pp. 37–50). International Sociological Association.

Stacey, J., & Thorne, B. (1985). The missing feminist revolution in sociology. *Social Problems, 32*(4), 301–316. Retrieved from https://www.jstor.org/stable/800754

True, J., & Mintrom, M. (2001). Transnational networks and policy diffusion: The case of gender mainstreaming. *International Studies Quarterly, 45*(1), 27–57.

UNDP. (2009). *E-discussion: Gender – Overcoming unequal power, unequal voice*. UNDP Regional Centre for Asia Pacific.

PART 3

Youth, Schooling, and Social Context of Education

CHAPTER 9

Framing the Early School Leaving Policy Problem: Indonesian Rural Youth Engagement in Transnational Labour Migration as a Test Case

Isabella Tirtowalujo

Abstract

Despite Indonesia's commendable achievements in expansion of education participation in the last few decades, significant proportions of high-school-going age adolescents and 19–21-year old youths remain either out-of-school (OOS) or have not completed 12-year compulsory education. Further, contextual factors contributing to rural youths opting out of schooling toward alternative means to realise their perceptions of successful adulthood lead to an overrepresentation of rural youth in the OOS children population in Indonesia. Contributing to existing literature on studies conducting meta-analyses which map the terrain of research and policy analysis work addressing education access and participation in international contexts, this chapter presents a policy document analysis, making explicit three frameworks used to organise existing national policies and programs that address the OOS issue in Indonesia, and discussing underlying assumptions behind each framework. The analysis then employs insights from an ethnographic case study—to serve as a test case—involving international labour force participation of Indonesian youth in a rural community at the expense of their completion of secondary education. The case study featuring a phenomenon of the entanglement of rural communities and youths in state-driven transnational labour migration systems serves to consider the policy frameworks' assumptions, potentials, and limitations.

Keywords

early-school leaving – out-of-school – policy analysis – rural youth – labour participation – rural ethnography

1 Introduction

Over the decades Indonesia has experienced major progress in the expansion of education participation among larger groups of children and youth, and at higher levels of education. However, despite commendable achievements in various education development indicators, challenges remain abound. Between 2010 and 2018 junior secondary Net Enrolment Rate (NER) has largely stagnated averaging at about 78% (MoEC, 2019). Furthermore, among primary and secondary school-age children (7–18 years), about 7.6% are not in school nor accessing any education services, and among senior secondary school-age children (16–18 years) alone, 22.8% are out-of-school (Ministry of National Development Planning/National Development Planning Agency [Bappenas], 2019). Considering the population size of Indonesia, this is equivalent to about 4.1 million school-age children who are out-of-school, 3 million among whom are those between 16–18 years old.

These statistics represent a major obstacle toward positioning the nation to fulfil the 2030 Agenda of reaching the Sustainable Development Goals and ensuring education participation for all citizens. While in most recent years the out-of-school children ratio has been in a steady decline (Bappenas, 2019), there is still a significant number of older children who are out-of-school, and as a corollary, a large proportion of youths who enter the labour force without senior secondary education completion. These youths contribute to the existing issue of low labour productivity and individuals remaining in low-wage, low-skill work (Manning & Pratomo, 2018).

In the effort of addressing these two major issues, the Government of Indonesian through Bappenas has drafted a national strategy to address the out-of-school children (OOSC) issue in Indonesia, or *Strategi Nasional Penanganan Anak Tidak Sekolah di Indonesia* (*Stranas ATS*),[1] with the support of UNICEF as a development partner. The national strategy document maps existing and gaps in policies and programs that directly address issues of out-of-school children and of youth early school leavers.

This chapter critiques the national strategy document's offering by investigating the multiple framings of the policy problem (Dumas & Anderson, 2014) inherent in the frameworks used in the national strategy document to map public policies addressing this issue. The analysis focuses on the potentials of the Stranas frameworks in addressing real-life situations, particularly in cases of labour force participation of early school leavers. Folded into this analysis is a test case based on findings from an ethnographic case study conducted in 2014 in Lampung province on rural youth overseas work aspirations. The case study serves to consider the policy frameworks' assumptions, potentials, and limitations. In doing so, the author foregrounds the role of ethnography in not only informing policy design and evaluation but also in providing nuance to the policy problem definition with the potential of disrupting dominant framing of the issue.

The analysis argues that the phenomenon of early school leaving youth exemplified in the ethnographic study is rooted in the entanglement of rural communities and youths in a state-driven transnational labour migration system targeting those willing to enter low-skill or manual work overseas. Existing policies countering common economic barriers to education participation will face challenges in addressing the issue of early school leaving involving overseas work aspirations. The analysis shows that the Stranas frames youth labour migration at the expense of secondary education completion as a socio-cultural barrier lowering education participation, and discusses policies in place meant to address this barrier. The discussion also highlights tensions in mapping the phenomenon of youth international labour force participation onto the policy expectations of the 12-year compulsory education.

2   Research on Education Access and Participation In Indonesia

Research on education participation at secondary levels in Indonesia predominantly has two aims. Firstly, there are studies that focus on investigating the determinants and what hinders or contributes to participation. These studies highlight a range of contributing factors such as cost, poverty, and child work impacting enrolment (Frankenberg, Smith, & Thomas, 2003; Sim, Suryadarma, & Suryahadi, 2017; Suryadarma, Suryahadi, & Sumarto, 2006; Suryahadi, Priyambada, & Sumarto, 2005), access or school distances and parental education background (Alisjahbana, 1994), academic achievement (Zuilkowski, Samanhudi, & Indriana, 2019), and various combined effects of economic and sociocultural factors, such as gender, ethnicity, migration, and cultural value systems (for example, Quisumbing & Otsuka, 2001; Rammohan & Robertson, 2012; Resosudarmo & Suryadarma, 2014; Suryadarma et al., 2006). Secondly, other studies seek to evaluate and understand the impacts of national policies and interventions on access and participation measures. Policies and programs analysed range from the massive primary school construction program (*SD Inpres*) in the 1980s throughout Indonesia (Duflo, 2001), the public scholarship program through the Social Safety Net program (*Jaring Pengaman Sosial, JPS*) implemented immediately following the 1998 economic crisis in Asia at large (Cameron, 2009; Ha & Mendoza, 2010), public spending policies

(Lanjouw & Pradhan, 2001), and community-driven development and conditional cash transfer programs (Rahayu, Toyamah, Hutagalung, Rosfadhila, & Syukri, 2008; Voss, 2008; World Bank, 2017).

In service of these two aims, studies have used a variety of variables or proxies to analyse access and participation measures, such as enrolment, attendance, absence, and dropout rate, and—denoting sustained participation—transition to higher education levels, completion, and attainment. Expressing a dominant perspective of a "schooled society" (Baker, 2014) and the spirit of Education for All, research highlighting non-participation at secondary levels have framed the issue using terminologies such as "dropout", "early school leaving", and "out-of-school", and subsequently, the subjects of interest as school dropouts, early school leavers, and out-of-school children or youth (for example, UNESCO, 2017; Utomo, Reimondos, Utomo, McDonald, & Hull, 2014).

There is also a segment of the literature on these issues covering international contexts that present a meta-analysis and have taken on the task of mapping the terrain of research and policy analysis work addressing education access and participation. These reports seek to distil important policy lessons from cross-country reviews and summarise key insights on crucial contextual factors for consideration by researchers, policy-makers, and practitioners (Ganimian & Murnane, 2016; Hunt, 2008; UNESCO, 2017; UNESCO & UIS, 2014). For example, since the launching of the Global Out-of-School Children Initiative at the beginning of the 2010, the UNESCO Institute for Statistics (UIS) and other branches of the UN system have produced reports analysing and categorising root causes of non-participation issues globally, while developing profiles of the OOSC demography in the world and in particular regions or countries (see for example UNESCO, 2017; UNESCO & UIS, 2014). In another example, a review of 223 studies by Alejandro Ganimian and Richard Murnane (2016) provides a comprehensive mapping and systematic categorisation of research carrying out a rigorous impact evaluation of education policy interventions in low- and middle-income countries. The authors map and categorise the policies and interventions on the basis of the policy's theory-of-action (such as policies reducing direct costs of schooling, improving school amenities, providing children with vital medications, expanding schooling options, and so on).

The chapter contributes to this segment of the literature by featuring and critiquing the frameworks used to categorise and map policies within the Stranas document. Few studies have engaged in meta-analysis with the aim of summarising and comparing ways of categorising existing policies addressing education participation issues—whether on the basis of the policy's theories-of-action or thematic grouping—to make explicit underlying assumptions in the framing of the policy problem. Further, few policy studies on issues of enrolment, drop-out, attainment, or completion feature interventions or policies categorised as addressing aspects of governance and policy implementation, a categorical framework included in the Stranas. The following section presents the frameworks of policy mapping used in the Stranas and discusses the multiple framings of the policy problem.

3 Three Policy Mapping Frameworks and the Early School Leaving Problem

Three frameworks are presented and discussed here. The combination and integration of the three frameworks serve as an organising structure for the national strategy document.[1] The first framework is a close adaptation of UNICEF's comprehensive global out-of-school initiative (OOSCI) studies framework (UNICEF, 2011, 2015), which foregrounds the notion of key issues posing as barriers to education participation. The second framework conceptually organises the policies on the basis of target beneficiaries. The beneficiary groups, in turn, are groups targeted by various existing social protection and welfare policies in Indonesia. The third framework represents a governance perspective, organising policies on the basis of implementation phases of the overall national strategy to this complex issue.

3.1 *Framework One: Barriers to Participation*
The framework categorises policies and programs addressing the issues of out-of-school children and early school leaving among youth utilising the notion of barriers to education participation. The framework is a close adaptation of the Global Out-of-School Children Initiative (OOSCI) framework (UNICEF, 2015). Based on economic terms, participation is described as an outcome of the meeting of supply of and demand for education. Policies are then categorised on the basis of whether they address supply- or demand-side barriers (see Figure 9.1).

The supply-side of education is characterised through notions of availability or accessibility, as well as of quality and relevance of education services or programs. As a direct corollary, supply-side barriers to participation, therefore, are issues linked to lack of access to education services, low education quality, or to education programs that fail to serve the educational needs or interests of children and youth.

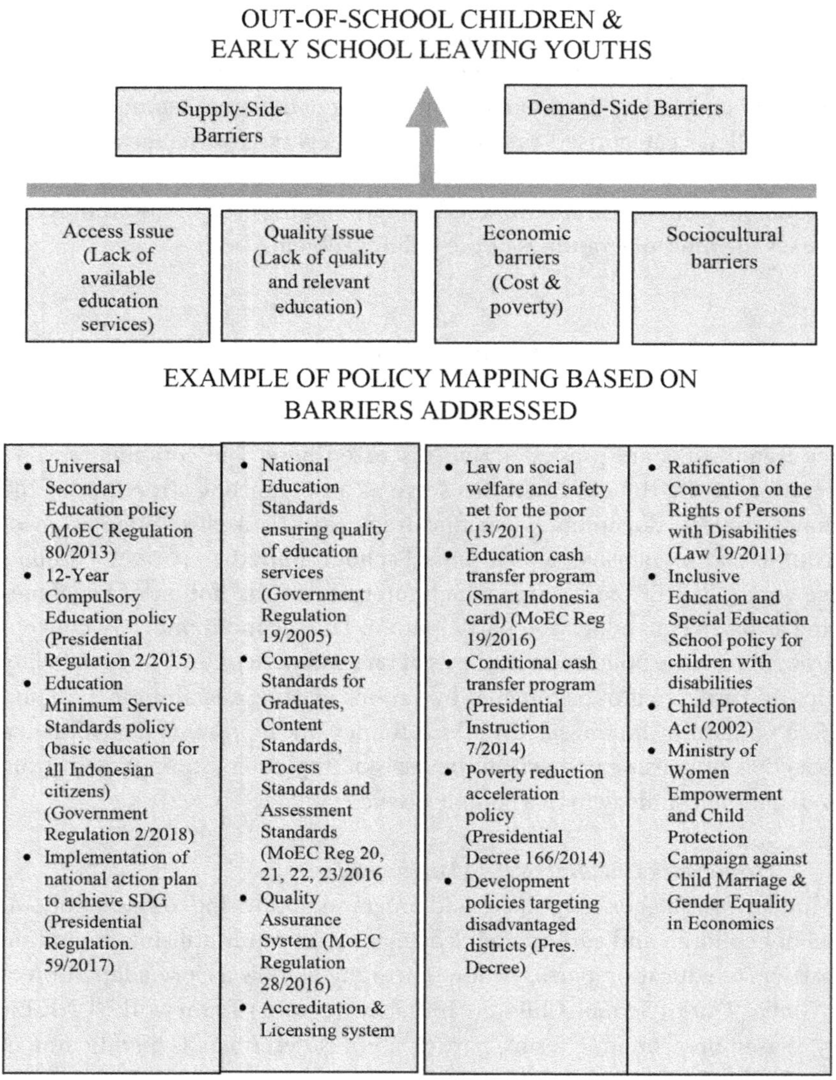

OUT-OF-SCHOOL CHILDREN & EARLY SCHOOL LEAVING YOUTHS

Supply-Side Barriers		Demand-Side Barriers	
Access Issue (Lack of available education services)	Quality Issue (Lack of quality and relevant education)	Economic barriers (Cost & poverty)	Sociocultural barriers

EXAMPLE OF POLICY MAPPING BASED ON BARRIERS ADDRESSED

• Universal Secondary Education policy (MoEC Regulation 80/2013) • 12-Year Compulsory Education policy (Presidential Regulation 2/2015) • Education Minimum Service Standards policy (basic education for all Indonesian citizens) (Government Regulation 2/2018) • Implementation of national action plan to achieve SDG (Presidential Regulation. 59/2017)	• National Education Standards ensuring quality of education services (Government Regulation 19/2005) • Competency Standards for Graduates, Content Standards, Process Standards and Assessment Standards (MoEC Reg 20, 21, 22, 23/2016) • Quality Assurance System (MoEC Regulation 28/2016) • Accreditation & Licensing system	• Law on social welfare and safety net for the poor (13/2011) • Education cash transfer program (Smart Indonesia card) (MoEC Reg 19/2016) • Conditional cash transfer program (Presidential Instruction 7/2014) • Poverty reduction acceleration policy (Presidential Decree 166/2014) • Development policies targeting disadvantaged districts (Pres. Decree)	• Ratification of Convention on the Rights of Persons with Disabilities (Law 19/2011) • Inclusive Education and Special Education School policy for children with disabilities • Child Protection Act (2002) • Ministry of Women Empowerment and Child Protection Campaign against Child Marriage & Gender Equality in Economics

FIGURE 9.1   Conceptual illustration of the barrier-to-participation framework (Framework One)

3.1.1   Underlying Assumptions in Framing the Policy Problem

The two supply-side barriers of access- and quality-related factors assume the following. Some children are out-of-school because they simply cannot access education services. This is exemplified in cases where there are no schools or education services accessible within a safe distance from where a child resides. And yet, school availability or accessibility does not guarantee participation. A school may be available, however, the school may face serious issues that compromise the quality of its operations or services, for example, a high rate of teacher absenteeism. These issues would stand in the way of families seeing any benefit in enrolling their children despite their ability to do so.

Quality-related supply issues may also manifest in cases where available education programs are perceived as irrelevant to the interest or needs of youths and the community. For example, while informal education programs offering general education completion courses are available and affordable within a community, not all youth early school leavers and their families see the need or relevance to gain their senior secondary diploma, and would seek instead for example programs offering entrepreneurial education.

This framework acknowledges an ideal level of demand, which in light of the 12-year compulsory education policy is universal at both the primary and secondary levels.[2] Demand-side barriers are categorised into economic and sociocultural factors. Economic barriers are related to education costs. Direct and indirect costs to education and poverty remain one of the main factors hindering enrolment and sustained participation (Castillo, Salem, & Sarr, 2014; Suryahadi et al., 2005; UNESCO, 2017).

Economic barriers are at times deeply entangled with sociocultural barriers to participation. Sociocultural factors barring education participation are rooted in perceptions and beliefs or shared values linked to cultural norms, tradition, or interpretation of religious teachings that devalues the educational participation of children on the basis of their social identities, such as gender, social status, marital status, (dis)ability status, ethnic/racial background, economic background, and others.

The framework acknowledges a need for a comprehensive or holistic understanding of what contributes to non-participation in education. Supply-side barriers attribute shortcomings to providers of education services, while demand-side barriers place the burden of behavioural and attitude change on children, youth, families, and the communities in which they live and learn. The barrier-to-participation framework allows for the analysis of the combinatory effects of multiple barrier factors, making the out-of-school issue in some contexts an extremely complex problem to address. The framework suggests a need to address participation issues from multiple angles and avoid stand-alone policies of, for instance, building more schools, providing scholarships to poor students, or launching a back-to-school campaign or program.

3.2 Framework Two: Sub-Groups of Out-of-School Children and Youth Early School Leavers

This framework maps and organises policies and programs by utilising a categorisation of groups of children and youth who are policy beneficiaries of various social welfare and development policies and programs. Within the Stranas document, the major sub-groups included are children and youth in disadvantaged, outermost, and border areas; children with disabilities; children in conflict with the law; working children/victims of child labour; children in child marriage and adolescent mothers; street children and abandoned children; and a general category of other out-of-school children including children in disaster areas, victims of abuse, and many others (see Figure 9.2).

3.2.1 Underlying Assumptions in Framing the Policy Problem

This framework recognises the need to, firstly, name the specific conditions or circumstances faced by children, which necessitate government's intervention or assistance toward offsetting the educational disadvantages that the children suffer. According to this framework, the OOSC or education non-completion problem is mediated by the named condition—whether disability, child labour, remote or isolated communities, homelessness, victimhood, etc. Secondly, mapping OOSC policies on the basis of categories or sub-groups of out-of-school children and youth highlights the vast differences and variety of contextual factors of non-participation. The framework assumes the need for a more targeted approach to developing priorities, policies, and programs to address the out-of-school or early school leaving issue.

Related to this, the sub-grouping framework is made meaningful as it is overlaid with the (supply-demand) barrier framework discussed in the previous sub-section. For each sub-group of out-of-school children and youth, this framework maps existing and gaps in policies and programs that seek to minimise barriers to participation faced by the sub-group. The sub-grouping of policy beneficiary framework, therefore, assumes the need for differentiated foci of intervention when it comes to returning children and youth to a path of learning. For example, while children in juvenile detentions predominantly face supply-side barriers to participation—due to detention centres lack adequate education services, girls in child marriage or adolescent mothers face predominantly demand-side sociocultural factors hindering them from enrolling or transitioning to higher levels of education.

Lastly, the sub-grouping framework utilises existing categorisation of beneficiaries of government policies and programs, acknowledging that education

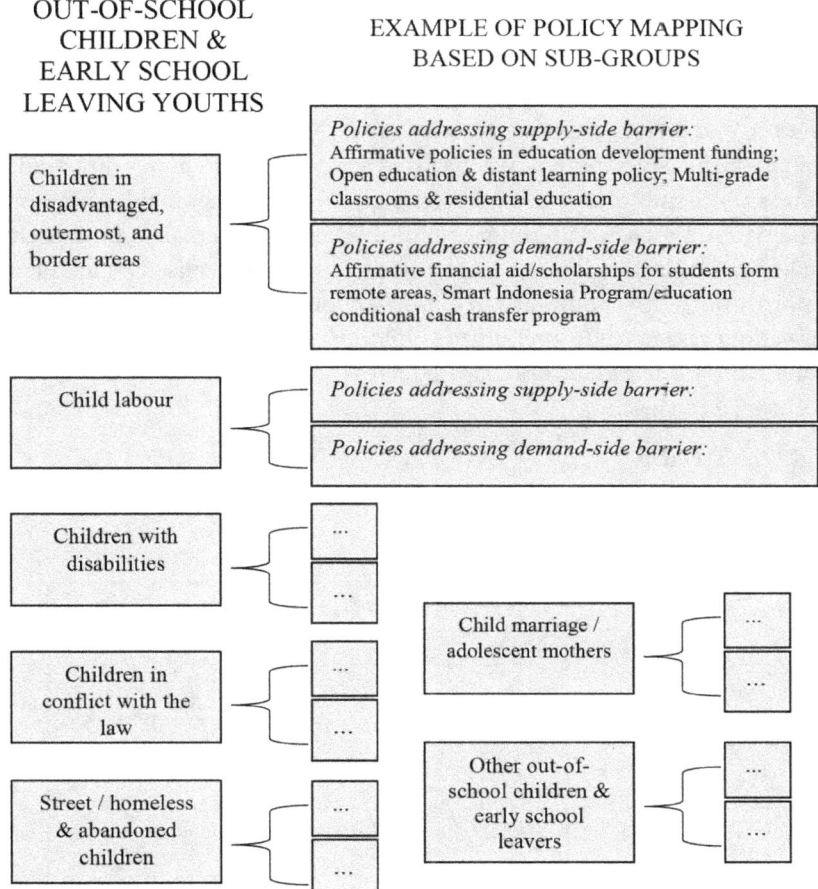

FIGURE 9.2   Conceptual illustration of the sub-grouping framework (Framework Two)

interventions targeting early school leavers are a component of a larger social welfare and assistance policies for these various groups of marginalised or disadvantaged children.

3.3   *Framework Three: Governance and Policy Implementation*

This third framework categorises policies on the basis of phases of the implementation of strategies to reduce the out-of-school rate in a particular locale in the context of a decentralised government. The first phase is the development of enabling conditions and supporting governance structures for a district-wide effort to address the out-of-school issue, predominantly by building and securing political commitment and local political capacity to allow for the mobilisation of resources. The second phase involves the development of a knowledge basis on the local out-of-school children and early-school leaver population, and a shared database or information management system. The third phase is the development of a localised action plan and policy directions to address the issue toward minimising (supply- and demand-side) barriers to participation for each sub-group of out-of-school children and youth early school leaver. The last phase is an implementation of the localised action plan including through direct outreach to out-of-school children and their families, and providing assistance to support the children's (re-)integration back into a path of learning. The framework maps policies that enact the processes of the phases (see Figure 9.3).

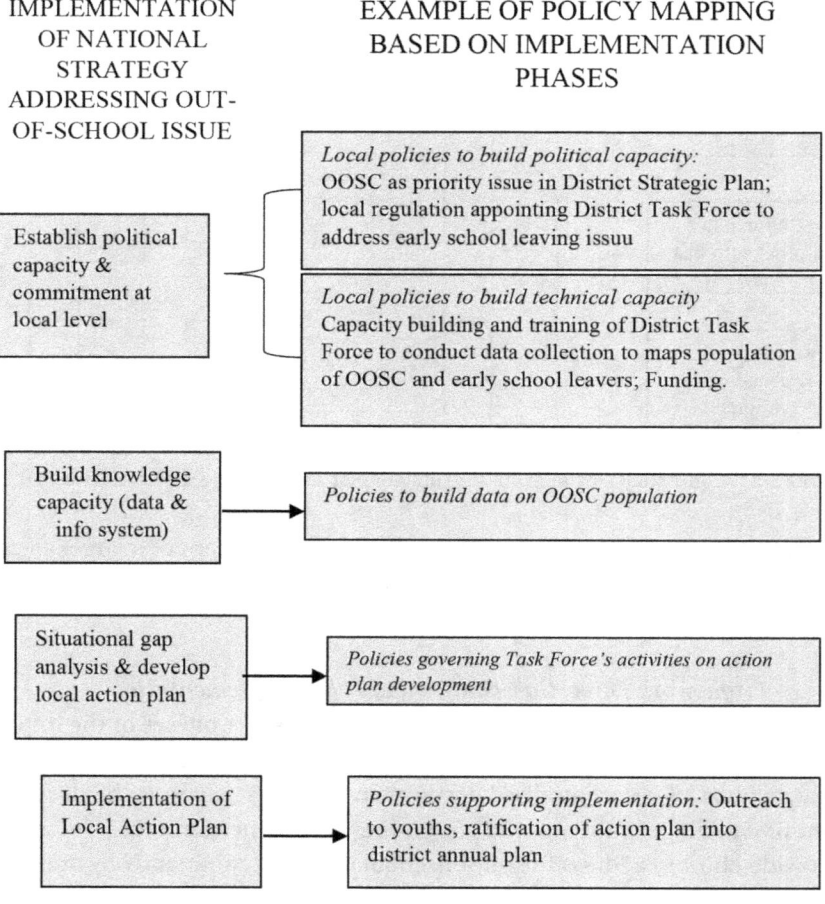

FIGURE 9.3   Conceptual illustration of the governance framework (Framework Three)

3.3.1 Underlying Assumption in Framing the Policy Problem

This framework defines the policy issue as a pragmatic problem of governance at the local government level. Expressed through the phases of strategy implementation above are four domains of governance: development of political capacity and will, development of knowledge capacity, development of technical (including fiscal) capacity, and execution of an action plan.

Policies toward developing political capacity and will at the local level, in this case include, for example, securing the commitment of the highest governing local office to reduce out-of-school children and increase completion rates at primary and secondary levels. In Indonesia, a secured public commitment would take the form of the issuance of a regulatory framework, as well as a special appointment of a task force to oversee the development and implementation of a local action plan to reduce OOSC.

Actions toward developing knowledge capacity include demographic survey and mapping to gain a knowledge basis on the out-of-school and early school leaver population within the local community—how many children and youth there are, where they live, reasons for leaving school, the highest education level completed, and so on. Further, knowledge capacity at the local level involves an understanding then of what the most predominant causes of the out-of-school problem are; what (supply- and demand-) barriers need to be addressed locally; what local policies and programs exist and are needed.

Policies toward developing technical capacity include guidelines for allocation of fiscal and human resources, in this case, including the recruitment and equipping of the district technical team to both develop and implement an action and budgetary plan, and dispatch teams who will work in and with local communities to identify out-of-school children and youth, issues faced by the communities, and when necessary, implement a case-by-case plan to reintegrate children and youth into education and training.

The integration of the three frameworks structures the national strategy to address the out-of-school and early school leaving issues in Indonesia. Upon the document's approval and issuance as government regulation, the Stranas serves as both a legal reference and guideline for local governments to address these issues as they manifest in each district and municipality.

Having discussed the frameworks and how they differently define the policy problem, the next section brings into the analysis a brief test case drawn from an ethnography study on the education and work aspirations of rural youths, captured through the concept of "narrative of success". The goal is to further discuss the potentials and limitations of the framings of the Stranas policy problem in addressing complex real-life situations involving early school leaving, which based on the case study, is linked to labour migration. The proceeding section briefly summarises one particular narrative of success that have animated rural youths' decision to leave schooling to enter overseas work, as a more extreme and complex case of youth labour participation at the expense of education completion.

4 Rural Youth (International) Labour Force Participation and Education Non-Completion

While child work is both a rural and urban phenomenon, children from rural communities are overrepresented within the population of working children. Based on the 2009 National Labour Force Survey data, 58% of children aged 7–14 years work in agriculture (Understanding Children's Work Programme [UCW], 2012). Studies on the relationship between child work, labour market, and education attainment do not similarly characterise how they correlate or are linked to each other. They do largely support the findings that both higher employment opportunity in a community and child employment adversely impact participation measures (Sim et al., 2017; UCW, 2012). Data evidence based on the 2015 national household survey does show an overrepresentation of rural youth (61%) among all senior secondary out-of-school youth population (16–18 years) (Ministry of Education and Culture [MoEC] & UNICEF, 2018).

In the case of Indonesia, since the 1960s labour migration has been promoted, regulated, and facilitated by the government of Indonesia through bilateral agreements (Hugo, 1995). This meant an expansion of international labour force participation opportunities for workers from rural communities. While there are no data displaying actual numbers and proportions of Indonesian overseas workers (*Tenaga Kerja Indonesia,* or *TKI*[3]) according to their rural-urban communities of origin, a majority of Indonesian overseas workers are from rural areas (Hugo, 2012).

In light of the historical and current prevalence of labour participation among children and youth in rural communities, as well as the state-facilitated transnational labour migration opportunities above, both the universal secondary education (USE) policy and the 12-year compulsory education policy made official respectively in 2013 and 2015 have created most tension in rural communities, where it is common for children and youth to be involved in economic activities and productive functions within and outside the family—and among youths, this includes international work destinations—at the expense of secondary education completion.

4.1 Ethnography Case Study: Insights on Education and Work Aspirations of Rural Youth

As mentioned, the test case is based on a larger and previously reported ethnographic case study (Tirtowalujo, 2016) based on fieldwork conducted in 2014 in three villages in East Lampung regency in the Southern part of Sumatra, Indonesia. Qualitative data included field ethnographic observations from a brief five-week stay in four villages with four different community-member hosts. Data were constructed based on multiple semi-structured single and pair interviews with 16 youth participants with varying backgrounds—including gender, religion, and whether or not they were in school, and six teacher participants from one private school, through which the author established local contacts and arranged the fieldwork. One focus-group interview was also conducted involving five of the youth participants. Youths were predominantly recruited by the author through her daily encounters with members of the community, or through the facilitation of the author's varying hosts.

Based on interviews and ethnographic observations, there is a narrative of success where success is mediated through temporary transnational labour migration.[4] In other words, youths and adults involved in the study recognised existing beliefs about pathways to successful adulthood and a phenomenon of youths within their community—both younger and older than 18 years old—aspiring to become a TKI or overseas workers in countries such as Malaysia, Taiwan, South Korea, and Hongkong, where they would enter predominantly low-skill work. The youths and adults in the study, which included students, out-of-school youth, university students, teachers, and community elders, had varying perspectives and standpoints with regard to youths aspiring and becoming migrant workers.

4.1.1 Lampung and Transnational Labour Migration

Between 2013 and 2018, Lampung consistently ranked fifth as the largest labour-exporting province in Indonesia, averaging about 17 thousand new TKIs leaving the province to work abroad (BNP2TKI, 2019). According to data released by the National Board for the Placement and Protection of Indonesian Overseas Workers (BNP2TKI) (2019), in 2018 alone of the 18,900 workers from the Lampung province placed overseas, more than one third (about 6,891 individuals) were from East Lampung regency. These statistics emerged from my data in the form of common discourses surrounding aspiration to become a migrant worker.

4.1.2 A Narrative of Success through Labour Migration

Out of the 16 youths interviewed in the study, three of them—two males and one female—were considering becoming a TKI in the near future. The two males were Febri, a 20-year old high who was a part of the focus-group interview, and Elya, the 21-year old who at the time of the interview were working in Jakarta as a security guard. They strongly expressed their TKI aspiration and planned on beginning the application process in the subsequent year or two. Citra, who was 20 years old and the only female among the three, was the least enthusiastic about the thought of becoming a TKI, and merely stated that she had thought of it.

Youths' statements regarding the origins of their TKI aspirations suggest that social and family networks have a significant role in the development of migratory aspirations, reflecting a known characteristic of a strong network factor involved in transnational migration (Hugo, 2012). Family members and relatives may proactively encourage those to consider becoming a TKI, in addition to displaying or pointing to the visibility of success derived from becoming a TKI through the accumulation of wealth. TKI friends, acquaintances, or family members were ubiquitous within the social networks of youths in this study.

Citra expressed that her mother and grandmother had both repeatedly urged her to consider the TKI path. Elya similarly formed his TKI aspirations by observing an older sibling who four years prior had become a TKI in Malaysia, as well as his cousin who then in 2014 had recently left for Taiwan. His cousin periodically notified him of work vacancies abroad. This cousin had attended university for one year but decided to leave to be a TKI. Elya had mentioned that he planned to do the same.

4.1.3 A Narrative of Success through Labour Migration

Youth participants expressed that being a TKI helps them achieve a range of important life goals and definitions of success. This included most importantly the ability to provide care for various family members, gaining further income-generating capabilities, and gaining respect and social status in the community.

Within a narrative of success through becoming a TKI, labour migration enables accumulation of wealth in a relatively short period of time. The sacrifice of being away from one's family and community over a period of three to five, or even ten years, pays off upon one's return through increased purchasing power and consumption capacities. TKIS receive a wide range of income on the basis of types of employment. According to one of the village leaders I interviewed, female domestic workers then may earn between Rp. 6–7 million per month, about 4 times the Lampung minimum wage at the time. Males who are predominantly factory workers may earn up to Rp. 10–20 million a month.

Success in this rural community is visible and tangible in the renovated and modern looking houses built on remittance money, plots of farmlands acquired, and labour-migrant owned businesses, all of which were present throughout the community and surrounding villages of the research sites. This phenomenon has been recorded in various studies on remittance-based development in overseas workers' villages of origin (Hugo, 1995, 2012; Lindquist, 2012; Silvey, 2007). The "visibility" of success works to strengthen the power of the TKI or labour migration narrative of success. Further, the renovated and newly constructed homes, farmland, and businesses acquired while workers are abroad express intentions of returning to one's home community. Youths confirmed that TKIs leave in order to succeed at home.

Citra's comments below pointed to this, as she explained the rationale behind her consideration of becoming a TKI:

> I thought of working abroad because I will be able to succeed. I can buy farmland and have money to open a business. I can have a car and work. Staying and working here, won't get you anywhere. I thought of working abroad because my *mbah* [my grandmother], and my mother already told me to. My grandma has seen that one of her granddaughters in Taiwan is successful. She built the house, the one that you are staying in, that's where the money is from.

Here, Citra reiterated the familiar pessimistic tone about staying in the community and the chances of, in her words, getting "anywhere in life".

For some TKIS, working abroad also enables them to ensure that their family—particularly parents, younger siblings, or children—are cared for and have their needs met (Tirtowalujo, 2016). This includes affording them access to health care and education.

In sum, within a narrative of success through labour migration, becoming a TKI yields economic empowerment which holds an encompassing potential for success, as it gives youths the ability to provide and care for their families, gain respect from increased social status within their community, and succeed in their home community.

5 Discussion: Youth Overseas Workers and Early School Leaving

Currently, two sets of policies are at odds with each other: the universal secondary education policy which supports the 12-year compulsory education policy, and the standing law on TKI recruitment and placement (39/2004), which set the minimum educational attainment level at junior secondary education and the minimum age at 18 years old. The TKI Law has contributed to evidence of a vast majority of TKIs from Lampung placed overseas having only completed junior secondary education or lower. For example, between 2011 to 2018, 70% of new Lampungese TKIs placed had only a junior secondary education or lower (Badan Nasional Penempatan dan Perlindungan Tenaga Kerja Indonesia [BNP2TKI], 2019), In absolute terms, this represents more than 2.1 million TKIs from Lampung placed abroad within the 8-year period.

The data suggest that, while the three particular youths featured in the ethnographic case study aspiring to become overseas workers had all completed 12-year education, many among their counterparts from Lampung and elsewhere have not and instead choose to enter overseas work. Moreover, insights from the ethnographic study and from data on the education completion rate among overseas workers suggest that there may be a significant population of youth TKIs younger than 21 years old, who have not completed 12-year education. Since there is no available data on TKIs by age or age groups, the size of this population remains unknown. Further, with each known or reported case of under-age overseas worker—whether involving commercial recruitment agencies recruiting underage workers, or adolescents lying about their age on paper,[5] there are multiple unreported cases of children under 18-years old working abroad illegally (for example, Andrevski & Lyneham, 2012; Silvey, 2007). Some of them similarly would not have completed 12-year education. As mentioned, no data is available that can definitively establish the size of this population.

5.1 *Promises and Challenges of Policies Addressing Real-Life Situations Involving Early School Leaving*

To reiterate, the groups of children and youth-targeted by the mapped Stranas policies are children ages 7–18 years[6] who are out-of-school, and youths up to 21 years[7] old who have not completed 12-year education. Findings from the ethnographic study on the narrative of success involving international labour migration in a rural community present a case of a phenomenon that contributes to the out-of-school and early school leaving issue. In the following, the three policy mapping frameworks and their framing of the out-of-school problem are staged against the test case described above.

The first framework interprets the education non-participation issue as rooted in failures to overcome education participation barriers. In the case of international youth labour participation, the issue is not predominantly rooted in access (supply) or economic (demand) barriers to participation. In some locales, young people may be driven to overseas work because there are no schools or relevant educational programs available in their communities, representing supply-side barriers. Findings from the study (Tirtowalujo, 2016) suggest that this is not necessarily the case. In other cases, youths may also opt to become a TKI because they are not able to afford education, which represents a case of the demand-side economic barrier. However, similarly, this is not a necessary factor in driving youths toward overseas work. Despite the ability to access and afford education, some youths opt-out of schooling.

In this case, the out-of-school issue is rooted in the entanglement of a rural community and their youths in a state-driven transnational labour migration system targeting those willing to enter low-skill or manual work. From a push/pull theory of education participation (Borgna & Struffolino, 2017; Bradley & Renzulli, 2011; Hunt, 2008), these youths are not necessarily barred from education participation nor pushed out of the education system. However, they are pulled out of schooling into labour migration by the promises of economic empowerment.

Policies countering economic barriers to participation will insufficiently address non-participation issue rooted in aspiration to participate in labour migration. In other words, the major policies targeted to minimise economic barriers, such as the School Operational Assistance (*Bantuan Operasional Sekolah*, BOS) school grant program providing operational funding for all schools in Indonesia, and education cash transfer programs targeting poor students such as the Smart Indonesia Card (*Kartu Indonesia Pintar*), will have limited potentials in turning some adolescents away from developing their migratory work aspirations.

The Stranas barrier-to-participation framework (Framework One) would interpret labour migratory aspirations among younger youths as a socio-cultural barrier lowering education participation rates. The narrative of success involving overseas work is a shared communal belief about an efficacious path enabling youths to realise common conceptions of successful adulthood. Again, this was expressed in Citra's comments regarding her "successful" cousin who was working in Taiwan and the house built on their remittance. This belief also underpinned Citra's grandmother's nudging for her to follow suit. This narrative of success expresses a value system and shared beliefs about rural youth identities and the relative importance or necessity of formal education in their lives to bring about desirable outcomes.

In many cases, sociocultural barriers faced by other disadvantaged children and adolescents—such as children with disabilities, children in conflict with the law, children who are married or pregnant teenage girls—are more actively directed at the individuals. For example, there are principals and teachers who would expel or refuse to enrol pregnant adolescents; Some parents of children with disabilities may not enrol their child due to assumptions that the child would not be able to lead independent lives nor be a contributing member of the community, and therefore, would not need to pursue education past a certain basic level. These social norms and beliefs are actively barring children from education participation. In contrast, the narrative of success through labour migration do not actively make parents, relatives, or community members bar youths from going to school. As further expounded on the report of the larger ethnographic study, through discourse, particular actions, and inactions, some member of the community allow for and contribute to the development of overseas work aspirations among youths (Tirtowalujo, 2016). In cases where rural youths participate in the international labour force without completing 12-years of education, the TKI narrative of success then hinders universalisation of 12-year education.

5.2 Policies to Counter Labour Migration Aspirations among Youths

The Stranas barrier framework suggests that labour migration aspirations among young adolescents serve as a socio-cultural barrier to participation. In light of this, the most seemingly straightforward policy solution is to increase the educational attainment requirements for overseas workers to senior secondary education. Considering the BNP2TKI data, the change in education requirements may deter a vast majority of individuals—as mentioned, about 2.1 million or 70% of all new TKIs placed between 2011 and 2018—from going overseas for work. Legally requiring applicants to hold a high school diploma holds the potential of delaying youths' aspiration to become TKIs until they have completed secondary education. This policy recommendation is currently not included in the national strategy document. Further, the discussion of the feasibility and favourability of amending the law in this regard is beyond the scope of this chapter.

The Stranas would also highlight a strategy of curbing the development of labour migration aspiration among youths by disrupting wider iteration of the narrative of success through overseas work and shaping local conversations to underline the importance for all children and youth to remain in paths of learning until at least completion of secondary education. As a policy direction, this takes the form of social campaigns, advocacy, and social persuasion methods conducted to encourage (secondary) education completion among all children. This can be done through national and local back-to-school movements, and through outreach activities or family and community education programs. It also takes the form of direct implementation of preventive measures by developing school monitoring systems, focusing on students who are at-risk of dropping out and on helping students transition from one education level to the next. This is a policy direction espoused by the government and is included in the national strategy document currently under development and review. However, as a policy direction, it puts the burden of change—in this case, of behaviours, attitudes, and discourse—on communities, families, and youths. It would have to be compensated with an acknowledgement that schooling and existing education programs are simply not meeting the learning, financial, and social needs of some rural youths and families.

An alternative strategy put forth by the Stranas is to provide attractive alternative programs and education services that recognise and affirm rural youth's labour migration aspirations, but prioritise on helping them gain essential skills, competencies, and knowledge basis that may benefit them while they are still present in the community and regardless of whether they eventually leave to pursue overseas work. As a policy direction, it takes the form of restructuring existing education programs, perhaps more feasibly, through the platform of informal education targeting 16–21 years old youth who have completed junior secondary education but do not prefer to experience mainstream senior secondary education. The emphasis of the alternative education approach is in equipping youths with essential entrepreneurial skills (and particularly agri-preneurial skills), basic financial literacies and skills, and a knowledge basis of the economic and social potentials of the local community, all of which will benefit them whether or not they become TKIs, while increasing their ability to capitalise on the outcomes of their time abroad if they do leave. Through reform and restructuring of informal education specifically targeting rural youths and the next generation of rural entrepreneurs, the central and local governments can send the message to Indonesian rural youths that remaining in a path of learning and upskilling oneself remains a sustainable option that can help them realise their future aspirations. This policy would demand increased levels of technical capacities at the local level in communities in which rural youths live, which are not necessarily readily available. To implement this policy, innovative cross-sectoral collaborations will be required, most importantly involving the central and local governments, international and regional development partners, private sector, education and research institutions, as well as community-based organisations and village learning canters. A version of this policy recommendation, in fact, is included in the national strategy document.

It is important to note that these policy solutions which address the development of labour migration aspirations among younger adolescents are preventive in nature. They seek to prevent younger adolescents from becoming overseas workers. They do not target adolescent and youths who are early school leavers who are already abroad and working. The Stranas sub-grouping framework (Framework Two) would recognise this population but has not officially done so. In other words, overseas worker youths (younger than 21 years old) who have not completed secondary education are currently not a recognised sub-group of out-of-school children and early school leavers and are not specially targeted by any policies. The Stranas could and arguably should include them as target beneficiaries of specific education intervention policies.

Lastly, as a policy mapping framework which interprets the out-of-school and early school leaving problem as a governance issue, Framework Three may similarly be limited in addressing cases of youths who are living abroad as TKIS but have not completed 12-year of education. Framework Three maps policies required to implement a local action plan to address the out-of-school and early school leaving issue within a district or municipality, down to the village level. As youth TKIS living and working abroad, they would be beyond the reach and jurisdiction of their local governments.

6   Conclusion

In light of the prevalence of labour participation among children and youth in rural communities, as well as the state-facilitated transnational labour migration opportunities, efforts and commitments to universalise secondary education in Indonesia face tensions in addressing cases of rural youths choosing to engage in overseas work at the expense of completing secondary education.

The policy mapping frameworks presented in the government's national strategy to address out-of-school and early school leaving issues in Indonesia summarise key ways that the policy problem is defined. The Stranas would define youths' engagement in transnational work migration as rooted in sociocultural factors barrier to education participation. The ensuing discussions are on policies that would be able to address or curb the development of these aspirations among youths who have not completed up to secondary education. The Stranas would also define Indonesia's youth overseas workers without secondary education completion as a sub-group of early school leavers in need of specific interventions and assistance.

The Stranas frameworks remain limited in countering beliefs and arguments constructing the narrative of success involving labour migration—of the relevancy and efficacy of transnational labour migration to enable youths to realise conceptions of successful adulthood, especially to gain economic empowerment and the ability to provide care for family and to gain respect and social status within their home communities. The analysis in this chapter points to the need for further research and discussions on how to address the gap between the 12-year compulsory education policy mandates and the limitation of schooling and education services in many predominantly rural contexts to meet the learning, financial, and social needs of some youths, families, and communities.

Notes

1   The combined frameworks were adopted by the UNICEF-Bappenas teams who carried out the planning, drafting, and rounds of technical consultation work during the document's development between 2017–2019. As mentioned, during the time of this writing, the Stranas and an accompanying technical operational district implementation guideline are undergoing technical and legal reviews. As a living document, the Stranas document will be piloted for implementation in select districts and municipalities, and revisions will ensue.
2   The 2030 agenda of Sustainable Development Goal for education (SDG 4) includes an indicator for universal education participation at junior secondary level.
3   More recently, the Indonesian Ministry of Labour has more often used the official term *Pekerja Migran Indonesia* (PMI) to refer to Indonesian overseas or migrant worker.
4   The larger study aimed to understand this narrative of success as they are constructed and iterated through discourse and are enacted through decisions made by youths. It did not investigate the processes by which this and other socially constructed narratives of success are adopted, adopted, and personalised by individual youths.
5   Captured in local news reporting and through BNP2TKI data of TKIs expatriated back to Indonesia (BNP2TKI, 2019–2014).
6   Representing official age of entry to primary education and official age of completion of senior secondary education.
7   Representing 1–3 years after official age of completion of senior secondary education.

References

Alisjahbana, A. S. (1994). *Demand for child schooling in Indonesia: Intrahousehold allocation of resources, the role of prices and schooling quality.* University of Washington. Retrieved from http://80.64.63.173/research/finn-websites-reproduced-permission-copyright-owner-further-reproduction-prohibited-without-permission/

Badan Nasional Penempatan dan Perlindungan Tenaga Kerja Indonesia [BNP2TKI]. (2019). *Data penempatan dan perlindungan PMI.* BNP2TKI.

Baker, D. P. (2014). Minds, politics, and gods in the schooled society: Consequences of the education revolution. *Comparative Education Review, 58*(1), 6–23. https://doi.org/10.1086/673973

Borgna, C., & Struffolino, E. (2017). Pushed or pulled? Girls and boys facing early school leaving risk in Italy. *Social Science Research, 61,* 298–313. https://doi.org/10.1016/j.ssresearch.2016.06.021

Bradley, C. L., & Renzulli, L. A. (2011). The complexity of non-completion: Being pushed or pulled to drop out of high school. *Social Forces, 90*(2), 521–545. https://doi.org/10.1093/sf/sor003

Cameron, L. (2009). Can a public scholarship program successfully reduce school drop-outs in a time of economic crisis? Evidence from Indonesia. *Economics of Education Review, 28*(3), 308–317. https://doi.org/10.1016/j.econedurev.2007.09.013

Castillo, L. L., Salem, D. S., & Sarr, L. R. (2014). The effect of poverty, gender exclusion, and child labor on out-of-school rates for female children. *Journal of Research in Childhood Education, 28*(2), 162–181. https://doi.org/10.1080/02568543.2014.884028

Duflo, E. (2001). Schooling and labor market consequences of school construction in Indonesia: Evidence from an unusual policy experiment. *American Economic Review, 91*(4), 795–813. https://doi.org/10.1257/aer.91.4.795

Dumas, M. J., G. A., & Anderson, G. (2014). Qualitative research as policy knowledge: Framing policy problems and transforming education from the ground up. *Education Policy Analysis Archives, 22*(11), 1–25. Retrieved from http://e-resources.perpusnas.go.id:2048/login?url=http://search.ebscohost.com/login.aspx?direct=true&db=eric&AN=EJ1032019&site=eds-live

Frankenberg, E., Smith, J. P., & Thomas, D. (2003). Economic shocks, wealth, and welfare. *The Journal of Human Resources, 38*(2), 280–321.

Ganimian, A. J., & Murnane, R. J. (2016). Improving education in developing countries: Lessons from rigorous impact evaluations. *Review of Educational Research, 86*(3), 719–755. https://doi.org/10.3102/0034654315627499

Ha, W., & Mendoza, R. (2010). The intended and unintended consequences of social protection on school dropout in post-crisis Indonesia. *Journal of International Development, 55,* 1115–1133. https://doi.org/10.1002/jid.1750

Hugo, G. (1995). Labour export from Indonesia: An overview. *ASEAN Economic Bulletin, 12*(2), 275–298. https://doi.org/10.1355/ae12-2k

Hugo, G. (2012). International labour migration and migration policies in Southeast Asia. *Asian Journal of Social Science, 40*(4), 392–418.

Hunt, F. (2008). *Dropping out from school: A cross country review of literature* (Create Pathways to Access, Research Monograph No. 16). Centre for International Education, Sussex School of Education. Retrieved from http://www.create-rpc.org/pdf_documents/PTA16.pdf

Lanjouw, P., & Pradhan, M. (2001). *Poverty, education and health in Indonesia: Who benefits from public spending?* (World Bank Policy Research Working Paper 2739). World Bank Group.

Lindquist, J. (2012). The elementary school teacher, the thug and his grandmother: Informal brokers and transnational migration from Indonesia. *Pacific Affairs, 85*(1), 69–89. https://doi.org/10.5509/201285169

Manning, C., & Pratomo, D. (2018). Labour market developments in the Jokowi years. *Journal of Southeast Asian Economies, 35*(2), 165–184. https://doi.org/10.1355/ae35-2d

Ministry of Education and Culture [MoEC]. (2019). *APK/APM Kemdikbud dan Kemenag Indonesia* [Ministry of Education and Culture & Ministry of Religious Affairs] data on net/gross enrolment rate]. Retrieved from http://apkapm.data.kemdikbud.go.id/index.php/cberanda/apkapmsekolahmadrasah?kode_wilayh=000000&tahun=2018

Ministry of Education and Culture [MoEC] & UNICEF. (2018). *SDG4 baseline report for Indonesia*. Kemdikbud & UNICEF.

Ministry of National Development Planning/National Development Planning Agency [Bappenas]. (2019). *Republic of Indonesia Voluntary National Reviews (VNR): Empowering people and ensuring inclusiveness and equality*. Bappenas.

Quisumbing, A. R., & Otsuka, K. (2001). Land inheritance and schooling in matrilineal societies: Evidence from Sumatra. *World Development, 29*(12), 2093–2110. https://doi.org/10.1016/S0305-750X(01)00086-9

Rahayu, S. K., Toyamah, N., Hutagalung, S. A., Rosfadhila, M., & Syukri, M. (2008). Qualitative baseline study for PNPM Generasi and PKH: The availability and use of the maternal and child health services and basic education services in the provinces of West Java and East Nusa Tenggara. Retrieved from http://www.smeru.or.id/sites/default/files/publication/cct_eng.pdf

Rammohan, A., & Robertson, P. (2012). Do kinship norms influence female education? Evidence from Indonesia. *Oxford Development Studies, 40*(3), 283–304. https://doi.org/10.1080/13600818.2012.711303

Resosudarmo, B. P., & Suryadarma, D. (2014). The impact of childhood migration on education attainment: Evidence from rural-urban migrants in Indonesia. *Asian Population Studies, 10*(3), 319–333. https://doi.org/10.1080/17441730.2014.942954

Silvey, R. (2007). Unequal borders: Indonesian transnational migrants at immigration control. *Geopolitics, 12*(2), 265–279. https://doi.org/10.1080/14650040601168917

Sim, A., Suryadarma, D., & Suryahadi, A. (2017). The consequences of child market work on the growth of human capital. *World Development, 91*, 144–155. https://doi.org/10.1016/j.worlddev.2016.11.007

Suryadarma, D., Suryahadi, A., & Sumarto, S. (2006). *Causes of low secondary school enrollment*. The SMERU Research Institute.

Suryahadi, A., Priyambada, A., & Sumarto, S. (2005). Poverty, school and work: Children during the economic crisis in Indonesia. *Development and Change, 36*(2), 351–373. https://doi.org/10.1111/j.0012-155X.2005.00414.x

Tirtowalujo, I. (2016). *Narratives of success: Indonesian rural youth as success subjects in a schooled society* (Doctoral dissertation), Michigan State University. The MSU Libraries Electronic Theses & Dissertations (ETD).

Understanding Children's Work Programme. (2012). *Understanding children's work and youth employment outcomes in Indonesia*. Retrieved from http://www.ucw-project.org/attachment/child_labour_Rwanda20110630_120902.pdf

UNESCO. (2017). *Situation analysis of out-of-school children in nine Southeast Asian countries* (Vol. 18). UNESCO.

UNESCO, & UIS. (2014). *Global initiative an out-of-school children: Eastern and Southern Africa regional report*.

UNICEF. (2015). *Global out-of-school children initiative. Operational manual*. Retrieved from http://allinschool.org/wp-content/uploads/2015/12/F_UNICEF1017_OOSCI_manual-web.pdf

Utomo, A., Reimondos, A., Utomo, I., McDonald, P., & Hull, T. H. (2014). What happens after you drop out? Transition to adulthood among early school leavers in urban Indonesia. *Demographic Research, 30*(1), 1189–1218. https://doi.org/10.4054/DemRes.2014.30.41

Voss, J. (2008). *Impact evaluation of the second phase of the Kecamatan Development Program in Indonesia*. Jakarta.

World Bank. (2017). *Towards a comprehensive, integrated, and effective social assistance system in Indonesia*. World Bank Group.

Zuilkowski, S. S., Samanhudi, U., & Indriana, I. (2019). 'There is no free education nowadays': youth explanations for school dropout in Indonesia. *Compare, 49*(1), 16–29. https://doi.org/10.1080/`03057925.2017.1369002

CHAPTER 10

Significance of Sociocultural Factors in Attribution of Educational Outcomes and Motivation Goals

Novita W. Sutantoputri, Aries Sutantoputra, Isabella Tirtowalujo, Juliana Murniati and Margaretha Purwanti

Abstract

In the Indonesian contexts, ethnicity, religion and gender are extremely important identifiers or components of one's identity (Sutantoputri, 2013), and are strong sources of a value system that young individuals bring into the pursuit of education. Contributing to the gap in this area of research, this study explores the hypothesis that individuals' sociocultural backgrounds bare some significance to their perceptions regarding educational or academic success and failures, as well as to their motivations through the academic experience. The analysis adds nuance to an understanding of sociocultural factors that directly and indirectly impact students' attribution of outcomes and motivational goals, utilising measures of religiosity and ethnic identity. Through a quantitative study involving 1006 Indonesian students from three public universities, differing ethnicities and religions of participants were found to not affect their educational outcomes significantly, whereas gender significantly affects the extent to which a student exerts themselves academically and the subsequent responses from the community.

Keywords

cultural study – motivation – attributions – educational aspiration – ethnic background

1   Introduction

Education can be perceived as one of the means to a better life. In many contexts including Indonesia, having higher education still leads to better opportunities to accessing better paying jobs. And yet, participation at higher levels of education, especially at the secondary level, and even more so at the tertiary, has been limited. For example, according to the National Socioeconomic Survey data for the year 2015, only slightly more than half (56%) of Indonesian youths between the ages 19–21 years have completed senior secondary education (Ministry of Education and Culture & UNICEF, 2018, p. 29), when the official age for completion of that level is at 18 years old. Further, educational participation at higher levels vastly differ among different groups of children and adolescents. It may suggest that education aspiration and motivation for achievement in academic settings—or achievement motivation—differ greatly among different groups of youth. This in turns means that one's likelihood or potentials to access better paying jobs differ among these groups of Indonesian youth.

It is well known that one's cultural background has a significant impact on one's motivation, and a wide range of individual's behaviour are formed and influenced by their surroundings and cultural context (Banks, 1993; King & McInerney, 2016). Affiliation to a cultural heritage, and as such, adoption and practice of a particular set of values, traditions, and language, also shape one's motivational goals (Oyserman, Harrison, & Bybee, 2001; Sutantoputri, 2012; Guay, 2016), and attributions to causality (Peng & Knowles, 2003; Sutantoputri & Watt, 2012, 2013a). As such, different cultural values emplace different meanings to education and academic achievement (Fuligni, Witkow, & Garcia, 2005). Studies have shown how one's cultural background can have a bearing on various academical factors such as on achievement goals (Woodrow & Chapman, 2002) and academic achievement (Hau & Ho, 2008). Further, experiences of discrimination—as experiences possibly rooted in one's cultural belonging or background and social identities—have also been linked to external attributions of negative outcomes (Crocker & Major, 1989). Relevantly, negative stereotypes have been found to affect students' academic performance (Steele & Aronson, 1995).

Studies exploring the differing educational and academic engagements among Indonesian students have largely focused on disparity in participation and outcomes, published in national reports produced by government entities and international or transnational development organisations such as the World Bank, UNICEF, and others. Few studies have integrated sociocultural perspectives to further understandings on impacts of social identities and cultural background on students' schooling experiences, and academic aspirations and motivations. There is a dearth of empirical studies establishing relationships between sociocultural factors to achievement motivation in education in the Indonesian context. The exceptions have contributed to an understanding of motivational differences among Chinese Indonesian and non-Chinese Indonesian students (Santoso, 2015; Setiawan, 2013); and on student academic ambitions and perception of the future importance of enrolment in senior secondary school among junior secondary students of various ethnic backgrounds in Indonesia (Murniati, Purwanti, & Sutantoputri, 2014; Sutantoputri, Murniati, & Purwanti, 2015). Avoiding generalisations among whole cultural (such as, ethnic-) groups, other studies have looked into individual-oriented versus social-oriented achievement motives—as shaped by cultural contexts—among Indonesian students, and their links to academic motivation and achievements (Liem, Martin, Porter, & Colmar, 2012).

In the Indonesian contexts, ethnicity, religion and gender are extremely important identifiers or components of one's identity (Sutantoputri, 2013), and are strong sources of a value system that young individuals bring into the pursuit of education. Contributing to the gap in this area of research, this study explores the hypothesis that individuals' sociocultural backgrounds bare some significance to their perceptions regarding educational or academic success and failures, as well as to their motivations through the academic experience. The analysis adds nuance to an understanding of sociocultural factors that directly and indirectly impact students' attribution of outcomes and motivational goals, utilising measures of religiosity and ethnic identity.

The proceeding section explores the significance of ethnicity, religion, and gender as meaningful and important cultural factors in contemporary and historical Indonesia, as well as in the study of students' motivations and achievements. The section that follows describes the study and its findings, and presents a discussion on some of the inquiry's most salient points of interest.

2   An Overview of Ethnicity, Religion, and Gender In Indonesia

2.1   *Ethnicity, Religion, & Gender as Significant Cultural Factors*
Classified as a lower-middle income country (The World Bank, 2013), Indonesia has a population of more than 260 million inhabiting the largest archipelago in the world with more than 17,000 islands, among which are the five major islands of Java, Sumatra, Kalimantan, Sulawesi, and Papua. Various ethnic groups are vastly dispersed among the islands, speaking various languages and practicing a diverse set of cultural values. The largest ethnic group is the Javanese, making up 40.2% of the population. Among each Indonesian ethnic group are sub-ethnic groups. For example, there are at least nine sub-ethnicities among Javanese, such as Osing, Tengger, Samin, (Na'im & Syahputra, n.d.) and others.

Among the various ethnic groups are those considered non-indigenous to Indonesia, or people groups who migrated to the archipelago over the last few centuries, including Chinese Indonesians, Indian Indonesians, and Arab Indonesians. They have lived amidst native Indonesians for many years, however, there remain difficulties to obtain demographical data on especially Indian- and Arab-Indonesians. The latest 2010 census included only demographical information on native Indonesians ethnic groups and Chinese (Na'im & Syaputra, n.d). The census reports that of 1.2% of the population are Chinese Indonesians.

Religion also plays an extremely important role in Indonesia. Indonesian citizens have historically been, and currently are still, required to declare a religious affiliation on their national identification card (*Kartu Tanda Penduduk*, KTP) (see Ong, 2005; Suhandinata, 2009). There were five state recognised religions: Islam, Catholicism, Christian Protestantism, Buddhism, Hinduism. In 2008, Confucianism was added into the list of officially recognised religion by the state.

Ethnicity and religion are intimately and intricately interlinked. In Indonesia and elsewhere, one's religious beliefs are often tied to one's ethnic belonging. For example, Chinese Indonesians are most likely to be perceived to be Buddhist or Christians (Suryadinata, 2010; Ong, 2005) whereas native Indonesians mostly as Muslims (Ananta, Arifin, & Bachtiar, 2008). Bataknese people from Sumatra Island are often identifiable as Christians or Muslims based on their family name, as the names trace them back to their ancestors' birth place and religions. Manadonese, an ethnic group in Sulawesi, are most likely perceived to be Christians, while Minang people from Sumatra may often be taken as Muslims. There have also been incidents of ethnic-/religion-based conflicts in Indonesia. Identity politics related to ethnicity and religion is thought to have been in display most recently on the political stage, as may be exemplified by the imprisonment of Jakarta's Christian and Chinese Indonesian Governor, Basuki Tjahaja Purnama on charges of religious blasphemy (Rikang, Nurita, & Putri, 2018).

Similarly, in Indonesia gender relations and gendered living experiences are significantly shaped by religion and ethnicity. The Syariah-based laws implemented in some regions in Indonesia exemplify how religion and gender are strongly linked in Indonesia, including for instance the implementation of local regulations instituting curfew hours for women (Baskoro et al., 2011). In another example, custody and inheritance rights and practices in Bali were historically governed by cultural laws observed by Balinese Hindu families and favoured males, resulting in divorced women not being entitled to any marital assets (Hidayat & Hasan, 2011). Further, as the largest Muslim nation in the world, Indonesia has promoted a largely patriarchal perspective on gender and sexuality (Blackburn, 2004; Clark 2010).

2.2 Cultural Factors Shaping Education Achievements and Motivations

One's level of educational aspiration is strongly tied to the culture in which one was raised (Murniatis, 1998). The complexities of relationships among ethnicity, religion, and gender in Indonesia further warrant an investigation of how they impact differences in educational aspirations, experiences, and performances among students with different ethnic backgrounds. This means that a young person's educational aspiration is a subjective view on education and its importance for their future in the society where they live. Educational aspiration then is shaped by a set of values, social norms and habits held and enacted by the community in which one lives, which then are expressed or manifest in one's behaviours and decisions regarding education (Muluk & Murniati, 2007).

The current chapter focuses on understanding whether these sociocultural variables would affect Indonesian students' perceptions of their educational outcomes and motivational goals, building on an existing larger study (Sutantoputri & Watt, 2012; Sutantoputri, 2013). The current study identifies whether religion, gender, and particularly having a Chinese minority ethnic background, affect students' attributions of educational outcomes or their perception of the causes of their academic successes and failures, their motivational goals, their sense of self-efficacy, as well as beliefs on intelligence.

3 The Study

3.1 Ethnicity, Gender, and Religion as Factors Affecting Attribution of Educational Outcomes and Motivational Goals

The study focuses on understanding whether sociocultural background factors affects students' attribution of educational outcomes, or their perception of the nature of the causes of one's educational successes and failures; and educational motivations. This section lays out the concepts and framework used for the analysis and discussion.

Attribution or the perceived cause of one's educational outcomes can be understood in terms of three dimensions (Weiner, 1986, 2010): (1) locus of control, which refers to whether the causes are internal in nature and can be self-attributed, versus external in nature and relate to something other than the self; (2) stability, which refers to whether the causes are stable and permanent, or are circumstantial and can change; and (3) controllability, which refers to perceptions of whether one can control or manipulate the causes.

Motivational goals can be understood in terms of the following components: (1) learning goal or a mastery orientation, referring to one's propensity to strive to develop one's competence; (2) performance approach goal, referring to one's propensity to strive to demonstrate one's competence; (3) performance avoidance goal, which is striving to protect oneself from being perceived as incompetent (see Dweck 1986; Pintrich & Zusho, 2002 for learning, performance approach and performance avoidance goals); and (4) work avoidance goal, referring to one's tendency to seek to minimise the amount of effort or work they need to do, or in this case to limit their engagement in the learning process (Archer 1994; Dowson McInerney, 2001). One additional concept, avoidance of novelty, was included as novelty avoidance predicts tendencies toward a mastery orientation (Vogler & Bakken, 2007). High avoidance of novelty might indicate a tendency toward learned helplessness, which has been established to be in opposition of mastery orientation (Dweck, 1986).

One's self-efficacy or beliefs about one's abilities has been found to affect one's choice, persistence, and performance (Eccles, 2005; Pajares, 2002). It is a concept that is closely related to motivational goals and attributions of outcomes, including in education. Lastly, students' beliefs on intelligence (Dweck, 1986) refers to one's beliefs of intelligence as something that is stable and uncontrollable—also referred to as having an "entity mindset", or as something that can be developed gradually—an "incremental mindset".

Reflecting the framework used above, the main question that guided the analysis is as follows: Are there differences on the basis of ethnicity, religion, and gender in students' attribution to education outcomes, motivation goals, sense of self-efficacy, and beliefs on intelligence?

Enriching the study, the analysis also utilised two relevant notions: religiosity, to compliment the categorical variable of religion; and ethnic identity, to compliment the categorical variable of ethnicity. Religiosity as a factor can be categorised into: (1) religious behaviour, referring to a spectrum of overt or public to private nature of religious practices, for example, going to church or mosque versus private reading of scripture; and (2) intrinsic religiosity, referring to application of one religious beliefs in one's daily life expressing a practical commitment to one's beliefs (Koenig, Meador, & Parkerson, 1997).

Ethnic identity as a factor is understood through measures of: (1) perceived similarity, which is a subjective assessment of the degree to which one is a prototypical member of the self-categorised group; (2) private regard, which is one's (positive or negative) evaluation regarding one's ethnic group; (3) explicit importance, referring to whether a collective identity is important to overall sense of self, and (4) social embeddedness, or the degree to which one's identification with one's group is embedded in one's everyday ongoing, social relationships (see Ashmore, Deaux, & McLaughlin-Volpe, 2004 for ethnic identity).

3.2 Study Context

The study involved 1006 university students in Indonesia from three public universities in the provinces of Central Java and East Java, and two private universities in Jakarta. Highlighting the study's interest to investigate differences in perceptions on educational outcomes and motivation particularly between Chinese minority students relative to native Indonesian students, for the purposes of the study, the categorical variable of ethnicity refers to two groups: those who identified as Chinese Indonesian and as native Indonesian. Six categories for the variable of religion are used: Islam, Catholicism, Christian Protestantism, Buddhism, Hinduism, Confucianism, and "Other".

Among the student participants in all three public universities, only 2.2% of the students identified as Chinese Indonesian. In reverse, the two private universities samples had only 25.3% of participants identifying as native Indonesians, which means that almost 75% identified as Chinese Indonesians. This discrepancy in the proportions of Chinese minority students in the sample participants from different types of higher education institutions—public versus private—is telling of the gaps in distribution and representation of higher education students on the basis of their diverse ethnic backgrounds, and may signal other forms of inequities, social dynamics and tensions.

4 Results

The study showed no significant differences found based on ethnicity on students' attributions and motivational goals, self-efficacy, and beliefs on intelligence. However, there are interesting findings that complexify our understanding of sociocultural background as factors that directly and indirectly impact students' attribution of outcomes and motivational goals. Table 10.1 discusses them one by one.

4.1 Religiosity, Motivation, and Ethnic Differences

The statistical analysis found that while intrinsic religiosity positively predicted learning and performance approach goals, it negatively predicted performance avoidance goals. This meant that the more students applied their religious beliefs to their daily life, the more likely they were to hold learning or performance approach goals, and the less likely they were to hold work avoidance goals. Further, students with high religious behaviour were more apt to

TABLE 10.1 Regression for attribution, ethnic identity, religiosity, self-efficacy, intelligence beliefs on motivational goals

Independent variable	Dependent variable	B	SE(B)	β	p
Mid test score	Learning Goals	−.00	.00	−.06	.02
Attribution:					
Locus of control		.02	.02	.03	.34
Stability		.03	.02	.03	.19
Personal control		.00	.03	.00	.81
External control		−.04	.02	−.05	.09
Self-efficacy		.46	.02	.47	.00
Intelligence beliefs		.03	.02	.03	.18
Religiosity:					
Religious behaviour		.07	.03	.06	.04
Intrinsic religiosity		.21	.07	.09	.00
Racial/ethnic identity:					
Private regard		−.03	.05	−.02	.49
Ethnic importance		−.01	.04	−.01	.75
Social embeddedness		.00	.04	.00	.87
Mid test score	Performance Approach Goals	.00	.00	.01	.72
Attribution:					
Locus of control		−.03	.03	−.03	.34
Stability		.12	.03	.12	.00
Personal control		−.03	.04	−.02	.46
External control		.06	.03	.05	.09
Self-efficacy		.14	.04	.11	.00
Intelligence beliefs		.05	.03	.04	.14
Religiosity:					
Religious behaviour		−.06	.04	−.04	.22
Intrinsic religiosity		.27	.09	.09	.00
Racial/ethnic identity:					
Private regard		.06	.07	.03	.38
Ethnic importance		−.28	.06	−.17	.00
Social embeddedness		−.14	.06	−.07	.01

(cont.)

TABLE 10.1 Regression for attribution, ethnic identity, religiosity, self-efficacy, intelligence beliefs on motivational goals *(cont.)*

Independent variable	Dependent variable	B	SE(B)	β	p
Mid test score	Performance	.00	.00	.04	.15
Attribution:	Avoidance Goals				
Locus of control		.02	.03	.02	.46
Stability		.06	.03	.06	.03
Personal control		−.08	.04	−.07	.04
External control		.05	.03	.05	.10
Self-efficacy		.25	.03	.23	.00
Intelligence beliefs		−.02	.03	−.02	.44
Religiosity:					
Religious behaviour		−.07	.04	−.05	.11
Intrinsic religiosity		.17	.08	.06	.05
Racial/ethnic identity:					
Private regard		.00	.06	.00	.95
Ethnic importance		−.15	.05	−.10	.01
Social embeddedness		−.08	.05	−.05	.13
Mid test score	Work Avoidance Goals	.00	.00	.06	.05
Attribution:					
Locus of control		−.01	.04	−.00	.80
Stability		.05	.04	.04	.20
Personal control		−.14	.05	−.08	.01
External control		.00	.04	.00	.83
Self-efficacy		−.29	.05	−.19	.00
Intelligence beliefs		−.02	.04	−.01	.66
Religiosity:					
Religious behaviour		−.11	.06	−.06	.05
Intrinsic religiosity		−.47	.12	−.12	.00
Racial/ethnic identity:					
Private regard		.12	.08	.05	.16
Ethnic importance		−.01	.08	−.00	.86
Social embeddedness		−.19	.07	−.08	.01

(cont.)

TABLE 10.1 Regression for attribution, ethnic identity, religiosity, self-efficacy, intelligence beliefs on motivational goals (*cont.*)

Independent variable	Dependent variable	B	SE(B)	β	p
Mid test score	Avoiding Novelty	.00	.00	.04	.12
Attribution:					
Locus of control		−.02	.03	−.02	.41
Stability		.07	.02	.08	.01
Personal control		−.07	.03	−.07	.04
External control		.06	.03	.07	.03
Self-efficacy		−.19	.03	−.18	.00
Intelligence beliefs		−.12	.03	−.12	.00
Religiosity:					
Religious behaviour		−.11	.04	−.09	.00
Intrinsic religiosity		.07	.08	.02	.37
Racial/ethnic identity:					
Private regard		.04	.06	.02	.48
Ethnic importance		−.06	.05	−.04	.28
Social embeddedness		−.09	.05	−.05	.07

learn new things. Perhaps by bringing the divine into their daily life, students had a sense of security and were more likely to have their academic pursuits align with their religious beliefs, constructing the inner desire and motivation to develop or demonstrate their competence. In other words, doing well in school is framed as an act of worship or religious piety.

In terms of differences with regard to intrinsic religiosity, there were in fact significant differences based on ethnicity. Here, native Indonesian students had significantly higher intrinsic religiosity than Chinese Indonesian students. This aligns with a previously published report based on the larger study (Sutantoputri, 2013), which explored the interaction effect between ethnicity, religion, and gender and reported that female native Indonesian participants were found to display the highest intrinsic religiosity, while females from those ethnically identifying as "Other" scored the lowest. However, as established from the main finding of this study, ethnicity-based differences in intrinsic religiosity does not translate to a significant ethnicity-based difference in motivation goals between Chinese and native Indonesian students. Further analysis may be warranted to contribute to the understanding of the relationship between intrinsic religiosity and learning and performance approach goals.

4.2   Ethnic Identity and Differences in Attribution of Educational Outcomes

In general, ethnicity-based differences do not predict students' attribution of educational outcomes. However, further probing showed that students' sense of explicit importance—referring to students' subjective appraisal of the degree to which a collective identity is important to their overall sense of self—did predict perception of whether they can control the causes of failure, or the controllability dimension of attribution of education outcomes. In this case, students who had high regard for being a member of their ethnic group were less likely to perceive the causes of their success as controllable by themselves. Further study on the mechanisms through which one's sense of collective ethnic identity interacts with or shapes one's attribution of educational outcomes, both failure or success, is much needed.

4.3   Gender Differences in Motivation Goals

There is a significant relationship between gender and perception on the stability of causes of educational success or failures, or the stability dimension of attribution of outcomes. Male participants were found to perceive the causes of their failure to be more permanent than their female counterparts.

Gender differences were also found on work avoidance goals. Female participants scored lower on both scales compared to their male counterpart. This seems to suggest that female participants were more likely to put effort in their work and were more engaged in the learning process.

The aforementioned previously published study (Sutantoputri, 2013) reported that when both gender and ethnicity were set as independent variables, the results showed that there were tendencies among male participants to have a higher avoidance of novelty compared to their female counterparts. This meant that male participants were more likely to display a tendency toward learned helplessness by choosing to do more familiar tasks rather than doing something new. Further, when gender and religion are set as independent variables, the results showed that there were significant differences on participants' locus of control attribution and intrinsic religiosity. Females had the highest locus of control attributions, meaning they were most likely to perceive the causes of their academic success and failure to be internal (caused by oneself), with male Chinese Indonesian participants had the lowest score.

4.4   Self-Efficacy and Beliefs on Intelligence

Reiterating the main finding, there were no statistically significant differences based on gender, religion, and ethnicity on self-efficacy and beliefs on intelligence. However, self-efficacy was found to predict performance avoidance goals, learning goals, and performance approach goals. In other words, students with high sense of self-efficacy in this particular study had the tendency not only to adopt a learning goal or performance approach goal, but also more likely to adopt a performance avoidance goal. This is in contrast to previous studies that found self-efficacy as negatively predicting performance avoidance goals (Bong, 2001; Elliot & Church, 1997).

In terms of beliefs on intelligence, this study found that beliefs on intelligence do not predict motivational goals. This too, however, stands in contrast to previous studies which showed that it predicted motivational goals (Dweck, 1986; Vogler & Bakken, 2007).

Previous study by Woodrow and Chapman (2002) found that Indonesian students scored higher on performance avoidance goals compared to other students from Europe, Vietnam, South America, and Japan. This may be explained through the notion of "saving face", where even Indonesian students who had high beliefs of their own abilities still chose to avoid looking incompetent, should they not perform at their levels of aspiration.

5   Discussion: Cultural Background of Learners

Along with one's socioeconomic backgrounds on the basis of family wealth or income as well as rural/urban location, the triad of ethnicity, religion, and gender, arguably serve as strong identifiers of one's identity which fundamentally shapes one's lived experiences and perceptions, including in the context of education in Indonesia. Unlike one's economic background and rural/urban residence, someone's ethnicity, religion, and gender are part of one's identity that are socially, legally, and practically hard, if not impossible, to change. Further, the three factors are so closely intertwined and interwoven into the fabric of Indonesian's complex and dynamic historical and contemporary political contexts. Students' sociocultural background as defined by their gender, religion, and ethnicity are factors that may fundamentally shape educational aspirations, experiences, and outcomes.

5.1   *Ethnicity*

Despite preliminary assumptions, this study found no significant differences based on ethnicity related to student attribution of educational outcomes, motivation goals, self-efficacy, and beliefs on intelligence among Chinese and native Indonesian students.

The authors acknowledge two significant explanatory factors. Firstly, it should have been noticed that ethnic identity changes over time and context

(Marcia, 1980; Kroger et al., 2010). The notion of a changing nature, assessment, and impacts of one's ethnicity-based self-identification complexifies any investigations involving ethnicity as a categorical variable. Secondly, the study's interest of exploring the difference of attributions of outcomes and motivation goals among Chinese and native Indonesian higher education students forfeited the analytical decision to further differentiate native Indonesian students on the basis of their diverse ethnicities, such as Javanese, Sundanese, Bataknese, Manadonese, and many others. In other words, due to the grouping of non-Chinese Indonesian students as one, more appropriately termed as, "supra-ethnic" group of "native Indonesians", the analysis missed investigations of general ethnicity-based differences. As such, the analysis did not capture the significance of ethnicity-based differences on student perceptions and educational aspiration at large.

5.2   *Gender*

This study found gender differences with regard to stability dimension of attribution of outcomes and avoidance goals. Male students scored higher in avoidance goals. In a largely patriarchal society like Indonesia, this phenomenon may well be stemmed from the need to protect the male-ego, self-worth or "academic self-concept". Adopting avoidance goals might be a form of defence mechanism, which may include self-handicapping strategies to minimise one's efforts in light of social pressures of the need to exert dominance and signal competence. Avoidance goals may give males the chance to save face by the default of dismissal.

In reverse, the study showed that females consistently had more propensity to exert themselves, as shown in significantly lower scores on both work avoidance and novelty avoidance goals. In addition, females tend to own more the outcomes of their educational experiences due to their belief that neither are causes of their success guaranteed, nor causes of their failures unchangeable, as shown in scoring lower on stability dimension of attribution of outcomes.

Indonesia has achieved gender parity in education participation up to tertiary education level. As the study's findings suggest, females seem to continue to respond to and against the contexts of their subjugation in a largely patriarchal society, as exemplified by existing beliefs that women do not need tertiary education and domicile women are considered virtuous (Blackburn, 2004, 2009; Lim, 2000).

It might be a common concern that due to the cultural perceptions of gendered roles still prevalent among different families and communities in Indonesia that young women might be hindered from pursuing higher levels of education or might themselves perceive having high academic achievement or pursuing higher education as something less useful or worthy than being domicile. There is validity and evidence warranting this concern, such as the phenomenon of child marriage where more often girls enter marriage at younger, school-going ages than males, and they are often barred from returning to formal education after marriage.

This study's findings and current education statistics for Indonesia regarding learning outcomes, such as test scores; and regarding participation, such as net enrolment, out-of-school rates, and completion rates, however, suggest the opposite. Nationally, females are on average testing better. Further, often more of them than males are participating at all levels of education (see Indonesia Ministry of Education and Culture & UNICEF, 2018; The World Bank, 2019). This, however, does not disregard gendered experiences of education as well as gender-based differences in education statistics. For example, female university students were found to be more likely to develop their social competence, which would affect the quality of their relationship (Sutantoputri, Evanytha, & Putri, 2014). Gendered norms and roles may also explain existing gender disproportions and under-representation of female students in university departments or faculties in particular areas of concentration, such as STEM fields.

5.3 *Religion*

This study did not find significant differences on the outcomes, namely on students' attribution, motivation goals, self-efficacy, and beliefs on intelligence based on students' religious background. However, as mentioned, the analysis did find that intrinsic religiosity is positively related to learning goal, performance approach goal, and negatively related to performance avoidance goals. Further, students with high religious behaviours were apt to learning new material While this study does not attempt to address whether particular religious backgrounds would contribute to higher or lower degrees of intrinsic religiosity and religious behaviour, the conclusion that students' religious life or religiosity shapes their attribution of success and failures and motivation goals is important for educators. As mentioned, the notion that doing well in school aligns with religious piety as empirically verifiable at least through this study involving more than one thousand university students, may signal to Indonesian educators and policy-makers entrenched in the discourse of character or value education that their mindset and approaches have been fruitful. Character education based on religious values has been championed as a crucial and necessary component in the nation's collective education agenda of building a future generation that is smart, capable, competent, and *berakhlak mulia,* or noble and having sound character.

Further investigation is needed to understand the combinatory effects of students' gender and religion on students' perception of educational outcomes, motivation goals, sense of self-efficacy, and beliefs on intelligence.

6 Conclusion

One's cultural background has been found to affect motivational goals, and in turn, learning processes (Li, 2012). Cross-cultural differences do affect motivational processes (Liem et al., 2012). This means who students are when they enter the classroom—in terms of their ethnicity, religion, and gender—may strongly affect their academic engagement and achievements.

This study on the role of students' sociocultural backgrounds in shaping their educational motivation and attribution of outcomes has implications for policy-makers, education practitioners and educators, and the society at large at the family or community level.

Culturally relevant pedagogies, including instructional materials incorporating local content, may help students to develop healthy perceptions or attributions of their educational outcomes and good motivational goals, eventually helping them to achieve well in academic settings and construct higher educational aspirations. In addition, having role models whose backgrounds are similar to the students has been known to also contribute to increasing students' academic motivations. This is also why it is important for diversity to be represented among teachers and educators, whether at the primary, secondary, or tertiary level. A push toward integrating more culturally-relevant teaching and materials within the classroom and the national curriculum may help more children and adolescents develop higher motivation, engagement, and education aspiration. In addition, ideally all teachers need to have be professionally equipped to facilitate students' learning processes through approaches that take into consideration how their sociocultural backgrounds impact their work ethics and academic engagement. For example, teachers may pay specific attention to increasing the awareness of gendered roles and expectations, and how that affects males and females differently, and what detriments the act of "saving face" or avoidance of novelty do to a student's potential growth. Through proper training, teachers can be taught to inspire more constructive ways so that all students may develop good learning habits and motivation goals, healthy beliefs on intelligence and their self-efficacy, and the causes of their and others' failures and successes.

References

Ananta, A., Arifin, E. N., & Bachtiar. (2008). Chinese Indonesians in Indonesia and the province of Riau archipelago: A demographic analysis. In L. Suryadinata (Ed.), *Ethnic Chinese in contemporary Indonesia*. Institute of Southeast Asian Studies and Chinese Heritage Centre.

Archer, J. (1994). Achievement goals as a measure of motivation in university students. *Contemporary Educational Psychology, 19*, 430–446.

Ashmore, R. D., Deaux, K., & McLauglin-Volpe, T. (2004). An organizing framework for collective identity: Articulation and significance of multidimensionality. *Psychological Bulletin, 130*(1), 80–114.

Banks, J. A. (1993). The canon debate, knowledge construction, and multicultural education. *Education Researcher, 22*(8), 4–14.

Blackburn, S. (2004). *Women and the state in modern Indonesia*. Cambridge University Press.

Blackburn, S. (2009). *Perempuan dan negara dalam era Indonesia Moderen* [*Women and state in modern Indonesia*] (E. Aritonang, Trans.). Kalyanamitra.

Bong, M. (2001). Between- and within-domain relations of academic motivation among middle and high school students: Self-efficacy, task value and achievement goals. *Journal of Educational Psychology, 93*(1), 23–34.

Clark, M. (2010). *Maskulinitas, culture, gender and politics in Indonesia*. Monash University Press.

Crocker, J., & Major, B. (1989). Social stigma and self-esteem: The self-protective of stigma. *Psychological Review, 96*(4), 408–430.

Dowson, M., & McInerney, D. M. (2001). Psychological parameters of students' social and work avoidance goals: A qualitative investigation. *Journal of Educational Psychology, 93*(1), 35–42.

Dweck, C. S. (1986). Motivational processes affecting learning. *American Psychologist, 41*, 1040–1048.

Guay, F. (2016). The virtue of culture in understanding motivation at school: Commentary on the special issue on culture and motivation. *British Journal of Educational Psychology, 86*, 154–160.

Fuligni, A. J., Witkow, M., & Garcia, C. (2005). Ethnic identity and the academic adjustment of adolescents from Mexican, Chinese, and European backgrounds. *Developmental Psychology, 41*(5), 799.

Hau, K., & Ho, I. T. (2008). Editorial: Insights from research on Asian students' achievement motivation. *International Journal of Psychology, 43*(5), 865–869.

King, R. B., & McInerney, D. M. (2016). Culturalizing motivation research in educational psychology. *British Journal of Educational Psychology, 86*, 1–7.

Koenig, H. G., Meador, K., & Parkerson, G. (1997). Religion index for psychiatric research: A 5-item measure for use in health outcome studies. *American Journal of Psychiatry, 154*, 885–886.

Kroger, J., Martinussen, M., & Marcia, J. E. (2010). Identity status change during adolescence and young adulthood: A meta-analysis. *Journal of Adolescence, 33*, 683–698.

Liem, G. A. D., Martin, A. J., Porter, A. L., & Colmar, S. (2012). Sociocultural antecedents of academic motivation and achievement: Role of values and achievement motives in achievement goals and academic performance. *Asian Journal of Social Psychology, 15*, 1–13.

Lim, Y. (2000). *Prasangka terhadap etnis Cina: Sebuah intisari* [*Prejudice toward Chinese ethnic group: An essential summary*]. Penerbit Djembatan & Penerbit Pena Klasik.

Marcia, J. E. (1980). Identity in adolescence. *Handbook of Adolescent Psychology, 9*(11), 159–187.

Ministry of Education and Culture, & UNICEF. (2018). *SDG4 baseline report for Indonesia*. MoEC and UNICEF.

Morris, M. W., & Peng, K. (1994). Culture and cause: American and Chinese attributions for social and physical events. *Journal of Personality and Social Psychology, 67*, 959–971.

Muluk, H., & Murniati, J. (2007). Konsep kesehatan mental menurut masyarakat etnik Jawa dan Minangkabau [Mental health concept according to Javanese and Minangkabau ethic groups]. *Jurnal Psikologi Sosial, 13*(2), 167–181.

Murniati, J. (1998). Struktur kognisi diri lima suku di Indonesia [Cognitive structure of five ethnicities in Indonesia]. *Jurnal Psikologi Sosial, 4*(6).

Murniati, J., Purwanti, M., & Sutantoputri, N. W. (2014). *Pengembangan aspirasi pendidikan dengan pendekatan nilai budaya local: studi pada lima etnik besar di Indonesia (tahun ke-1)* [*Developing local educational aspiration with local values approach: A study on five big ethnicities in Indonesia (Year 1)*]. Unpublished report. Unika Atma Jaya: Faculty of Psychology.

Na'm, A., & Syahputra, H. (n.d.). *Kewarganegaraan, suku bangsa, agama, dan bahasa sehari-hari penduduk* [*Indonesia. Citizenship, ethnicities, religions, and common language of Indonesians*]. Badan Pusat Statistik.

OECD. (2015). *PISA 2015 results: Excellence and equity in education* (Vol. 1). Retrieved from http://www.oecd.org/education/pisa-2015-results-volume-i-9789264266490-en.htm

Ong, H. H. (2005). *Riwayat Tionghoa Peranakan di Jawa* [*History of Peranakan Chinese in Java*]. Komunitas Bambu.

Oyserman, D., Harrison, K., & Bybee, D. (2010). Can racial identity be promotive of academic efficacy? *International Journal of Behavioral Development, 25*, 397–385.

Peng, K., & Knowles, E. D. (2003). Culture, education, and the attribution of physical causality. *Personality and Social Psychology Bulletin, 29*, 1272–1284.

Pintrich, P. R., & Zusho, A. (2002). The development of academic self-regulation: The role of cognitive and motivational factors. In A. Wigfield & J. S. Eccles (Eds.), *Development of achievement motivation*. Elsevier Science & Technology.

Rikang, R., Nurita, D., & Putri, B. U. (2018, July 8–14). Duplikat Jakarta di Utara Sumatera. [Duplicating Jakarta in North Sumatra]. *Tempo*, 38–39.

Santoso, D. A. (2015). Perbedaan motivasi berpartisipasi dalam olahraga antara suku Jawa, Madura, dan Cina [Motivational difference in sports participation among Javanese, Maduranese, and Chinese]. *Jurnal Penjakora, 2*(1), 73–82.

Setiawan, D. C. (2013). *Hubungan parental expectancy dengan motivasi berprestasi pada etnis Cina dan Jawa* [Correlation of parental expectancy and achievement motivation between Chinese Indonesian and Javanese]. Retrieved from http://digilib.ubaya.ac.id/pustaka.php/233095

Statistics Indonesia/Badan Pusat Statistik. (2013). *Indikator Pendidikan tahun 1994–2011*. Retrieved from http://www.bps.go.id/tab_sub/view.php?kat=1&tabel=1&daftar=1&id_subyek=28&notab=1

Suryadinata, L. (2010). *Etnis Tionghoa dan nasionalisme* [Indonesian. Chinese ethnicity and Indonesian nasionalism]. PT Kompas Media Nusantara.

Sutantoputri, N. W. (2013). *Attribution and motivation: A cultural study among Native and Chinese Indonesian university students* (Doctoral dissertation). Faculty of Education, Monash University-Australia.

Sutantoputri, N. W., Murniati, J., & Purwanti, M. (2015). Educational aspiration, attributions and motivational goals: A comparative study of 5 sub-ethnicities in Indonesia. *Asian Journal of Educational Research, 3*(2), 76–85.

Sutantoputri, N. W., & Watt, H. M. G. (2012). Attribution and motivation: A cultural study among Indonesian university students. *International Journal of Higher Education, 1*(2), 1201–1229.

Sutantoputri, N. W., & Watt, H. M. G. (2013). Attribution and motivation: Gender, ethnicity and religious differences among Indonesian university students. *International Journal of Higher Education, 2*(1), 12–21.

The World Bank. (2019). *Gender statistics* [Genders_Indicators_Report]. Retrieved from https://databank.worldbank.org/Data/indicator/SE.ENR.TERT.FM.ZS?id=2ddc971b&report_name=Gender_Indicators_Report&populartype=series

The World Bank. (2019). *Indonesia*. Retrieved from https://data.worldbank.org/country/indonesia

Weiner, B. (1986). *An attributional theory of motivation and emotion*. Springer-Verlag.

Weiner, B. (2010). The development of an attribution-based theory of motivation: A history of ideas. *Educational Psychologist, 45*(1), 28–36.

Woodrow, L., & Chapman, E. (2002). Assessing the motivational goal orientations of international English for Academic Purposes (EAP) students. *Current Research in Social Psychology, 7*(15), 257–274.

CHAPTER 11

Successful Student Mobility: What Makes an Indonesian Alternative Education Beneficial for Internal Youth Migrants?

Ila Rosmilawati and David Wright

Abstract

The phenomena of residential mobility from rural to the urban area in Indonesia are often difficult to track, though there is no doubt that internal migrants are huge population. Internal migrant youth, who migrated individually or with their families are also engaged in child labour in the new cities without having high school qualifications. Many young people maintain their access to education in the host cities to gain the 21st-century skills which enable them to cope with and to compete in the globalised world. This chapter examines an effective educational function for Indonesian migrant youths in Equivalency Education context as part of non-formal education subsystem. The features of Indonesian Equivalency Program as an alternative education 'space' will be explored, which is successfully prevent Indonesian migrant youth from educational exclusion. The chapter also draws on the learning experiences in the new environments that transmitted by teachers and students via an explicit curriculum of a subject area or implicitly via hidden curricula such as attitudes, values, beliefs and behaviour. The chapter concludes with a discussion of how the Indonesian migrant youth get benefit from alternative school cultures that impact on student's engagement into a new learning environment.

Keywords

internal migration – student mobility – migrant youth – alternative education – transformation

1 Introduction

Raka is 24 years old and from Pemalang, in Central Java, Indonesia. He moved to Jakarta when he was 16 years old to find work. Before Raka, his cousin and other friends also travelled to the city from Pemalang, hoping for a better life for themselves and their families. This sort of travel is generally referred to as an 'internal migration'. Migration of this sort has become commonplace for young people in rural Indonesia.

Raka's first job in Jakarta was as a labourer on a construction site. He is now working as a cleaner in a music studio. Before coming to Jakarta, Raka discontinued his schooling (at senior secondary school level) because his parents could not afford to continue to support him. His father works as a farmer and according to Raka, preferred to send his children to work than to school, believing that hard work hard is the pathway to a better future. However, Raka does not agree with his father. After four years of working in Pemalang and Jakarta, he decided to return to the education system and joined an Equivalency Education Program in Jakarta. He had heard about this sort of alternative school from his cousin who enrolled in the program a year previously. It was not easy for Raka to get permission from his employer to enrol in this program due to his workload, but eventually, his employer decided to support his ambition.

Raka's story is one among many. It illustrates the Indonesian experience, not uncommon in developing countries, of increasing numbers of young adults migrating from rural hometown regions to urban conglomerates in search of economic and social opportunity. In Indonesia, the term 'internal migration' is used to refer to this movement and the resulting redistribution of population. Those involved in the process are commonly referred to as an 'in-migrant'.

In Indonesia, the preferred destinations of young in-migrants are large cities such as Jakarta and Surabaya. These cities are seen to offer better opportunities for employment, education and an enhanced lifestyle. In this respect, internal migration is seen as a tool for upward social mobility, especially in the communities that people leave (Easthope & Gabriel, 2008; Morrison & Clark, 2011). However, while it is clear that very large numbers of people are involved in this movement, the impact of large-scale migration from rural to urban areas in Indonesia has been difficult to monitor and measure. Even though internal migration is motivated by the desire to improve standards of living, and migrants move to places assumed to have better social and economic opportunities, this is not always the outcome. Internal migration can lead to social and economic distress, isolation from extended families and long-standing community connections, difficulties in paying rent in new places and unsafe, unaffordable and otherwise unacceptable living and working conditions can be detrimental for the individuals and families who choose to make this shift (Schafft, 2006). In such circumstances, education could be viewed as a lesser consideration.

In 2011, the Statistics Indonesia reported that 30% of the internal migrant population were aged 15–24 (Statistics Indonesia, 2011). These young people move to the cities either with family or individually. Thus 'individual migration' and 'family migration' are differentiated. This chapter, which addresses education opportunities in cities for in-migrant youth, focuses on both individual and family migration.

While a 2018 Organisation for Economic Co-operation and Development (OECD) report stated that the employment rate of young adults in Indonesia without senior secondary education is relatively high (68%), education continues to be inaccessible to many young people. Again, while many of the young internal migrants continue their education in their new city locations, not all of these young people can re-enter mainstream education. This chapter illuminates an alternative educational pathway for Indonesian migrant youth through non-formal education. Features of the Indonesian Equivalency Education Program will be discussed here, along with the capacity of the program to prevent Indonesian migrant youth from being refused opportunities in education. This chapter refers to both the explicit content-based curriculum and the implicit or hidden curriculum provided through Indonesia's equivalency education programs: the attitudes, values, beliefs and behaviour young people can acquire through participation in these programs, in addition to subject-based learning. The chapter concludes with a discussion of ways in which the Indonesian migrant youth benefit through their engagement with learning in this alternative learning environment.

2   Magnifying the Often 'Underserved': On Methodology

Fifteen life histories of young in-migrants, aged of 15–25, were gathered through interviews in two non-mainstream schools in Jakarta and Depok City (immediately south of Jakarta). Both these schools offer schooling pathways that operate as alternatives to that available through mainstream education systems. One is categorised and funded as a public institution and the second is categorised as belonging to the community with only some of its funding needs met by the local government. Data were collected over a six-month period and each of the 15 participants was interviewed at least three times. A criterion sampling strategy was used to select participants. All were over 15 years of age and all had migrated to the city from rural locations (individually or with family) more than one year before. Life history interviews were used to gather in-depth data on these students' perspectives of their educational experiences. The transformative learning theory, with a focus on perspective transformation (Mezirow, 1991) shaped through structural-developmental processes (Daloz, 2012, Kegan, 2000), was applied to these histories.[1]

TABLE 11.1   Age, educational profile and employment status of in-migrant youth

Participant	Sex	Age	Grade	Employment	In-migration type
Sinta	F	17	11	Shopkeeper	Individual
Mika	F	18	9	Housemaid	Individual
Raka	M	24	11	Office boy	Individual
Dimas	M	23	11	Office boy	Individual
Risma	F	22	11	Housemaid	Individual
Aminah	F	17	10	Housemaid	Individual
Laili	F	17	10	Housemaid	Individual
Neneng	F	22	11	Housemaid	Individual
Siti	F	21	11	Housemaid	Individual
Sri	F	17	11	Works at internet café	Individual
Iman	M	17	11	Toy seller	Family
Rizal	M	15	8	Snack Peddler	Family
Ria	F	17	11	Toy Seller	Family
Ajeng	F	20	10	Housemaid	Individual
Eva	F	18	12	No-job	Family

The 15 migrant youths are a combination of school-age and post-school age students. Their ages range from mid-teens to early twenties. There are similarities in the factors that influenced these in-migrant students to exit mainstream schooling in their city of origin. For most, family financial difficulties contributed to these students' inability to continue the study. As in many other nations and regions, families of low socioeconomic status (SES) in Indonesia often lack a commitment to education and prefer, and sometimes force, their children to enter the workforce. The search for financial security, for self and family, is, therefore, a major contributor to the decision to travel to the city to find work. This is a consistent cultural pattern in disadvantaged rural regions. Some who move to the city continue their education in their newly adopted location. While some enrol in regular formal education, others opt for non-formal education programs. This study gathered narratives of in-migrants who decided to re-enter education through an alternative route of non-formal education: the equivalency education pathway. The study sought to gain insight directly from individuals who made the decision to re-engage with education in this way. Polkinghorn (1988) offers insightful perspectives on the role of narrative in research:

> We live immersed in narrative, recounting and reassessing the meanings of our past actions, anticipating the outcomes of our future projects, situating ourselves at the intersection of several stories not yet completed. We explain our actions in terms of plots, and often no other form of explanation can produce sensible statements. (p. 160)

A narrative study can be seen to utilise story as discourse, to understand how individuals make sense of events in their lives. It enables attention to be focussed on perspectives upon incidents that represent an episode in one's life that influences their worldview. This allows the person to integrate past experiences with present situations and orientations towards the future through reference to those transformative moments or experiences. As Polkinghorne (1988) suggests, "the purpose of narrative knowing is not to produce a representation of reality as it exists independent of the knower, rather, it is a display of a type of meaning that life events have for (those who) experience them" (p. 82).

The concept of transformation, as used in this study, refers to a change from one state or condition to another. This notion was applied to learning by North American education researcher Jack Mezirow in the 1970s. His work has been extended by a series of scholars who have asked further challenging questions about the ways in which understanding—and perspectives upon the experience that are modified as a result of changes in understanding—is transformed. The structural development approach, developed by Daloz (2012) and Kegan (2000), builds on Mezirow's analysis to identify transformation through reference to a developmental process. These processes enable young people to perceive, feel, understand, act and relate through newly integrated perspectives in accordance with a structure of development. While this requires conceptual integration and understanding, Taylor and Elias (2012) argue that imagination is also a necessary part of this process.

Internal migration requires young people who make this transition to perceive themselves in new ways. Clearly, their new life circumstance cannot be managed with the learning they relied on upon before migration. This new learning has the potential to include qualitative changes in the ways in which individuals' make meaning from their experience. Inherent in this sort of developmental perspective is the understanding that in-migrant youth will experience change. These processes of change, which comprise in part adaptation to new circumstances, also invite reflection and interpretation. Accordingly, it is argued that the capacity to appreciate processes of change or adaptation overtime in an ever-changing environment enables conscious engagement with the learning associated with the experience (Ivey & Ivey 2001). This feedback system builds awareness of and commitment to conscious participation in social and cultural experiences. Daloz (2000) argues that human growth is not merely a matter of physical maturation. It incorporates mental, emotional and spiritual growth. Life span or psychological interpretations of experience, such as those described through this perspective, align culturally significant encounters with stages in life. This suggests that young people who consciously engage with this form of learning will function with more equanimity as they gain perspectives from insight into their earlier experiences.

3 Indonesian Internal Youth Migrants at a Glance

United Nations Economic and Social Commission for Asia and the Pacific (UNESCAP) (2016) numbers the Indonesian population at just under 261 million, with a fertility rate of 2.4% and an annual population growth rate of 1.1%. While 54% of the total population live in urban areas, this ratio is expanding rapidly and it is expected that 68% of the total Indonesian population will be living in cities by 2025 (World Bank, 2016). In-migration to city areas is contributing to a situation where urban employment has now overtaken rural employment. Ginting and Aji (2015) report that the Indonesia agricultural sector lost 900,000 jobs in the decade preceding 2015 while the informal employment sector in urban areas has increased rapidly in the same time period (with minimal oversight and regulation). It is likely that many of the in-migrants will be living and working in problematic, if not unsatisfactory, conditions in the cities they have travelled to. Indeed, the United Nation (2017) reports that as much as 21.8% of Indonesia's urban population lives in slum areas.

Evidence gathered through in-migrant interviews identifies important factors that are often combined in the lives of these young people. They include family dysfunction, early marriage, extreme poverty and low levels of income. For example, 18-year-old Mika left her family in Purbalingga, Central Java and moved to Jakarta to find work as a housemaid. Like her five siblings, Mika graduated from elementary school but did not enrol in junior secondary school, limited by the low income of her parents and their lack of enthusiasm for education for their children. She now lives alone in Jakarta (and has re-engaged with education through an equivalency education program).

Internal migrants in Indonesia constitute a significant population. Sukamdi and Mujahid (2015) reported that in 2010 nearly 9.8 million individuals were estimated to be internal migrants, with cities on the island of Java being the most attractive destinations. Data suggests that most in-migrants view their move to the city as temporary, at least initially. Statistics Indonesia (2011) categorised this migrant type as *migrasi risen* (recent migrants). Most of the *migrasi risen* are aged 15–19, while the second largest group are aged 20–24. Females form 47.6% of this population (Sukamdi & Mujahid, 2015). Though ubiquitous, young adult in-migrants can be easily overlooked in the economic and social analysis as they tend to fall into one or more of the following categories: undocumented youth, unaccompanied minors, disconnected youth or low-wage workers. United Nations International Children's Emergency Fund (UNICEF) estimates at least 2.7 million in-migrants, predominantly female, work in domestic service in Indonesia (UNICEF, 2011).

Many young people from rural areas think that migration is something they need to do to gain greater opportunity. This can also be interpreted as a response to family or community pressures. Family and peer networks can be integral to migration decisions, especially for those who migrate individually. Prior connections can smooth integration upon arrival and facilitate access to the job market.

Raka is an in-migrant youth who followed friends and relatives to Jakarta. His cousin is a 'gate' for Raka to find a place in the city. They live together in a small rented room. By contrast, Siti says her migration to the city as a consequence of unexpected social pressures. Her mother forced her to marry a mature man just after she graduated from junior high school. Siti was very upset with this and decided to leave home in Solo, Central Java and travel to Jakarta with only Rp. 100,000 ($7). Since then, Siti has not returned to her family home and now studies while working as a housemaid.

Sukamdi and Mujahid (2015) argue that in-migrants do not always face difficulties finding employment. They report that 50.2% of in-migrant youth, aged 15–19, are working, mostly in the services sector (e.g. casual worker, unpaid family worker, own-account worker, employee), tough questions need to be asked about the reliability of this figure given the undocumented status of most youth employment. In this respect, Sukamdi and Mujahid (2015) point out that 13% of in-migrants, aged 5–14 (four million in number), are involved in child labour. Interestingly, UNESCO (2017) observes that educational opportunities and outcomes are worse for those migrants under the age of 18 who stay in rural areas than those who migrate. The same source also shows that young people who migrate individually and with family have generally also received incomplete schooling in their place of origin.

TABLE 11.2   Education attainment of the in-migrant population (by percentage)

	Male		Female	
Age	5–15	16–24	5–15	16–24
Never attended school	15.8	0.7	14.8	0.6
Not completed primary	57.9	1.6	55.6	1.6
Primary school	19.7	12.5	21.1	13.8
Junior high school	6.6	27.2	8.5	29.0
Senior high school	0.0	45.1	0.0	44.5
Vocational high school	0.0	9.1	0.0	5.4
Diploma I/II	0.0	0.6	0.0	0.9
Diploma III/Academy	0.0	1.4	0.0	1.9
Diploma IV/Undergraduate	0.0	1.8	0.0	2.5
All levels	100	100	100	100

SOURCE: SUKAMDI AND MUJAHID (2015)

Based on these data, a significant proportion of males and females aged 16–24 (45.1 and 44.5% respectively), who migrated from rural areas completed their senior high school. In addition, 27.2% of male in-migrants and 29.0% of female in-migrants, aged 16–24, only completed junior high school. Overall, this means that the majority of young in-migrants did not finish schooling completely from kinder to senior high school, and a large proportion completed significantly less schooling. Therefore, there is a very large pool of under-educated young in-migrants in Indonesian cities. These people are not yet adults, but in many cases are managing independent life with limited education, while undertaking or seeking employment. For these young people, the lack of education represents an additional complexity in an already troubled life.

4   Accessing Alternative Education Program

Evidence suggests that it is difficult for mainstream school systems to meet the educational needs of in-migrant youth (Rosmilawati 2016). This is especially the case for in-migrant youth in part- or full-time work. The needs of such students are influenced by two principal factors: their prior experience of school and the complexities of their current experience. For many in-migrant youths, the school has been a disillusioning or alienating experience. This, separate from or in association with family financial problems, has contributed to the high numbers of students leaving school before completion.

In the city, the demands of work, including the hours required to work, the physical demands of work, and ongoing responsibilities for family and personal and financial insecurity, combine to make mainstream schooling impractical. Greater flexibility in methods of teaching and learning is required. Alternative schooling such as the Equivalency Education Program (*Pendidikan Kesetaraan*) provides educational opportunities, up to and including pathways to graduation, for young people who want to re-enter education. Equivalency education programs consist of Packages A & B, which are equivalent to primary and junior secondary level, and Package C which covers senior secondary levels. The curriculum is designed to help learners attain similar competencies and recognition equivalent to that provided to students who complete formal or mainstream schooling. Furthermore, equivalency education programs provide additional subject matter designed to provide an education in life skills (such as knowledge about the local economy, workplace roles and responsibilities and basic work skills) that will benefit all learners, but particularly those from disadvantaged backgrounds. The equivalency programs are managed by both government and Community Learning Centres (CLCs) under the Ministry of Education and Culture (MoEC) supervision. These flexible learning and teaching methods (UNESCO, 2013) have been designed to meet the needs of diverse target groups. This means that, regardless of duration, mode and place of delivery, the equivalency education program is required to adapt to context-specific sensitivities of particular students and locations that are not taken into consideration in mainstream schooling. In this respect, equivalency education programs take different forms and use different methods to reach different cohorts. In-migrant youth is only one of (though one of the most significant of) those cohorts, and enrolments are growing. Research participant Shinta said that when she first enrolled in her program there were only 20 students in her class. One year later, there are more than 40 students enrolled. Unlike in traditional schooling, students in equivalency education programs can enrol anytime. This provides great flexibility for youth with unconventional work-life schedules.

Numerous influences have an impact on in-migrant youth's schooling life. The transition between the old and the new life in the new location can be very demanding. Accommodating this alongside the demands of the workplace and responsibilities associated with re-entering school can be very stressful for the young people involved. For in-migrant youth who have moved with family, parents supportive of their children continuing their education can be important influences. Those who migrate individually might find that peers and employers can help with this transition. Mika, who only graduated from the primary school in her city of origin said that for six years, since migrating to Jakarta, she could only find work as a housemaid. Finally, she decided to enrol in an equivalency education program. Her employer helped her to find a school in the neighbourhood and helped her to arrive at an effective balance between her workplace responsibilities and her schooling. This support was both unexpected and appreciated. It has helped Mika to consider new possibilities in life.

The flexibility available through the equivalency system can also have an impact on student motivation. Twenty-three-year-old Dimas, who works as a cleaner, struggled to get permission from his employer to attend school. At one point, Dimas' employer demanded him to work additional hours. Other students who also work describe instability at school as causing some of the frustrations they experience at the workplaces. Workload, exhaustion and emotional uncertainty in the workplace can become major reasons for worker students to experience tension at school. This presented considerable difficulties. Dimas told his interviewer that only his experience in different jobs, his ambition, and his resilience enabled him to both respond to his employer's demands and continue at school. This was made easier by his school's flexibility; his school's program, like most in equivalency education, is 'open' in terms of admission, age, mode, duration, pace and place of delivery. Flexibility around hours of schooling, face-to-face delivery and/or distance education, and low-cost tuition fee (some equivalency schools are free) provide opportunities for students inconvenienced by circumstance to continue to access learning. However, different occupations have different challenges to access equivalency education. Those who work in informal sectors such as housemaids, babysitters, casual workers at coffee shops, shop keepers and snack peddlers have more opportunity in terms of time management between working and schooling.

The re-engagement in the education of in-migrant youth in programs developed in response to their experience of under-education, caused by either poverty and alienation, or both, has the potential to construct a new form of critically engaged students. While approximately 75% of the content of the curriculum of equivalency education programs draws on the mainstream subject matter, students also get the benefit of training in functionally relevant life and work skills (UNESCO, 2013). Work skills programs such as basic automotive and screen-printing workshops are useful in the job field as it enables students to improve their careers in their work. Mostly, the implementation of these programs depends on the availability of funds from donors or local government.

Graduates of non-formal education programs also have the opportunity to pursue higher education after completing the program, thereby enhancing their prospects even further. Moreover, equivalency education programs systematically seek to change their young students' sense of self; who they are and how they can contribute. This is both a social necessity—in that it is what is required to ensure students can maintain their commitment to education, as well as a transformative agenda.

Non-formal education challenges prior assumptions related to formal schooling and perceptions of learning. It also holds the potential of changing students' perspectives and their life decisions and courses of action. This is an empowering form of individuation (Cranton, 1994).

The transition from dependent childhood to insightful and responsible adulthood is difficult for many people. For those who have experienced significant and sustained disadvantage, it could be seen to be even more difficult. Life skills in such activities as critical thinking, decision-making and self-esteem are extremely valuable for young people determined to make positive choices and avoid high-risk behaviours.

5 Improving Integration in Schools for Working Students

Most in-migrant youths understand that participating in education leads to change. As suggested, such learning can also increase the capacity of in-migrant youth to adapt to life in the city. This is a sort of "trans-*form*-ative" learning in which the form of knowledge is part of that which is changed. It is different from "in-form-ative" learning, which seeks only to bring new content, [and] to extend existing forms of knowing (Kegan, 2009, p. 42).

Seventeen-year-old Aminah entered equivalency education knowing that she wanted a better future instead of being a housemaid. During her interview, she said she often asked herself, "how did I come to be living this way?" She proceeded to reflect on her schooling, asking "and why is this school so important to me?" This form of critical analysis, which incorporates critical self-reflection, is a rational process. The self-reflection enabled Aminah to recognise that her previous belief that "working as a housemaid in the city is better than staying in the village with no life prospects", is no longer sufficient. Further education has led Aminah to understand that she can change her expectations. In an interview, Aminah stated, "I want a job with clear work rules". Through this understanding, a clear grievance is supplanted by the imagination of a preferred work future: one governed by agreed workplace rules.

The transformation of Aminah's considerations around what is possible in a workplace is evidence of considerable learning. In transformative learning theory (Mezirow, 2000; Cranton, 1994), transformation occurs when an individual opens his or her frame of reference, discards a habit of mind, perceives alternatives, and as a result of this new understanding, acts differently in the

TABLE 11.3   The integrating and inhibiting factors

Integrating factors	Inhibiting factors
The presence of peers and sound peer relationships	A lack of attention and care from teachers, including a lack of effective communication between teachers and students.
A school culture that encourages flexible modes of teaching and learning and class structures designed to fit the complexities of students' work-life.	Educational experiences that alienate or isolate students from their community and the interests and needs of community members.
The influence of educational leaders, who are seen as role models because they understand the ways in which students understand and experience work-life.	Lack of inspiration from educational leaders.
Students' share disillusion with past-experience; provoking them to imagine new avenues and opportunities.	Low self-esteem of students, leading to self-deprecation and lack of critical insight into the possibilities of the equivalency education program.
Negative comments about Equivalency Education Program from others prompts students to defend their equivalency program and in so doing appreciate the ways it has influenced their thinking.	Negative comments from community members about the equivalency education program that contributes to student's self-deprecation.
Students' valuing of the non-formal educational setting (place) through which they are learning.	Discipline issues in the classroom (students not valuing the learning)
Personal (and often shared) orientation towards future goals after graduation.	Inability to utilise the program to develop critical insights that suggest future opportunities.

world. Cranton (1994) argues that the new learning of this kind is most likely to happen through discourse. It is important that young people have support from others to help them realise the transformative within their learning. Dialogue between students, teachers or mentors can assist in developing different points of view about the value of an equivalency education program. In this regard, we can consider the factors that contribute to the integration of students into equivalency education programs and those that inhibit such participation.

Every in-migrant youth comes with a "learning past". This is an important ingredient in each student's present and future learning. These students have also usually experienced some form of hardship or trauma, such as Neneng who was forced into marriage at a young age. Nonetheless, large numbers of students remain on track to graduate senior high school through equivalency education programs. In 2015, of 101.002 students who took equivalency education national exams, 85.172 were successful and graduated with the Package C certificate (Ministry of Education and Culture, 2016). Indonesian in-migrant youth enrolled in equivalency education programs display the sort of resilience that shapes efforts to achieve positive outcomes. Interviews revealed that a sense of personal responsibility provides many with hope for the future, which could explain their resilience. Mika says "In school days, I am busy; managing time for working and studying. I get home at 7:30 after school and continue my work ... gardening or washing dishes until 9 pm". Studying and working simultaneously makes these young people very busy, but some say that learning in these circumstances is not necessarily onerous. Ajeng stated, "school days are a wonderful time as I can socialise with friends at school, away from my daily routine as a housemaid, where I often feel lonely and bored".

A widely shared sense of community is crucial to engaging and motivating students to learn in school. Young people need to spend time with peers to develop their identity and prepare for a role as a member of an expanded network. Relationships with teachers, as well as those between students, contribute to the determination of a sense of belonging within the school community. This sense of belonging provides psychological support and contributes to a commitment to learning with others who share the challenges of learning in difficult circumstances. Before Ajeng could make progress towards her academic goals, she said she needed people around her to understand her life situation and to be willing to "treat her better...like a family". In disadvantaged circumstances, support of this kind can make a critical difference to a student's success. As suggested in the interviews conducted with students enrolled in equivalency education programs; teachers, guest speakers, alumni, fellow students and peers can act as role models who offer inspiration. They can, in diverse ways, provide ongoing encouragement and nurture student achievement.

6 Conclusion: Prevailing Alternative School Practices for Addressing Concerns of the Working Youth

The Indonesian equivalency education system gives young people the attention and the support they need to succeed. This is often attention and support they could not find in the traditional school system. Unlike traditional schools, where students are predominantly from the same region, equivalency schools in urban areas like Jakarta and Depok City are full of in-migrant youth, bought together from all over the country. In such environments, in-migrant youth and youth communities are trying to rebuild personal identity and social connection. This enhances their motivation to learn. Young adult learning of this kind is a process of problem-finding and problem-solving which often starts with the questions, "where we are now" and "where to from here".

The decision to re-enter education through an equivalency education program is a consequence of individuals' own perception of their own needs: their understanding of their life situation and the need to build capacity for the future. Therefore, in Indonesia, there is consensus that equivalency education programs should welcome and orient newcomers at that time of need, rather than a time that is administratively convenient for the school. Equally, there is consensus that there should be equivalency education opportunities in all cities of destination for in-migrant youth. Recognising and harnessing the education of working youth aids those students to realise their potential and enhance their opportunity to contribute to personal and national development.

In this regard, internal migrant youth workers who have not completed their entire schooling from kinder to senior high school in their city of origin must be identified as an 'at risk' group in regional or local development policies and planning frameworks. To support this policy and practice, it is necessary to highlight some consistent features of successful equivalency education programs.

First, flexible learning strategies are crucial to the promotion of lifelong learning for working youth. Inclusivity and program flexibility are the foundation of learning strategies that are able to respond to the diverse needs of working youth. Successful programs aim to bring education to students rather than getting students to go to school. Flexible aspects include a teaching schedule that is appropriate to students working hours and that maximises interaction between teachers and learners (UNESCO, 2013, p. 4).

Second, flexibility in the assessment of prior learning of working students is a good way to fast-track studies towards a high school degree. Unlike students in traditional schooling, a large percentage of students in equivalency education programs have dropped out of school or are continuing their education after an extended time gap. They often have a considerable bank of life experience. This experience could be interpreted as advanced standing sufficient to allow them to re-enter an equivalency education program at a level higher to that which they last studied in a mainstream school. Various testing methods or portfolios could assist to determine appropriate entry levels.

Third, distance education through e-learning models can be used to make equivalency programs more accessible and available anywhere, at any time, without time constraints. Using this method, programs can be developed to work for youth who are physically unable to get to school.

Lastly, as working students or members of other disadvantaged groups often have minimal time to study because of demanding personal lives, self-paced courses need to be developed for these busy but determined young people.

Designers of equivalency education programs need to be strategic to meet the needs of the largest number of students possible. This requires attention to links between equivalency education, academic content, vocational training methodologies, and workplaces. Every equivalency institution should be required to build partnerships with local enterprises, to seek out and provide labour market information and appropriate job-specific skills to prepare students for employment. Furthermore, life skills training needs to be emphasised because of their essential relationship in preparing working students for the demands of everyday life and employment. Such programs should be appropriate to each region and locally designed and operated to best serve students. Further life skills training could include education in areas such as attitude, communication skills, time management, self-awareness and balancing work and life demands. An approach of this kind reflects the fact that modern social environments benefit from the provision of individuals ready with the knowledge, skills and confidence to shape a better future for themselves and the nation that recognises and nurtures their potential.

Note

1   All names of participants are pseudonyms.

References

Cranton, P. (1994). *Understanding and promoting transformative learning: A guide for educators of adults*. Jossey-Bass.

Daloz, L. A. (2000). Transformative learning for the common good. In J. Mezirow (Ed.), *Learning as transformation: Critical perspectives on a theory in progress*. Jossey-Bass.

Daloz, L. A. (2012). *Mentor: Guiding the journey of adult learners* (2nd ed.). Jossey-Bass.

Easthope, H., & Gabriel, M. (2008). Turbulent lives: Exploring the cultural meaning of regional youth migration. *Geographical Research, 46*(2), 172–182.

Ginting, E., & Aji, P. (2015). *Summary of Indonesia's economic analysis* (Asian Development Bank Papers on Indonesia, Vol. 2). Asian Development Bank. Retrieved from https://www.adb.org/sites/default/files/publication/177010/ino-paper-02-2015.pdf

Ivey, A. E. O., & Ivey, M. B. (2001). Developmental counseling and therapy and multicultural counseling and therapy. In D. C. Locke, J. R. Myers, & E. L. Herr (Eds.), *The handbook of counseling* (pp. 219–239). Sage.

Kegan, R. (2000). What form transforms? A constructive-developmental approach to transformative learning. In Mezirow (Ed.), *Learning as transformation: Critical perspectives on a theory in progress*. Jossey-Bass.

Kegan, R. (2009). What form transforms? A constructive-developmental approach to transformative learning. In K. Illeris (Ed.), *Contemporary theories of learning: Learning theorists in their own words*. Routledge.

Mezirow, J. (1991). *Transformative dimensions of adult learning* (1st ed.). Jossey-Bass.

Mezirow, J. (2000). *Learning as transformation: Critical perspectives on a theory in progress*. Jossey-Bass.

Ministry of Education and Culture. (2016). *Non-formal education statistics in 2015*. Ministry of Education and Culture Data Centre and Statistics, Jakarta.

Morrison, P. S., & Clark, W. A. V. (2011). Internal migration and employment: Macro flows and micro motives. *Environment and Planning, 43*(8), 1948–1964.

Polkinghorne, D. E. (1988). *Narrative knowing and the human sciences*. State University of New York Press.

Rosmilawati, I. (2016). *Disadvantaged youth in alternative schooling: Investigating Indonesian young people's re-engagement with education* (Unpublished PhD thesis). Western Sydney University, Australia.

Schafft, K. A. (2006). Poverty and student transiency within a rural New York school district. *Rural Sociology, 71*, 212–231.

Statistics Indonesia. (2011). *Internal migration of the Indonesian population: The results of the 2010 population census*. Statistics Indonesia.

Sukamdi and Mujahid, G. (2015). *Internal migration in Indonesia* (UNFPA Indonesia Monograph Series, Vol. 3). UNFPA. Retrieved August 7, 2018, from https://indonesia.unfpa.org/sites/default/files/pub-pdf/FA_Isi_BUKU_Monograph_Internal_Migration_ENG.pdf

Taylor, K., & Elias, D. (2012). Transformative learning: A developmental perspective. In E. W. Taylor & P. Cranton (Eds.), *The handbook of transformative learning: Theory, research, and practice.* Jossey-Bass.

UN Data. (2017). *UNdata | record view | Slum population as percentage of urban, percentage* [Online]. Retrieved May 23, 2018, from http://data.un.org/Data.aspx?d = MDG&f = seriesRowID%3 A710

United Nations Economic and Social Commission for Asia and the Pacific (UNESCAP). (2016). *ESCAP population data sheet* [Online]. Retrieved July 22, 2018, from https://www.unescap.org/sites/default/files/SPPS%20PS%20data%20 sheet%202016%20v15–2.pdf

United Nations Educational, Scientific and Cultural Organisation (UNESCO). (2013). *Flexible learning strategies: Country case report.* UNESCO. Retrieved July 4, 2017, from http://www.unescobkk.org

United Nations Educational, Scientific and Cultural Organisation (UNESCO). (2017). *Internal migration in Southeast Asia: Towards better inclusion of internal migrants.* UNESCO.

United Nations Children's Emergency Fund (UNICEF). (2011). *The impacts of climate change on nutrition and migration affecting children in Indonesia* [Online]. Retrieved June 18, 2018, from https://www.unicef.org/eapro/Indonesia_ climate_ change_report.pdf

World Bank. (2016). *The Indonesia Urban Story* [Online]. Jakarta, Indonesia. Retrieved September 1, 2018, from http://www.worldbank.org/en/news/feature/2016/06/14/indonesia-urban-story

CHAPTER 12

Participatory Action Research on Education for Self-Reliance for Rural Youth in Indonesia

Hasriadi Masalam

Abstract

Based on the author's educational and Participatory Action Research (PAR) engagement in a remote mountainous village in South Sulawesi, Eastern Indonesia, this chapter reflects on educational practices that can initiate self-reliance activities and projects in a rural community in Indonesia. The chapter begins with a brief conceptual genealogy of the education for self-reliance (ESR) and Participatory Action Research (PAR) to show the pertinent of the methodology adopted in this inquiry. The next section discusses the analysis on learning, schooling processes, content and organisation of formal education, learning spaces in the rural community, vision on education and the self-reliant practices in that village. The last segment discusses potentials and traits of education for self-reliance for the rural community, particularly in dealing with challenges of the deskilling of youth, and in attracting as well as retaining rural youth in the agricultural sector. This study argues that ESR can address the problem of the deskilling of rural youth and can contribute to their economic sustainability. The analysis shows how entrepreneurship and life skills education could be counterproductive when the obstacles to education for self-reliance, as rooted in factors contributing to the diminishing of rural youth agency, are not appropriately considered and addressed.

Keywords

rural youth – education for self-reliance – participatory action research

1   Introduction

As an agrarian country with a majority of the population lived and worked in rural areas, Indonesia is facing a paradox. Compared to the previous generation, the country now has the most educated rural youth population due to the compulsory basic education campaign. Yet at the same time, one-third of the rural youth (15–25 years old) are openly unemployed and walking away from agriculture (White, 2012). This is, partly, due to the mismatch of the employment opportunities and their formal education level, as the longer they stay at school the less relevant their new acquired skills to make rural life and family farming an attractive choice they have reason to value.

To remedy this dire situation, there has been a policy shift targeting rural youth from employment creation to promotion of entrepreneurship and life skills to address the unemployment spectre (Naafs & White, 2012). Some scholars, however, are critical on the over-emphasis of the role of entrepreneurship and life skills education in solving the issue of the deskilling of rural youth and ensuring their economic mobility. They call for further scrutiny of the structural failures of neoliberal education and development policies (Sukarieh & Tannock, 2015). This begs a question of the systemic deficits of formal schooling in rural areas, and what educational or communal practices can instead encourage self-reliance in rural communities.

Based on the author's educational and Participatory Action Research (PAR) engagement in a remote mountainous village in South Sulawesi, the eastern part of Indonesia, this chapter reflects on educational practices that can initiate self-reliance activities and projects in a rural community in Indonesia. The rest of the chapter is organised as follows. The chapter begins with a brief conceptual genealogy of the education for self-reliance (ESR) and Participatory Action Research (PAR) to show the pertinent of the action-oriented participatory methodology adopted in this inquiry. The next section discusses the analysis—conducted jointly involving the author and the PAR participants—on learning, schooling processes, content and organisation of formal education, learning spaces in the rural community, vision on education and the existence of self-reliant practices in that village. The joint analysis on these issues prepares the basis for the discussion on the initiatives to nurture youth agency in self-reliant activities where the author involved as a facilitator for a food and energy sovereignty project in that community. The last segment discusses potentials and traits of education for self-reliance for the rural community, particularly in dealing with challenges of the deskilling of youth, and in attracting as well as retaining rural youth in the agricultural sector.

This study argues that education for self-reliance can address the problem of the deskilling of rural youth and can contribute to their economic sustainability. It highlights the shortcomings of formal schooling as well as adverse unintended consequences of development projects targeting rural communities. The analysis shows how entrepreneurship and life skills education could be counterproductive when the obstacles to education for self-reliance, as rooted in factors contributing to the diminishing of rural youth agency, are not appropriately considered and addressed.

2   Thirdworld-Ist Genealogy of Education for Self-Reliance (ESR) and Participatory Action Research (PAR)

Education for self-reliance (ESR) was introduced by Julius Nyerere (1922–1999), the founding father and first president of Tanzania who was also known as *Mwalimu* (teacher). Through his renowned article using the same title (1968), he laid out the strategic plans to redirect the elitist nature of the British colonial education system into one that "foster[s] the social goals of living together, and working together, for the common good" by "inculcat[ing] a sense of commitment to the total community" (1968, p. 273). Nyerere's pedagogical praxis is often equated with Paulo Freire's (1979, 2000) conscientisation and cultural works in Latin America, and continues to inspire today's' educationalists to reinvigorate the self-reliance praxis (Mulenga, 2001). In Indonesian context today, the direct impact of this elitism and urban bias is reflected in the educational policy in Indonesia today, where the exclusive education with elitist curriculum could only be grasped by 30% of the students (Kompas, 2004).

Similar to education for self-reliance, the historical emergence of the Thirdworld-ist PAR (Fals-Borda, 1988; Freire, 1979, 2000) triggered by the attempts to acknowledge and even promote different epistemologies which stand for the interests of oppressed groups, continues to derive a contemporary significance from, for instance, small peasant and indigenous people struggles (Kapoor, 2017). The response to this appeal was taken up in different ways in different parts of the 'post colony' since the 1970s, often influenced by similar engagements of Fals-Borda (1988) with peasants in Nicaragua, Mexico and Colombia. From Africa, the work of Mwalimu Julius Nyerere in Tanzania through his concept of education for self-reliance that denounced the colonial legacies in the education system of post-colonial countries had a strong influence on the formulation of early ideas of PAR. From South Asia, the work of Bhoomi Sena (Land Army) movement and the early work of the Society for Participatory Research in Asia (PRIA) are some of the important lineages of a loosely referenced Thirdworld-ist PAR.

With this perspective of Thirdworld-ist genealogy in mind, this PAR engagement was aimed to provide opportunities for the village members to rethink aspects of the current learning and knowledge reproduction practices in their village, located in the slope of Bulusaraung Mountain (1,353 meters above sea level), in the border of Bantimurung-Bulusaraung National Park, and administratively part of Pangkep District, South Sulawesi Province, eastern Indonesia. The area is rich with abundant mining resources; especially limestones cliffs also known as tower karts, the main material for cement and granite. Despite the remote location, this village has been "flooded" with development schemes either by the government or by the international development organisations through local NGOs.

The encounter with this rural community began in 2006 when the author was working as a coordinator of an interdisciplinary fieldwork training organised by Foundation for Advanced Studies on International Development (FASID), a Tokyo-based think tank, and attended by graduate students and young development professionals mostly from Japan and Southeast Asian countries. Throughout the three weeks homestay in this village, the author was facilitating the logistical engagement and day to day interactions with the host families and community members.

The brief encounter was re-established when the author returned to this village to do a three months action-oriented inquiry (January–March 2008) for graduate thesis research, where part of this chapter draws on. Through the dialogical interviews, the PAR participants (47 villagers from mixed age, gender, education level, and income sources, selected through purposeful sampling strategy) were involved in joints analysis and collective thinking processes on the research questions. Longer engagement with these PAR participants and wider community members took place in early 2009–2011, when the author worked as a facilitator for a Food Sovereignty and Alternative Energy program in this village. Through this initiative, organised under the umbrella of *Sekolah Rakyat Petani* (Farmers Folk School (SRP)) Payo-Payo,[1] a South Sulawesi-based rural community organising network, the author deepened the problem-posing praxis through "reflexive conversations" (Jordan, 2009, p. 21) with the villagers, which provided the opportunity to identify some central issues that they hope to tackle to improve their situation.

Throughout the series of PAR praxis, the individual and group conversations often turned into engaging discussions to exchange information and insights, and hence mutual learning and problem posing in Freirean terms. The political and pedagogical commitment of Thirdworld-ist PAR adopted in this study is potentially in keeping with the appeal to investigate reality to transform it (Fals-Borda, 2006), particularly through the problem-posing pedagogy to transform the banking education system that creates the culture of silence (Freire, 1979, 2000) and diminishes the self-reliant initiatives among the rural communities.

3   Rethinking Rural Education Praxis: A Joint Analysis

This PAR praxis was intended to ignite the involvement of the community members in rethinking the educational practices that could be more relevant with their social-cultural milieu. In line with the spirit of PAR as a process of transforming reality by investigating it (Fals-Borda, 2006), this study asked questions stimulating the collective thinking processes and emergence of generative themes (Freire, 1979, 2000) around learning and schooling, child-rearing, farming skills acquisition, learning spaces, and factors contributing and hindering self-reliant practices.

3.1   *Perceptions of Learning and Schooling*

To capture the perception of research participants on learning and schooling, it is important to comprehend the inner motives for sending their children to school, especially for basic education, in the first place. There were five reasons why parents sent their children to school: government imperative, aspiration to become civil servant, parental obligation, expectation to improve living conditions and to prevent themselves from getting deceived. Among those motivations, one of the most often reiterated was obeying the government's program, as a father of an elementary school girl said bluntly in one of the interviews *"Isse'i do' ka nasuroki pammarenta"* (I don't know. It's the government who ordered us to do so) (Fieldnote, Jan 2008).

Another reason that stood out were the aspirations to become a civil servant and the opportunity to improve their lives. These responses implied underlying beliefs that schooling can serve as a ladder to climb up to higher social stratification. The relatively affluent lives of their fellow villagers who served as civil servants attested their assumption. One research participant said, "It's nice to be a civil servant as they can save their salary from the government, while they can still earn from farming or other business". The possibility to gain a surplus of wealth seems to be the main motivation for this aspiration.

Despite the high expectation of schooling for socio-economic mobility, there are mixed messages about their perception of *"to macca"* (educated person), the term used by the villagers throughout the conversations. There were two main categories of responses: applicability of knowledge and being helpful to others. The typical response could reflect their idealised conception as a communal agrarian community, where at times they need depend on each other and make use of importance of practical hands-on skills, such as farming, house construction, especially in facing difficult times, such as natural disaster or harvest failure. Interestingly, their analysis on *tau nia sikolana* (the schooled person) presented more negative paint, including the loss of hard work ethics, power-oriented, and focus on textbook-oriented theoretical knowledge. These observations could help to explain the contribution of schooling in the deskilling of rural young people, as one villager said, "They have been holding pens for too long, so they can't [stand] hold[ing] the hoes anymore". The statement reinforced the idealised traits of *to macca* as having practical skills and knowledge and use them to contribute to solutions of localised societal problems.

3.2   What Happens inside Schools

After revealing the perception of the villagers toward learning and schooling, this section will scrutinise the PAR participants joint analysis on the content and organisation of formal education system, both from teachers' and parents' perspectives. From teachers' point of view, there are four categories of concerns toward the institution they work with, i.e. lack of facilities, result-oriented curriculum, highly bureaucratic system and low motivation teachers.

The lack of facilities was obvious just by taking a short glance at the physical infrastructure of the schools in this village. During the research in 2008, there are four elementary schools, one kindergarten and one Open Junior High School, yet one doesn't have their building and use the classroom of one of the elementary schools in the afternoon. The condition of school buildings varied, the one located in the capital of the village has a relatively new building which was renovated about two years ago. It has six classrooms for grade one to six and one teacher office. The other school only has three classrooms, where each class was divided into two classes. The teachers' office was even shared with one of the classrooms. The availability of learning facilities like textbooks for instance also varied. The school in the centre of the village had more textbooks than the two other schools at the peripheries.

The highly bureaucratic system is another area identified by the teachers. Of the many issues within a complicated bureaucracy the teachers dealt with, the two areas most often pointed out were curriculum and administrative tasks. One senior elementary school teacher complained that "The curriculum keeps changing. We have not mastered the old curriculum yet, and now they launch a new one". Another teacher added that the upgrading workshop was very late. Even after two years from the commencement of the new curriculum, they had not attended any training yet. As for the administrative tasks, it was perceived as a daunting and exhausting burden. A teacher for sport class mentioned that he often spent more time filling all the required forms or preparing lesson plans than actually teaching it. Teachers seemed to function more as school administrators rather than as educators (Bjork, 2005; Buchori, 2007).

We have discussed at length about the teachers' evaluation of their institution. Now we will see what the parents say about the content and organisation of the formal education system. Parents viewed teachers as civil servants and school administrator rather than as educators. It is important to notice though that the negative image of teachers was not always that way. The older generation in the village had pleasant memories of the respectful figure of a teacher. The first elementary school in this village was established in 1964 when there was no road to this village, the only access was a small footpath that in the rainy season even their horse could not pass the small path. Therefore, the arrival of the first teacher was accepted as a blessing by the villagers.

Besides criticising teachers, parents also voiced their concern about the irrelevance of the subjects that their children learned at school. Other parents were concerned more with the fact that the longer their children at school the less possibility they would ever come back to live in the village. "School only prepares the children to leave the village not to stay", lamented one parent. He worried about the fact that what their children learned at school had nothing to do with their lives in the village

3.3 Schooling outside of the Village

Now, where do the children continue their schooling beyond the confine of their village? In terms of the geographical locations, the three most favourite cities were Makassar, Pangkep and Maros, the closest cities where the junior and senior high schools are located. In the past, when the road was still inaccessible the decision would be based on the availability of a relative in one of those places. As for the junior high school, the choices were Junior High School or Tsanawiyah, Islamic school equivalent to Junior High School. Most of the pupils in this village went to Junior High School.

After finishing this level, the choices of schooling became more complex. In many families, they first had to figure out whether they could afford to send their children to higher levels of schooling, especially if they had to send them to bigger and farther city, which meant spending more money. From this point, the most important consideration was which school could promise more access to jobs, especially white-collar ones. "If you are wealthy, go to high school, but if you are not rich enough, you better choose vocational school", one participant explained the parents' secondary school choice. There was a shared perception that Vocational School could promise easier access to jobs. However, the children from the relatively well-off families were reluctant to go to Vocational School and preferred Senior High School. This was due to the image that Vocational School was school for rudimentary jobs, such as welding and electronic services. They aspired for soft jobs, positions such as a teacher or an administrative staff at government offices.

3.4   *Learning Spaces in a Rural Community*
From conversations with villagers, the kinds of knowledge they share among themselves were skills as rural dwellers, such as livestock raising, weather forecasting, coffee planting, *ammile-mile* (rice breeding), brown sugar making, pig hunting, basket weaving, and house construction. Logically, people will learn what they need most to endure the given natural environment. A six years old boy, for instance, was so proficient in identifying all the names of the plants around his grandmother's house. Not only that, he could even tell me the function of each plant. Yet when the author asked him to identify the pictures in his school textbook he confused a postman for a medical doctor.

Where and how do learning processes take place? Contrary to the modern schooling method where learning is conducted in a confined, like a classroom, and during a predetermined period, the villagers passed their knowledge from generation to generation through "on the job training". "I learned to construct a house by observing my uncle who worked as a carpenter, and asked him about more sophisticated techniques", said one of the participants who assembled his first cupboard when he was 13 years old. Since then he kept improving his carpentry skills and become one of his main sources of income. He proudly claimed that most of the furniture that the people in Tompo Bulu used in their houses was his work.

In terms of social values, that the community embodied and arranged their interactions according to these set of values, the learning took place naturally in various community events. For instance, Puang Intang, the community elder (64 years), described how she reminded her fellow villagers to nurture "*passamuturukang*" (the sense of community). She said, "*punna nia tau a'gaukang pangngerangangngi berasa, areka pangngerangangngi ere, kaju, manna ce'laja*" (Whenever any community members have an event [such as wedding party, circumcision celebration] please bring them rice, or water, cooking wood, or even just a pinch of salt).

The issue here, as discussed in previous sections, is that the knowledge that children learn at school is not relevant to the practical challenges that they face, such as degrading environmental quality or lack of economic opportunities. Therefore, school becomes an alienating institution where children are disconnected from their wider world. Moreover, the knowledge that has been proven to be useful in solving their concrete problems is not valued by the school.

3.5   *Vision of Ideal Education*
This section will discuss what the villagers perceive as an ideal education, in the broadest sense. There are four categories of comments from the conversations.

The first and foremost expectation is that an educational institution will help young people to have livelihood skills. This is captured in a remark offered by a parent within the village, "Schooling for the lower-class people is supposed to enable children to gain *pakkatuhoang* (skills to earn a living)". This comment was based on their experience that schooling did not equip their children with the skills and mentality to creatively tackle the social-economic challenges in their community.

Not all villagers, however, put all their expectations of children's education solely on formal schooling. One parent had an idea to establish their own learning space. He was trying to secure some funding from the Village Fund to establish a carpentry learning centre in this village. He was concerned about the young people in his village who didn't know what to do after finishing their study in the city. Many of them failed to get a job in the city and when they eventually returned live in their home village, what they had learned in school was useless. That was why he made this plan to create apprenticeship opportunities for the villagers, targeting particularly the young people, to teach them construction and carpentry skills.

During interviews and in conversations, another typical framing of an ideal education was for learning to help improve and contribute to social cohesion within the community. For instance, one participant mentioned the initiative to develop a demonstration plot to produce organic fertiliser, which was used both as learning and production centre to meet the growing interest of the community members to reduce the intensive use of chemical agricultural inputs, and eventually could lead the strengthening of the collective work among the villagers. Some villagers suggested building more connections between the classroom activities and the daily work or activities of community members and make use of available resources. For instance, one idea raised was to invite the local Agriculture Extension Workers to teach students basic farming skills, as a part of the *muatan lokal* or Local Content class.

3.6 *Hindrance to Self-Reliance Initiatives*

The joint analysis on the existing the self-reliance practices focus on communal activities identified by the PAR participants, such as *gotong royong* (joint bearing of burdens), *kerja bakti* (community works), *ronda* (night watch), daily prayer in the mosque, socio-cultural gatherings, economic activities, like farming and brown sugar making, and even house construction. Some fundamental changes identified that discourage the practices of self-reliance in Tompo Bulu were increasing dependence on external resources, dependence on development projects, and widening economic gaps.

One example of increasing dependence on external resources mentioned by a mother who noticed that "[t]here are more things that we have to buy from the city these days. We even have to buy *pattapi* (rice winnow) from the city". Such dependence was exacerbated by growing consumerism among young people, for instance buying motorcycle or cell phone. Some families even sold their land or used it as a mortgage to buy a motorcycle. Driving a motorcycle became a symbol of social status among youth, both those who were attending school in the city and those who were staying in the village.

Another factor which has a significant impact on hindering self-reliance was the moral hazards of development projects. The fact that the majority of villagers have less say in how the development programs were designed and implemented, has created deep-seated apathy among them, especially the lower class. They learned that the lack of accountability enabled them to pursue taking personal benefits from public goods. One villager jokingly said, "They intentionally do the project in remote places, so there will be no traces afterwards", and therefore described the village as *"tempat jin buang buang proyek"* (colloquial term to describe unwanted or haunted place) (Batiran, 2011, p. 32). As an illustration, in 2000 alone some of the construction projects implemented in this village were: Elementary School Building, Village Road Construction, Community Centre, Grave Fencing, Clean Water Piping Project, tourism villa, to name a few. Not to mention various training projects from the National Park and the National Program for Community Empowerment (*Program Nasional Pemberdayaan Masyarakat*, or PNPM), a World Bank-funded project.

> Some of these projects bring benefits to the villagers, but a few of them seems "fishy", even strange. The Trading and Mining Office, for example, provided training for making *tempe*, although no farmers are planting soybeans in this village. Or the potato training and planting project from the Agriculture Office, where the altitude and temperature of the air the village is not suitable ... Or a project to build a dam for irrigating paddy fields which were already broken even before it was used ... revolving fund project, also called by the villagers as *uang mati* ["dead money"]. (Batiran, 2011, p. 30)

Last but not least, the contributing factor hindering the self-reliance practices in the village was the widening gap between the haves and the haves not. In the analysis of the PAR participants, there were three groups of people who can improve their livelihood in the village, the large landowners, the traders, and civil servants. Often the large landowners are also civil servants, therefore they can grow more prosperous than their fellow villagers as they can save their salary to accumulate more wealth and use the income from farming for their daily expenditures. In the villagers' analysis, these village elite groups were often also the village officials who use their positions to manipulate the supposedly participatory and accountable development project for their personal economic and political gains. The following typical comment by one villager summed the impact of this "elite capture" (Lucas, 2016):

> The loss of *gotong-royong* (joint bearing of burdens) began since the former head of the village. He often ordered us to do *kerja bakti* (community works), but we later found out that it was a funded project.

4 Countering the Deskilling of Rural Youth: Nurturing Agency

As "complexities are best understood through analysis of concrete situations" (Foley, 1999, p. 16), this section presents the author's engagement in what Foley described as learning in social action, through the Food Sovereignty and Alternative Energy project (2009–2011), particularly with a rural community in the mountainous part of Pangkep District, South Sulawesi, eastern Indonesia.

The earlier discussion has demonstrated how formal education and development interventions have contributed to making the villagers are gradually getting more dependent on external supports and slowly destroyed their self-reliance values and practices. Not to mention the impacts of green revolution since 1990s, which was not only affecting the physical environment through the extensive use of chemical agricultural inputs but also the division of labour and work ethic of the rural peasant, that had effectively banished the communal institutions especially in farming, and made them dependent to chemical agricultural inputs. At the same time, the rural youth are increasingly seeing the village life and agricultural livelihood as an unattractive choice for them.

The PAR participants also agreed to send to two young farmers (both males in the early twenties) from this village to join a three months hands-on training on organic farming and community organising in Solo, Central Java. After returning from the training, they were working with their fellow young farmers to initiate a small-scale rural livelihood project in their village. The informal conversations with some villagers provided the opportunity to identify some central issues that they hope to tackle to improve their situation. One of the most immediate problems identified was the scarcity of water for agriculture, and the solution proposed was building a small water reservoir.

After calculating the costs to construct the dam, the youth group found out it was way beyond their financial capacity, although the costs could be reduced if they were willing to contribute their time and energy. The community organisers agreed to support the idea with one condition, the whole processes of constructing and maintaining the dam should be geared towards shifting the charity paradigm of development projects. From positioning the villagers as passive recipients of projects handouts, into solidarity building, where the villagers become capable actors of mobilising their local resources to achieve their common vision. Practically, it means SRP Payopayo was in charge for the fundraising of start-up fund, while the villagers developed the work system to build and maintain the small dam and its irrigation utilising any available local resources that they have.

After more than three decades of being positioned as passive development beneficiaries, it was not an easy task to revive the communal work system. It took some time for the youth group to analyse their situations and to try out some practical strategies to mobilise their resources for the dam construction. The group eventually managed to organise "barefoot engineers" that utilised their vernacular knowledge to design how the water from the spring inside the mountainous forest could reach their rice fields. They also agreed to contribute their time every Tuesday morning for almost six months to work together in constructing the small dam, including collecting the constructions materials, such as sand and stones, from the closest river where the dam was going to be built.

Their success in constructing the dam gave them a sense of confidence in taking matters of their own hands. Built on their initial success, through their weekly meetings, the young farmers together with other more senior villagers also identified their dependence on external chemical agricultural inputs and seeds. Moreover, the findings from Participatory Action Research (PAR) demonstrated that food and energy were the biggest expenditures of the households in this village, as they buy more processed food from the city. The findings encouraged them to discuss why and since when was it the case, as well as to identify potential solutions of utilising local food and energy sources.

To continue their learning processes, the group built a "living laboratory" where they developed an integrated system involving permaculture, biogas, other forms of alternative energy, as well as the farmers' cooperative system. Based on insights from the living laboratory, they can document promising results and have started to publicise them in a campaign against chemical agricultural products promoted by the government and private companies. The research has been replicated in eight other villages and they have conducted exchange visits so they may learn from each other. To expand the impact of this project and contribute to supporting the rural food and energy sovereignty movement, findings from the research and lessons learned from the community organising work have been published into books and captured in various media forms, such as a photo essay, a documentary, and periodic newsletters produced with the support of SRP Payopayo community organisers.

Moreover, throughout their learning processes, the community organisers the questions of "who gains" and "who loses" in analysing their situation. In their language, they identified the impacts of green revolution and neoliberal development paradigm that the Indonesian government is pursuing by cutting agricultural subsidies and budget for basic social services, especially health and education, in rural areas. In addition, the soaring prices of fossil fuels have devastating impacts on the income level and purchasing power of these communities.

In light of their struggle to nurture their self-reliance, they continued to develop their capacity to invent "popular science", specifically hands-on/practical technology and to construct counter-argument to the mainstream chemical agricultural inputs promoted by the government through the local Agricultural Extension Officers. In 2009, the farmers' group established a community learning centre to discuss and debate their vision for local sovereignty over natural resources, especially over food sources and local energy, and sustainability of ecosystems. The learning centre also has gardening plots for women and young children to encourage them to use their house yard to plant vegetables and develop a herbal garden.

Through the farmers' field school developed according to the specific needs of the community as identified through the ongoing participatory action research, they were involved in joint learning and research on organic agriculture, alternative energy, soil and water conservation, and nutrition. The networks of field schools developed into joint researches among the farmers' groups where the learning processes were based on equality and solidarity through critical dialogue processes. Therefore, the ultimate goal of the field school was to enable local people to choose, decide and control its process and direction of social change they aspire, following their own needs and abilities, which will be the cornerstone to revitalise their self-reliance towards socio-economic, political, and cultural sovereignty.

The rural youth groups are continuously widening the spaces for communal learning to discuss and debate their vision for local sovereignty over natural resources, especially over food sources and local energy and sustainability of ecosystems. Through the process of communal "learning in social action" (Foley, 1999), they are now "making the road by walking" (Horton & Freire, 1990) towards a sovereign, equitable, dignified, and sustainable rural community life.

5 Discussion: Insights on Education for Self Reliance for Rural Youth

The previous two sections have presented the joint analysis and reflections of the PAR participants on their perception and practices on learning, education and schooling, and the factors contributing to the diminishing of self-reliance in their community. Despite the high parents' expectation on the schooling as means of securing social and economic mobility for their children, they also saw schooling as an alienating institution, where the hidden curriculum conveyed recurring messages of simplistic modernisation by equating certificate with knowledge, occupation as white-collar jobs and modernity with owning high-tech gadgets. The fact that educated rural youth unemployment is soaring does not negate this expectation.

Furthermore, the rural development interventions exacerbated the moral hazards and widening social differentiation in this village which further weaken their collective capacity to maintain the social fabric of the community. With this analysis in mind, this section proposes three key insights in facilitating ESR for rural youth: the need to address the alienating hidden curriculum of rural education and the interconnection with the structural failures of the education and development interventions and advancing collective action and commons in learning and knowledge production pertinent to the immediate issues they are facing as rural communities.

5.1 *Addressing the Alienating "Hidden Curriculum" of Rural Education and Development Interventions*

The schooling experience of the rural youth as discussed in the previous was characterised by their awkward engagement with the elitist and urban bias of the "hidden curriculum", which prompted the villagers to make a distinction between "*to macca*" (educated people) and "*tau nia sikolana*" (schooled people). For the villagers, often the schooling period that their children had gone through generated the mentality of the young generation who economically and culturally unfit any longer to rural livelihood and even look down on their self-reliant practices, particularly related managing resource and labour. The decreasing 'learning by doing' of domestic and farming tasks throughout their elementary and secondary education period exacerbates the disconnection between the young people and the practical challenges that they face in their community, such as degrading environmental quality or lack of economic opportunities. Therefore, school becomes an alienating institution where children are disconnected from their wider world. Moreover, knowledge and skills that have been proven to be useful in solving their concrete problems are not valued by the schooling standard. Moreover, their investment in ensuring their children to get formal education could go wasted as they learned the mismatch of the employment opportunities and their formal education level, and often led the rural young people to accept the last avenue, living in urban slums and working in unskilled jobs.

5.2 Advancing Collective Action and Commons in Generating Rural Youth Agency

At the same time, the long ignorance of rural and agricultural infrastructure development, as well as the impact of the green revolution, have increased the dependence of rural farmers to external agricultural inputs, which further deteriorate the productivity of their livelihood due to soaring production costs, climate change and volatile market dynamics. In addition, the fact that the majority of villagers have less say in how the education and development interventions were designed and implemented, has created deep-seated apathy among them, especially the marginalised groups, especially women and rural youth. As the second part of this section demonstrates, the women and rural youth could potentially exercise their agencies towards collective emancipatory and self-reliant vision through communal knowledge production that could address issues of rural youth deskilling, as well as attracting and retaining rural youth in the agricultural sector.

5.3 Connecting the Local Analysis with Wider Structural Failures of Neoliberal Education and Development Policies

To develop the rural youth agency in the learning in social action (Foley, 1999), an important part of developing sustainable solutions in these communities is establishing an atmosphere that allows people to draw on resources that they have, especially to address the crucial issues they face together. Such an atmosphere also provides a forum for people to analyse their situation more critically, and this may serve as the starting point for the construction of lasting relationships characterised by more equitable power relation, both with actors outside and inside the village.

To be more concrete, this revitalisation effort must begin with what they have, instead of what they "should" have. Introducing alternative livelihoods without considering the changes in farming culture and unfair agricultural commodities market cycles would only mean spreading the lure of prosperity for farmers. Revitalisation of agricultural knowledge and practices will be more effective if farmers themselves successfully identify strategies to overcome their problems by mobilising resources and the existing capacity around them.

Learning in social action means the process of revitalising local knowledge requires real engagement, not simply mobilisation, in safeguarding their environment, without putting the excessive burden of conservation agenda to their shoulders. It should be kept in mind that the revitalisation of local knowledge is not just an environmentalist romanticism. Local knowledge is needed to create a farming system based upon agricultural practices that can ensure their welfare, without sacrificing the carrying capacity of nature, which has become their main asset as farmers.

6 Conclusion

This chapter has demonstrated the potential of ESR and PAR to nurture the communal knowledge production and its subsequent impacts for agency generating towards self-reliance. The main principle is the struggle to revive the people's self-reliance should not primarily be based on the theory of the "*tau nia sikolana*" (schooled) people, but with muddy hands, by starting from the most pressing issue at play in a particular community and build the change from the very practical aspect. The majority of the efforts should be initiated by the community members themselves.

Inherited through the generations, people have the innate propensity to interpret their surrounding environment. For centuries, they have developed such capacities and used them to nurture their capacity to sustain themselves. Yet in many disadvantaged communities, their potentials as genuine knowledge producer have been seriously curtailed by modern science, through the green revolution, and modern nation-state capitalistic/neoliberalist development agenda.

The emancipatory paradigm and practices of PAR could potentially support marginalised groups to regain their capacity in making their community as learning centres and therefore a valid source of knowledge. The peasants are indeed not anti-theory; their perseverance to practice environmentally friendly farming, for instance, emerged from relentless research that brought them to the conclusion on the benefit of natural farming, for instance. This is the emerging point of the concrete experiences of the grassroots and the abstract knowledge of the intellectuals. The tasks of the external intellectuals are systematising the people's knowledge and wisdom and supporting genuine knowledge production by the peasants.

Note

1   SRP-Payo Payo is one the members of Komunitas Ininnawa, a network of five NGOs (SRP Payo-Payo, Tanete Institute (TANI), Active Society Institute (AcSI), Katakerja, and Ininnawa Publisher) promoting rural innovations, traditional market revitalisation, and youth and women empowerment in Eastern Indonesia.

References

Bjork, C. (2005). *Indonesian education: Teachers, schools, and central bureaucracy.* Routledge.

Buchori, M. (2007). *Evolusi Pendidikan di Indonesia: Kweekschool sampai ke IKIP: 1852–1998* [*Evolution of education in Indonesia from kweekschool to IKIP: 1852–1998*]. Insist-Press.

Fals-Borda, O. (1988). *Knowledge and people's power: Lessons with peasants in Nicaragua, Mexico and Columbia.* Indian Social Institute.

Fals-Borda, O. (2006). The north–south convergence: A 30-year first-person assessment of PAR. *Action Research, 4*(3), 351–58.

Foley, G. (1999). *Learning in social action: A contribution to understanding informal education.* Zed Books.

Freire, P. (1979/2000). *Pedagogy of the oppressed.* Continuum.

Horton, M., & Freire, P. (1990). *We make the road by walking: Conversations on education and social change.* Temple University Press.

Kapoor, D. (Ed.). (2017). *Against colonization and rural dispossession: Local resistance in South East Asia, the Pacific and Africa.* Zed.

Kompas Daily. (2004, September 4). Pendidikan Indonesia Alami Proses Involusi (*Indonesian Education is in Involution Process*). Retrieved June 6, 2006, from http://www.kompas.com/kompas-cetak/0409/04/utama/1248649.htm

Lucas, A. (2016, June 1). Elite Capture and Corruption in two Villages in Bengkulu Province. Sumatra. *Human Ecology: an Interdisciplinary Journal, 44*(3), 287–300.

Mulenga, D. C. (2001). Mwalimu Julius Nyerere: A critical review of his contributions to adult education and postcolonialism. *International Journal of Lifelong Education, 20*(6), 446–470. doi:10.1080/02601370110088436

Naafs, S., & White, B. (2012). Intermediate generations: Reflections on Indonesian youth studies. *The Asia Pacific Journal of Anthropology, 13*(1), 3–20. http://doi.org/10.1080/14442213.2012.645796

Nyerere, J. (1968). Education for self-reliance. In J. Nyerere (Ed.), *Freedom and socialism/Uhuru na Ujamaa: Essays on socialism* (pp. 278–290). Oxford University Press.

Prabowo, A., Batiran, K. B., & Mansyur. (2011). *Melawan ketergantungan kebijakan pangan dan pengalaman pengorganisasian tiga desa* [*Fighting dependence: Food policy and community organizing experience in three villages*]. INSISTPress.

Sukarieh, M., & Tannock, S. (2015). *Youth rising? The politics of youth in the global economy*. Routledge.

White, B. (2012). Indonesian rural youth transitions: Employment, mobility and the future of agriculture. In A. Booth, C. Manning, & T. K. Wie (Eds.), *Land, livelihood, environment, and the economy in Indonesia: Essays in honour of Joan Hardjono* (pp. 1–14). Yayasan Pustaka Obor Indonesia.

Index

7 E's Framework   13, 109, 111, 112, 117, 118, 121, 122

academia   147–149, 157
academic achievement   163, 186, 197
activists   62, 156
Adat, traditional   151
alternative education   179, 203, 205, 210
Association of Southeast Asian Nations (ASEAN)   125
Ausindo Educational (AE)   125, 128, 131, 134, 141
Australian AID, AusAID   149
authentic learning   128, 129, 131, 138
autonomy   23, 27, 52, 137

bachelor of education   7, 9, 90, 95, 146, 152, 155
Badan Nasional Penempatan dan Perlindungan Tenaga Kerja Indonesia (BNP2TKI), National Board for the Placement and Protection of Indonesian Overseas Workers   176
Badan Pemeriksa Keuangan (BPK) [State Financial Audit Agency]   156
Badan Pengawasan Keuangan dan Pembangunan (BPKP) [State Finance and Development Supervision Agency]   156
Bahasa Indonesia   29, 49, 70, 71, 96, 126, 131–133, 135, 136, 138–141, 144
banking education   223
Bantuan Operasional Sekolah (BOS) [School Operational Assistance]   7, 177
behaviour rubric   114, 122
belongingness   23, 27
benchmarking   125
berakhlak mulia [noble and having sound character]   199
boundary crossing   13, 89, 90, 93, 94, 100–102
boundary objects   94, 99, 100, 102
Buddhism, Buddhist   4, 69, 71, 74, 85, 188, 191
Building Relationships through Intercultural Dialog and Growing Engagement (bridge) Project   125, 126, 128, 131, 134, 135, 139, 141

Bupati, Head of district   57, 59, 60

career
  aspiration   10, 12, 66, 68, 70, 74, 76, 79, 82, 84
  plan   59, 68, 72, 74
Catholicism, Catholic   4, 12, 68, 69, 71, 74–83, 85, 116, 117, 119, 188, 191
character, types of
  building   108–111, 114–116, 121
  change   108, 114, 122
  development   109, 116, 121
  education   13, 107–113, 115, 116–123, 198
  moral character   109, 117, 119
  performance character   109, 117
child labour   168, 209
Chinese Indonesians   186–188, 191, 194, 195, 197
classroom management   12, 22–24, 27, 28, 30, 33–36, 38, 40–42, 98
Communications Studies Program (CSP)   146, 147, 150, 152–154, 156
Community Learning Centres (CLCs)   211
competence   23, 27, 69, 110, 116, 118, 119, 190, 194, 197, 198
Confucianism   69, 188, 191
constitutional court   55
contemporary theories of learning   23, 38
control variable   31, 32
Convention on the Elimination of all Forms of Discrimination Against Women (CEDAW)   152
coordination   93, 94, 99–101
covariates   32–34
cross-cultural understanding/intercultural understanding   13, 126, 127, 130, 136, 138, 141
cultural
  background   14, 186, 187, 189, 191, 196, 199
  heritage   186
  values   130, 137, 163, 186, 187
cultural appreciation   128
culture   13, 25, 40, 69, 91, 92, 108, 109, 111, 112, 126–128, 130, 137, 138, 141, 156, 189, 214, 223, 235

curriculum   3, 13, 15, 23, 26, 28, 57, 92, 108–111, 114, 130, 141, 146, 151, 152, 199, 205, 211, 212, 222, 225, 233

Dakwah [Islamic teaching]   69
decentralisation   6, 12, 50
democratisation   50, 52
Dewan Perwakilan Rakyat Daerah (DPRD)   53, 58, 60, 61
digital media   129 (*see also* ICT)
Directorate General of Higher Education   156
distance education   212, 217
district   6, 9, 12, 49, 50, 52, 53, 54, 56–63, 134, 169, 171, 180, 181
domain-general   24
domain-specific   24

education policy   52, 54, 164, 167, 172, 176, 181
early school leaving   14, 161, 163–165, 168, 171, 172, 176, 180
early school leaver   162, 164, 167–171, 180
Education for Self-Reliance (ESR)   221, 222, 233, 235
educational aspirations   14, 189, 196, 197, 199
emotional climate   22–24, 27, 28, 32, 39, 41
emotional support   30, 33–37, 39, 40
engagement/global engagement   2, 8, 13, 15, 58, 124, 126, 127, 129, 130, 134, 136–138, 141, 161, 180, 186, 190, 199, 205, 208, 221–223, 233, 235
English   71, 92–98, 102, 127, 129, 131–133, 135–138, 141
entity mindset   190
entrepreneurship   10, 221
equality   130, 146, 148, 232
equity   7, 12, 21, 22, 24, 25, 27, 40, 50, 72, 75, 130, 141
ethnicity   163, 187–191, 194–197, 199
ethnography   14, 163, 173
exchange programs   135, 136, 139

Factors Influencing Teaching Choice (FIT-Choice) framework   71, 85
faith   6, 13, 68, 69, 84, 110, 112, 113, 115, 117, 118 (*see also* religiosity)
fakultas, faculty   146, 150, 152, 154, 155
feminism   148, 156, 157
    radical   148

financial issues   6, 9, 84, 137, 211
flexibility   15, 108, 211, 212, 216, 217
founding mothers   153, 156

gender
    analysis   148
    awareness   148, 154
    diffusion   14, 146–148, 150, 152, 156
    inequality   146, 152
    knowledge   13, 14, 146–153, 155–157
    mainstreaming   13, 146, 157
    policies   145 (*see also* policies, gender)
    studies   13, 14, 145–151, 153–157
    Studies Program (GSP)   14, 149, 156
    role   83
generative themes   224
ghettoisation   14, 146–148, 150, 155
global   11–13, 124, 125, 127, 130, 136, 137, 141, 146, 149, 157, 164, 165
    citizen   130, 137, 141
globalisation   2, 124, 127, 136
Golongan Karya (Golkar) [Functional Group Party]   51
government regulation   56, 57, 59, 154, 171
grade repetition   31–33, 35, 38
Graduate Program of Gender Studies (GPGS)   146, 147, 150–157
guru [teacher]   48, 70, 90

hierarchical linear regression   32
Higher Education   13–15, 145–147, 149, 150, 153, 155–157, 164, 185, 191, 197, 198, 213
Hinduism/Hindu   4, 69, 71, 74, 85, 188, 191
homestay   137, 223

Identification   93, 98, 101, 188, 190, 197
Ignatian pedagogy   116, 118, 119
incremental mindset   190
independence   108, 111, 115
individuation   213
Indonesian youth   1, 8, 10, 67–70, 186
Information and Communication Technology (ICT)   129, 137, 138
inquiry-based instruction   24, 31–36, 38
institutional change   156, 157
instruction   12, 22–24, 27, 28, 30–36, 38–42, 92, 199
integrity   2, 108, 111
intelligence   96–98, 116, 189–196, 198, 199

INDEX   241

interactive instruction   12, 28, 30, 33–36, 38, 40–42
internal migration   14, 204, 207
International Monetary Fund (IMF)   52
Intraclass Correlation (ICC)   33
intrinsic religiosity   190–195, 198
Islam/Muslim   12, 13, 69, 71, 74–84, 117, 188, 191
Islamic missionising   69
item-response theory   29

Jaring Pengaman Sosial [Social Safety Net program]   163
jenis, jenjang, fungsi [type, level and/or function]   56

Kabupaten Cerdas [Clever District]   59
Kartu Indonesia Pintar   177
Kartu Tanda Penduduk (KTP) [national identification card]   188
Kementerian Perencanaan Pembangunan Nasional/Badan Perencanaan Pembangunan Nasional [(Bappenas) Ministry of National Development Planning/National Development Planning Agency]   7, 8, 17, 52, 162, 181
Kementrian Pemberdayaan Perempuan [Ministry of Women's Empowerment]   229
Komisi Nasional Perempuan (Komnas Perempuan) [National Commission on Violence Against Women]   58, 60, 63

labour migration   161, 163, 172–181
Laki-Laki Baru [New Man]   151
language learning   126, 128–130, 138, 140
language teaching   127, 131, 136
    English language education   71, 136
Law on Teachers and Lecturers   134
learning mechanism   93, 94, 98, 100, 102
life skills   213
    education   211, 217, 211

mainstream education   205
male-female participation
    in economics   97
    in education   76, 79, 195, 210
    in politics   145, 149, 151
Marxist/Marxian   148
migrasi risen [recent migrants]   209

Minister of Finance   53
Minister of National Education (*see* Ministry of Education and Culture)   53
Minister of Religious Affairs   53
Ministry of Education and Culture (MoEC)   3, 4, 15, 16, 59, 211
Ministry of Religious Affairs (MoRA)   3
Ministry of Research, Technology, and Higher Education (MoRTHE)   3
Ministry of Women Empowerment and Child Protection   154
motivation   9, 14, 26, 27, 31–36, 60, 68, 69, 71, 72, 76, 91, 102, 129, 138, 212, 225
    motivational goals   190
motto   115, 116, 118, 120
multidiscipline vs one-discipline   155
multilevel modelling   32, 33
Multivariate analyses of variance (MANOVA)   74
municipalities   6, 49, 54, 55, 61, 62, 134, 171, 180, 181
mutual cooperation   108, 111

narrative study   207
national education system   111
National Labour Force Survey   172
nationalism   111, 115, 118
native Indonesian   14c, 188, 191, 194, 196, 197
Net Enrolment Rate (NER)   7, 162
New Order, the   50–52, 150
Non-Governmental Organisation (NGO)   151, 153, 156, 223, 136

open junior high school   225
Organisation for Economic Co-operation and Development (OECD)   12, 28, 29, 31, 33, 205
out-of-field teachers   13, 89–92, 93–95, 99, 101–103
out-of-school children (OOSC)   162, 164, 168, 171

Participatory Action Research (PAR)   15, 220–225, 228–231, 233, 235
Pasca Sarjana [Graduate School]   155
patriarchy   84, 147, 152, 189, 197
pedagogical content knowledge   91, 95
peer evaluation   13, 121–123
Pegawai Negeri Sipil (PNS) [Civil servant]   56

Pekerja Migran Indonesia (PMI) [Indonesian overseas or migrant worker] 181, *see also* TKI
Pendidikan Kesetaraan [Equivalency Education Program] 211
Pendidikan Profesi Guru (PPG) [Teacher Professional Education Program] 67
Pengadilan Tata Usaha Negara (PTUN) [local state administrative court] 60
Penguatan Pendidikan Karakter (PPK) [Strengthening Character Education] 108–112
perception of teaching 83, 84
Persatuan Guru Republik Indonesia (PGRI) [the Indonesian Teachers Union] 51, 52, 58
Petunjuk Teknis (juknis) [technical guidelines] 56
policy
    agenda 54
    analysis 164
    design 14, 163
    education 52, 54, 164, 167, 172, 176, 181
    framework 60, 71, 93
    implementation 42, 53, 61, 107
    makers 15, 52, 68, 130, 139, 164, 198, 199
    mapping 165, 176, 180
    teacher management 50, 52, 61
political-economy 12, 48, 50, 53, 61
post-reformation 150
predictor variable 30, 34
problem posing 223
professional development 41, 42, 70, 72, 79, 81, 82, 84, 95, 99–102, 130, 136, 223
Professional Engagement and Career Development Aspirations (PECDA) scale 73, 81
Program Studi Kajian Wanita [Women's Studies Program] 149
Programme for International Student Assessment (PISA) 8, 12, 21, 22, 26, 28, 29, 38, 39, 42, 49, 67
Protestantism/Protestant 69, 188, 191
Pusat Studi Kajian Gender (PSKG) [Centre for Research on Gender Studies] 150

qualitative 13, 14, 112, 123, 132, 173, 207
quantitative 12, 14

Rapat kerja [working group meetings] 60

reflection 13, 25, 68, 93, 94, 100, 102, 117, 118, 208, 213, 233
reflexive conversations 223
regression 33, 37, 192–194
reliability 30, 31, 74, 209
religion 12, 64, 68–72, 76, 82–85, 92, 98, 108, 119, 121, 130, 151, 173, 187–191, 194–196, 198, 199
religiosity 69, 108, 111, 115, 187, 190–195, 198 (*see also* faith)
religious
    behaviour 190–194, 198
    beliefs 9, 12, 66, 68–71, 74, 75, 76, 79, 81, 82, 84, 85, 146, 188, 190, 191, 194
    groups 68, 70, 74–81, 83, 84
    influences 68, 70, 72, 75, 76
    practices 69, 71, 74, 190
Religious Commitment Inventory (RCI), the 71
Rencana Pembangunan Jangka Menengah Nasional (RPJMN) [National Mid-Term Development Plan] 1
resilience 212, 215
resistance 50, 51, 60, 148, 149
reward and punishment system 114, 118, 120, 121
Rintisan Sekolah Bertaraf Internasional (RSBI) [International Standards Pilot Schools] 132, 134, 139
rural areas 8, 54–56, 58, 133, 172, 209, 210, 220, 221, 232
rural communities 15, 115, 163, 172, 175–177, 180, 221, 223, 227, 230, 233
rural youth
    deskilling 11, 15, 221, 225, 230, 234
    unemployment 233

Satuan Pendidikan Kerjasama (SPK) schools [Joint Cooperation Schools] 13, 92–94, 97, 102
school
    level 26, 29, 31–35, 38–40, 42, 49, 58, 90, 110, 136, 140
    status 32
schools, levels of
    preschool 95, 96
    primary 3, 4, 7, 9, 56, 71, 95–98, 101, 108, 110–115, 119, 121, 122, 125, 126, 131, 135, 136, 162, 163, 167, 171, 181, 199, 210–212

INDEX

secondary   3–8, 10, 12, 15, 16, 21, 22, 31, 32, 34, 131, 136, 205
schools, types of
  Catholic   119
  Christian   119
science literacy   12, 28, 29, 32–36, 38–40, 42
Sekolah Dasar Instruksi Presiden (SD Inpres) [Primary school construction program]   4, 163
Sekolah Kajian Strategik dan Global [School of Strategic and Global Studies]   150
self-efficacy   25, 189–191, 195–199
self-evaluation   121, 123
sense of calling/to answer a calling   70
sister school partnerships   13, 124–141, 144
social power   148
socio-cultural   146, 163, 177, 178, 180, 228
Socio-Economic Status (SES)   12, 22–28, 31–38, 40, 42, 206
sociology   27
Southeast Asia   149
Southeast Asia Minister of Educational Organisation (SEAMEO)   125
spirituality   119
Strategi Nasional Penanganan Anak Tidak Sekolah (Stranas ats) [National Strategy for Out of School Children]   162
student-centred activities   30, 33
Sustainable Development Goals   162, 181

teacher
  distribution   12, 30, 48–52, 54–56, 58–61
  education student   9, 12, 66, 70, 73, 84, 85, 191, 197
  feedback   31, 33–37, 39
  maldistribution   49
  qualification/certification   7, 9, 22, 26, 67, 92
  redistribution   12, 50, 52–61
  shortage   56, 93
Teacher Law 2005, 7, 92, 102
teacher-student ratio   48, 49
teacher-directed instruction   28, 30, 33–36, 39
Tenaga Kerja Indonesia (TKI) [Indonesian overseas or migrant worker]   172–181
third world   222, 223
tolerance   111, 117, 119–121

transformation   93, 94, 101, 102, 206, 207, 214
transformative learning   206, 213, 214
Transnational labour migration   161, 163, 172, 173, 177, 180, 181
transition from youth to adulthood   213
Trends in International Mathematics and Science Study (TIMSS)   26, 38, 49

UNESCO   209
UNESCO Institute for Statistics (UIS)   164
Unit Pelaksana Teknis Daerah (UPTD) [community-level education agency branches]   55
United Nations Development Programme (UNDP)   146
United Nations Economic and Social Commission for Asia and the Pacific (UNESCAP)   208
United Nations International Children's Emergency Fund (UNICEF)   59, 162, 165, 181, 186, 209
United States Agency for International Development (USAID)   49, 52, 57
Universal Secondary Education (USE)   172
University of Indonesia (UI)   146, 149, 150, 155

value
  intrinsic   9, 71, 75
  personal utility   82, 216
  social utility   9, 227
Victorian Indonesian Language Teachers Association (VILTA)   131
vocational school   5, 6, 125, 226

women
  decade of   49, 231
  empowerment   148, 149, 154, 236
  movement   12, 148, 149, 156
  publishing agency   195
  studies   148–150, 156, 157
  voice (tutur perempuan)   149
  year   51
workshop   154, 212, 225
World Values Survey Association   69

youth, in-migrant   14, 203, 205, 206, 208–213, 215, 216

www.ingramcontent.com/pod-product-compliance
Lightning Source LLC
Chambersburg PA
CBHW070559300426
44113CB00010B/1325